Study Guide

for

Oltmanns and Emery

Abnormal Psychology
Sixth Edition

prepared by

Michele T. Martin
Wesleyan University

Prentice Hall

Boston   Columbus   Indianapolis   New York   San Francisco   Upper Saddle River
Amsterdam   Cape Town   Dubai   London   Madrid   Milan   Munich   Paris   Montreal   Toronto
Delhi   Mexico City   Sao Paulo   Sydney   Hong Kong   Seoul   Singapore   Taipei   Tokyo

Printed in the United States of America.

10 9 8 7 6 5 4 3 2 1   13 12 11 10 09

Prentice Hall
is an imprint of

www.pearsonhighered.com

ISBN-10: 0-205-69130-7
ISBN-13: 978-0-205-69130-2

CONTENTS

CHAPTER ONE

EXAMPLES AND DEFINITIONS OF ABNORMAL BEHAVIOR

CHAPTER OUTLINE

OBJECTIVES

You should be able to:

1. Define abnormal psychology.
2. Discuss the criteria used to define abnormal behavior.
3. Understand epidemiology, incidence, and prevalence.
4. Discuss the impact mental disorders have on people's lives.
5. Examine the relationship between culture and psychopathology.
6. Discuss the different mental health professions.
7. Discuss the importance of scientific research in the diagnosis and treatment of mental disorders.
8. Discuss the differences between the Hippocratic perspective and the moral treatment movement.
9. Understand the benefits and limitations of case studies.
10. Discuss the conservative approach in research, which leads to a reluctance to reject the null hypothesis.

MATCHING I

Answers are found at the end of this chapter. Match these terms and concepts with the definitions that follow:

a. Abnormal psychology
b. Case study
c. Comorbidity
d. Psychopathology
e. Psychosis

f. Epidemiology
g. Incidence
h. Prevalence
i. Lifetime prevalence

1. _____ the presence of more than one condition within the same period of time
2. _____ the scientific study of the frequency and distribution of disorders within a population
3. _____ the total number of active cases of a disorder present in a population during a specific period of time
4. _____ the total proportion of people in a population who have been affected by the disorder at some point in their lives
5. _____ a descriptive presentation of the psychological problems of one particular person
6. _____ a state of being profoundly out of touch with reality
7. _____ the manifestations and study of the causes of mental disorders
8. _____ the application of psychological science to the study of mental disorders
9. _____ the number of new cases of a disorder that appear in a population during a specific time

MATCHING II

Answers are found at the end of this chapter. Match these terms and concepts with the definitions that follow:

1. Insanity
2. Not guilty by reason of insanity
3. Nervous breakdown
4. Syndrome
5. Harmful dysfunction
6. *Diagnostic and Statistical Manual of Mental Disorders*
7. Culture

8. Moral treatment movement
9. Psychiatry
10. Experimental hypothesis
11. Null hypothesis
12. Clinical psychology
13. Social work
14. Flourishing
15. Psychosocial rehabilitation

a. _____ psychological functioning at the highest levels
b. _____ any new prediction made by a researcher
c. _____ a group of symptoms that appear together and are assumed to represent a specific type of disorder
d. _____ a specialization in medicine concerned with the study and treatment of mental disorders
e. _____ a legal term indicating a legal defense or finding that although a person committed a crime, he or she is not criminally responsible for the illegal behavior because of a mental disorder
f. _____ a movement founded on a basic respect for human dignity and the belief that humanistic care would be effective in the treatment of mental illness that promoted improved conditions at mental hospitals
g. _____ the alternative to the experimental hypothesis: predicts that the experimental hypothesis is not true
h. _____ currently, this is a legal term referring to a person's culpability for criminal acts if he or she has a mental disorder

i. _____ an approach to defining whether a condition is a mental disorder in terms of its harm to the person and whether the condition results from the inability of some mental mechanism to perform its natural function

j. _____ a specialization in psychology concerned with the application of psychological science to the assessment and treatment of mental disorders

k. _____ the values, beliefs, and practices that are shared by a specific community or group of people

l. _____ the official listing of mental disorders and their diagnostic criteria published by the American Psychiatric Association: updated regularly

m. _____ a profession concerned with helping people achieve an effective level of psychosocial functioning: focuses less on a body of scientific knowledge than on a commitment to action

n. _____ an old-fashioned term indicating that a person became incapacitated because of an unspecified mental disorder

o. _____ professionals who teach the severely mentally ill practical daily living skills

MATCHING III

Answers are found at the end of this chapter. Match these names with the descriptions of their contributions to the study of abnormal psychology.

a.	Jerome Wakefield	c.	Dorothea Dix
b.	Hippocrates	d.	Samuel Woodward

1. _____ an early advocate for the humane treatment of the mentally ill: promoted the creation of mental institutions for treatment

2. _____ saw mental disorders as diseases having natural causes, like other forms of physical diseases

3. _____ argued that mental disorders could be traced to immoral behavior, stress, or improper living conditions: optimistic about curing mental illnesses

4. _____ proposed the harmful dysfunction approach to defining mental disorder

CONCEPT REVIEW

Answers are found at the end of this chapter. After you have read and reviewed the material, test your comprehension by filling in the blanks or circling the correct answer.

1. Case studies are particularly important in understanding mental disorders that are

    _____.

2. Case studies can prove that a certain factor is the cause of a disorder: **true   false**

3. One limitation of case studies is that one person may not be_____ of the disorder as a

    whole.

4. There are several laboratory tests available to test for the presence of certain forms of mental disorders:

    true   false

5. An unusual behavior or symptom that goes away after a few days is not clinically significant; that is,

    does not indicate that a person has a disorder: **true   false**

6. What is the problem with defining abnormal behavior based on the individual's experience of
    personal distress? _____

7. What is the problem with defining abnormal behavior based on statistical norms of rarity?_____

8. The DSM-IV-TR defines mental disorder in terms of personal _____, impairment of
    _____, or significantly increased risk of suffering some form of harm.

9. Why was the behavior of the Yippie Party of the 1960s, whose members threw money off the balcony
    at a stock exchange, not considered to be a symptom of a mental illness?

    _____

10. Optimal psychological health is   **more than**   **equal to**   the absence of mental disorders.

11. The DSM-IV-TR is not influenced by social or cultural forces: **true   false**

12. What was a major force in the shift that led to homosexuality no longer being included in the DSM as
    a mental disorder?

    _____

13. Much of our current estimate of the prevalence of mental disorder is based on the
    _____study.

14. Most psychopathologists view mental disorders as being culture-free: **true   false**

15. Psychotic disorders are less influenced by culture than are nonpsychotic disorders: **true   false**

16. Epidemiological studies indicate that the following percentage of people have had at least one
    diagnosable condition sometime in their life: **6 percent   46 percent   83 percent**

17. People affected by severe disorders often qualify for the diagnosis of more than one disorder at the
    same time: **true   false**

18. The concept of disease burden combines which two factors?

    _____

19. Mental disorders cause 1 percent of all deaths but produce 47 percent of all
    _____ in economically developed countries.

20. Almost all mental disorders occur in Western countries: **true   false**

21. Most people who have a diagnosable mental disorder receive some form of treatment for it: **true   false**

22. Many ancient theories of abnormal behavior see as its cause the disfavor of the gods or demonic
    possession: **true   false**

23. Cutting patients to make them bleed and reduce the amount of blood in the body was a form of
    treatment for mental illness in the nineteenth century: **true   false**

24. Urbanization was one of the reasons that _____ were built.

25. What led to the creation of the specialization of psychiatry?

    _____

26. Samuel Woodward saw masturbation, among other "morally objectionable" behaviors, as the cause of _____.

27. Woodward claimed a success rate of: **about 30 percent**   **about 50 percent**

about 85 percent

28. Fever therapy involved infecting mental patients with _____ to cause a fever because symptoms sometimes disappeared in patients with a high fever.

29. What type of mental health professionals may prescribe medication?

_____

30. What type of mental health professionals are trained in the use of scientific research methods?

_____

31. A greater number of treatment providers for mental health services are professionals other than sphysicians: **true   false**

MULTIPLE CHOICE

Answers are found at the end of this chapter. These multiple choice questions will test your understanding of the material presented in the chapter. Read each question and circle the letter representing the best answer.

1. A type of formal thought disorder characterized by significant disruptions of verbal communication:
    a. depression
    b. schizophrenia
    c. psychosis
    d. disorganized speech

2. When literally translated, the term "psychopathology" refers to
    a. "deterioration of the psyche."
    b. "pathology of the mind."
    c. "pathology of the psyche."
    d. "deterioration of the mind."

3. A mental disorder is typically defined by
    a. a person experiencing the feeling that something is wrong.
    b. statistical rarity.
    c. a set of characteristic features.
    d. being out of contact with reality.

4. These two disorders are much more common in men than they are in women:
   a. alcoholism; antisocial personality disorder
   b. anxiety disorders; depression
   c. alcoholism; depression
   d. anxiety disorders; antisocial personality disorder

5. With the exception of _____, all of the following could be considered psychotic symptoms.
   a. delusions
   b. hallucinations
   c. disorganized speech
   d. depression

6. Eating disorders may be fatal if they are not properly treated because
   a. there is a high suicide rate among people with eating disorders.
   b. they affect so many vital organs of the body.
   c. people with eating disorders are often unaware of the disorder and therefore are prone to developing additional disorders.
   d. the majority of people with eating disorders do not view their behavior as problematic, and therefore do not seek treatment.

7. Cultural forces
   a. mostly affect people living in non-Western societies.
   b. do not change.
   c. only affect women.
   d. affect what we perceive as abnormal.

8. This is a general term referring to a type of severe mental disorder in which the individual is considered to be out of contact with reality.
   a. threshold
   b. syndrome
   c. psychosis
   d. schizophrenia

9. In order for a behavior to be considered abnormal, it must include all of the following with the exception of
   a. distress or painful symptoms.
   b. conflicts between the individual and society that are voluntary in nature.
   c. impairment in one or more important areas of functioning.
   d. increased risk of suffering death, pain, disability, or an important loss of freedom.

10. Which is true about the role of value judgments in the development of diagnostic systems?
   a. Values may be avoided with the use of scientific methods.
   b. Diagnosis is completely determined by values.
   c. Values have no place in the attempt to define disease.
   d. Values are inherent in any attempt to define disease.

11. Nancy grew up in a society where mourners pull out their hair, go into an emotional frenzy, and begin speaking in tongues. On a visit to the U.S., she did these things in public when she heard that a relative had died. According to DSM-IV-TR, this would be considered
    a. not psychopathology, because it is part of her culture.
    b. not psychopathology, because it caused no disruption in her social relationships.
    c. psychopathology, because of her personal distress.
    d. psychopathology, because it impaired her functioning.

12. Which of the following is not considered a criterion for defining a behavior as a form of mental illness?
    a. negative effects on the person's social functioning
    b. recognition by the person that his or her behavior is problematic
    c. personal discomfort
    d. persistent, maladaptive behaviors

SHORT ANSWER
Answer the following short answer questions. Compare your work to the material presented in the text.

1. Describe the criteria that need to be present in order for a behavior to be considered abnormal. Why is it important to have criteria to define abnormality?

2. Choose two case studies presented in this chapter and discuss how they illustrate abnormal behavior.

3. Discuss the history of institutionalization.

4. What is the importance of the null hypothesis? Provide one example.

ANSWER KEY

MATCHING I

1. c	4. i	7. d
2. f	5. b	8. a
3. h	6. e	9. g

MATCHING II

a. 14	f. 8	k. 7
b. 10	g. 11	l. 6
c. 4	h. 1	m. 13
d. 9	i. 5	n. 3
e. 2	j. 12	o. 15

MATCHING III

1. c	2. b	3. d	4. a

CONCEPT REVIEW

1. rare
2. false
3. representative
4. false
5. true
6. they may not have insight
7. something rare is not necessarily bad
8. distress; functioning
9. it was voluntary and was a political gesture
10. more than
11. false
12. political pressure from gay rights activists
13. National Comorbity Survey-Replication (NCS-R)
14. false
15. true
16. 46 percent
17. true
18. mortality and disability
19. disability
20. false
21. false
22. true
23. true
24. lunatic asylums
25. creation of institutions to treat mental patients
26. mental illness
27. about 85 percent
28. malaria
29. psychiatrists
30. clinical psychologists
31. true

MULTIPLE CHOICE

1. d	4. a	7. d	10. d
2. b	5. d	8. c	11. b
3. c	6. b	9. b	12. b

CHAPTER TWO

CAUSES OF ABNORMAL BEHAVIOR

CHAPTER OUTLINE

OBJECTIVES

You should be able to:
1. Describe the biopsychosocial approach. Explain how it is a systems approach.
2. Describe several breakthroughs that led to the modern scientific study of abnormal psychology.
3. Understand the biological, psychodynamic, cognitive behavioral, and humanistic paradigms.
4. Distinguish holism from reductionism.
5. Understand systems theory.

6. Discuss issues regarding etiology. Include information pertaining to multiple pathways, correlation versus causation, equifinality, and diathesis-stress.
7. Describe the functions of the hindbrain, midbrain, and forebrain.
8. Distinguish structural from psychophysiological problems.
9. Describe the functioning of the central and peripheral nervous systems, the voluntary and autonomic nervous systems, and the sympathetic and parasympathetic divisions.
10. Understand the research design used for twin studies, adoption studies, and family incidence studies.
11. Define evolutionary psychology and temperament and explain their significance in the etiology of psychopathology.
12. Describe some ways in which modeling, social cognition, and sense of self may affect abnormal behavior.
13. Understand how social relationships, gender roles, prejudice, and poverty can impact psychological well-being.

MATCHING I

Answers are found at the end of this chapter. Match these terms and concepts with the definitions that follow:

a.	Paradigm	l.	Ego
b.	Etiology	m.	Reality principle
c.	Biological paradigm	n.	Superego
d.	General paresis	o.	Neurotic anxiety
e.	Syphilis	p.	Defense mechanisms
f.	Psychoanalytic theory	q.	Projection
g.	Hysteria	r.	Psychosexual development
h.	Conversion disorder	s.	Oedipal conflict
i.	Psychodynamic paradigm	t.	Electra complex
j.	Pleasure principle	u.	Cognitive behavioral paradigm
k.	Id	v.	Moral anxiety

1. _____ an elaborate theory of personality based on the concepts of Freud
2. _____ a set of assumptions about the substance of a theory and the scientific method used to test the theory
3. _____ unconscious processes that reduce conscious anxiety by distorting anxiety-laden memories, emotions, and impulses
4. _____ the mode of operation for the ego, wherein the need to gratify impulses is balanced against the demands of reality
5. _____ Freud's concept that a stage boys go through involves having sexual impulses toward their mothers and aggressive impulses toward their fathers: resolved by identifying with their fathers
6. _____ a psychoanalytic diagnostic category involving the conversion of psychological conflicts into physical symptoms
7. _____ Freud's theory of development
8. _____ a sexually transmitted disease caused by bacteria, the end stage of which includes psychiatric symptoms: treatable with antibiotics
9. _____ a Freudian term for the part of personality that serves as the conscience, containing societal standards of behavior
10. _____ the modern diagnostic category for hysteria

11.   ____   a Freudian term for the part of personality that is the source of basic drives and motivations, including sexual and aggressive impulses
12.   ____   the cause of abnormal behavior
13.   ____   produced by conflict between the id and the ego
14.   ____   Freud's concept that a stage girls go through involves yearning for a penis, which they feel they must have lost
15.   ____   focuses on biological causation
16.   ____   a defense mechanism wherein the person perceives his or her own forbidden unconscious impulses as a characteristic of another person
17.   ____   views abnormal behavior as caused by unconscious conflicts arising out of early childhood experiences
18.   ____   the mode of operation for the id, whereby impulses seek immediate gratification
19.   ____   a disorder with delusions of grandeur, dementia, and progressive paralysis; progressively worsens, ending in death; caused by untreated syphilis
20.   ____   a Freudian term for the part of personality that deals with the realities of the world
21.   ____   asserts that behavior is learned and examines the processes underlying learning
22.   ____   produced by conflict between the ego and superego

MATCHING II

Answers are found at the end of this chapter. Match these terms and concepts with the definitions that follow:

1.	Medical model		14.	Humanistic psychology
2.	Classical conditioning		15.	Determinism
3.	Unconditioned stimulus		16.	Free will
4.	Unconditioned response		17.	Systems theory
5.	Conditioned stimulus		18.	Holism
6.	Conditioned response		19.	Reductionism
7.	Extinction		20.	Risk factors
8.	Operant conditioning		21.	Molecular
9.	Positive reinforcement		22.	Molar
10.	Negative reinforcement		23.	Levels of analysis
11.	Punishment		24.	Correlational study
12.	Response cost		25.	Correlational coefficient
13.	Behaviorism			

a.   ____   a neutral stimulus that, when repeatedly paired with a stimulus that elicits an automatic reaction, comes to produce that reaction itself
b.   ____   the idea that human behavior is not determined but a product of a person's choice
c.   ____   a statistic for measuring how strongly two factors are related: it ranges between -1.0 and +1.0
d.   ____   when the onset of a stimulus increases the frequency of a behavior
e.   ____   the use of different perspectives, subsystems, or "lenses" to conceptualize causal factors
f.   ____   when the removal of a stimulus decreases the frequency of behavior
g.   ____   viewing psychological illness as the same as physical illness
h.   ____   events or circumstances that are correlated with an increased likelihood of a disorder
i.   ____   a paradigm that emphasizes interdependence, cybernetics, and holism
j.   ____   Pavlov's form of learning through association of paired stimuli
k.   ____   a research design wherein the relation between two factors is studied

l. _____ when the cessation of a stimulus increases the frequency of a behavior

m. _____ a stimulus that elicits an automatic reaction

n. _____ the assumption that human behavior is caused by predictable and potentially knowable internal and/or external events

o. _____ an automatic reaction to an event

p. _____ the most general

q. _____ the belief within psychology that observable behaviors are the only appropriate focus of psychological study

r. _____ a learning theory asserting that behavior is a function of its consequences: that behavior increases if it is rewarded and decreases if it is punished

s. _____ the gradual elimination of a response when learning conditions change

t. _____ the idea that the whole is more than the sum of its parts

u. _____ the most reductionistic

v. _____ the perspective that the whole is the sum of its parts, and that the task for science is to divide the world into smaller and smaller components

w. _____ when the introduction of a stimulus decreases the frequency of a behavior

x. _____ a paradigm of abnormal behavior that rejects determinism and argues that human behavior is the product of free will

y. _____ a response that is elicited by a conditioned stimulus

MATCHING III

Answers are found at the end of this chapter. Match these terms and concepts with the definitions that follow:

a.	Positive correlations	n.	Prognosis
b.	Negative correlations	o.	Anatomy
c.	Third variable	p.	Physiology
d.	Diathesis-stress model	q.	Neuroanatomy
e.	Equifinality	r.	Neurophysiology
f.	Reciprocal causality	s.	Neurons
g.	Linear causality	t.	Soma
h.	Prognosis	u.	Dendrites
i.	Multifinality	v.	Axon
j.	Developmental psychopathology	w.	Axon terminal
		x.	Synapse
k.	Developmental norms	y.	Neurotransmitters
l.	Premorbid history	z.	Dopamine
m.	Reverse causality	aa.	Serotonin

1. _____ a predictable course for the future

2. _____ the study of brain structures

3. _____ a pattern of behavior that precedes the onset of the disorder

4. _____ trunk of the neuron that transmits messages toward other cells

5. _____ the idea that causality is bidirectional

6. _____ cell body

7. _____ predictions about the future course of a disorder

8. _____ the same psychological disorder may have different causes

9. _____ the study of biological structures

10. _____ an approach to abnormal psychology that emphasizes the importance of age-graded averages and determining what constitutes abnormal behavior
11. _____ the study of biological functions
12. _____ the end of the axon where messages are sent out to other neurons
13. _____ as one factor goes up, the other factor goes down
14. _____ age-graded averages
15. _____ as one factor goes up, the other factor goes up
16. _____ causation operates in one direction only
17. _____ branching cell structures that receive messages from other cells
18. _____ the possibility that causation could be operating in the opposite direction: Y could be causing X instead of X causing Y
19. _____ the same event can lead to different outcomes
20. _____ the study of brain functions
21. _____ a small gap between neurons that is filled with fluid
22. _____ a correlation between two variables could be explained by their joint relation with some unmeasured factor
23. _____ a neurotransmitter linked with schizophrenia
24. _____ chemical substances released into the synapse that carry signals from one neuron to another
25. _____ a view of the etiology of a disorder that assumes it is produced by an interaction of a predisposition and a precipitating event
26. _____ a neurotransmitter linked with depression
27. _____ nerve cells

MATCHING IV

Answers are found at the end of this chapter. Match these terms and concepts with the definitions that follow:

1.	Receptors	14.	Thalamus
2.	Reuptake	15.	Hypothalamus
3.	Neuromodulators	16.	Cerebral hemispheres
4.	Vesicles	17.	Lateralized
5.	Dualism	18.	Corpus callosum
6.	Hindbrain	19.	Ventricles
7.	Medulla	20.	Cerebral cortex
8.	Pons	21.	Frontal lobe
9.	Cerebellum	22.	Parietal lobe
10.	Midbrain	23.	Temporal lobe
11.	Reticular activating system	24.	Occipital lobe
12.	Forebrain	25.	Stroke
13.	Limbic system	26.	Alzheimer's disease

a. _____ a brain grouping including the medulla, pons, and cerebellum
b. _____ regulates emotion and basic learning processes
c. _____ sites on the dendrites or soma of a neuron that are sensitive to certain neurotransmitters
d. _____ the uneven surface of the brain just underneath the skull that controls and integrates sophisticated memory, sensory, and motor functions
e. _____ receives and integrates sensory information and plays a role in spatial reasoning
f. _____ controls bodily functions that sustain life, like heart rate and respiration

g. _____ the process of recapturing some neurotransmitters from the synapse before they reach the receptors of another neuron

h. _____ receives and integrates sensory information from the sense organs and from higher brain structures

i. _____ four connected chambers in the brain filled with cerebrospinal fluid

j. _____ each cerebral hemisphere serves a specialized role in brain function: the left hemisphere is involved in language and the right in spatial relations

k. _____ regulates stages of sleep

l. _____ connects the two cerebral hemispheres and coordinates their different functions

m. _____ helps coordinate physical movement

n. _____ processes sound and smell, regulates emotions, and is involved in learning, memory, and language

o. _____ controls a number of complex functions like reasoning, planning, emotion, speech, and movement

p. _____ the view that mind and body are separable

q. _____ regulates sleep and waking

r. _____ a brain grouping that evolved last and is the location of most sensory, emotional, and cognitive processes

s. _____ the two major structures of the forebrain and the site of most sensory, emotional, and cognitive processes

t. _____ chemicals that may be released from neurons or endocrine glands that influence communications of many neurons by affecting the functioning of neurotransmitters

u. _____ a brain grouping which controls some motor activities, especially fighting and sex, and includes part of the reticular activating system

v. _____ receives and interprets visual information

w. _____ controls basic biological urges such as eating, drinking, and sex

x. _____ structures which contain neurotransmitters

y. _____ a form of dementia characterized by tangles of neurons in the brain visible at autopsy

z. _____ blockage of blood vessels in the brain cutting of the oxygen supply and resulting in death of portions of brain tissue

MATCHING V

Answers are found at the end of this chapter. Match these terms and concepts with the definitions that follow:

a.	Psychophysiology	o.	Phenotype
b.	Endocrine system	p.	Alleles
c.	Hormones	q.	Locus
d.	Hyperthyroidism	r.	Polygenic
e.	Central nervous system	s.	Monozygotic (MZ)
f.	Peripheral nervous system	t.	Dizygotic (DZ)
g.	Somatic nervous system	u.	Concordance
h.	Autonomic nervous system	v.	Shared environment
i.	Sympathetic nervous system	w.	Nonshared environment
j.	Parasympathetic nervous system	x.	Probands
k.	Genes	y.	Gene-environment interaction
l.	Chromosomes	z.	Gene-environment correlation
m.	Behavior genetics	aa.	Individual differences
n.	Genotype	bb.	Species-typical characteristics

1. _____ the study of changes in the functioning of the body that result from psychological experiences
2. _____ an individual's actual genetic structure
3. _____ fraternal twins produced from separate fertilized eggs: the twins are as genetically related as nontwin siblings
4. _____ the voluntary nervous system that governs muscular control
5. _____ one's disorder is caused by a combination of one's genetic risk and an environmental stress
6. _____ the component of the family environment that offers the same or very similar experiences to all siblings
7. _____ a division of the human nervous system including all connections to the body's muscles, sensory systems, and organs
8. _____ the component of the family and non-family environment that is unique to that sibling
9. _____ a specific location on a chromosome
10. _____ a division of the human nervous system including the brain and spinal cord
11. _____ characteristics all people have in common as part of human nature
12. _____ units of DNA, located on the chromosome, that carry information about heredity
13. _____ caused by more than one gene
14. _____ chemical substances that affect the functioning of distant body systems
15. _____ the study of genetic influences on the evolution and development of normal and abnormal behavior
16. _____ a collection of glands located throughout the body that produce psychophysiological responses by releasing hormones into the bloodstream
17. _____ the involuntary nervous system that regulates body organs
18. _____ identical twins produced from a single fertilized egg: the twins have identical genotypes
19. _____ the expression of a given genotype
20. _____ agreement: when twin pairs either both have a disorder or both are free of the disorder
21. _____ alternate forms of a genetic trait
22. _____ how people are different from one another
23. _____ a disease in which the thyroid gland secretes too much of the hormone thyroxin, causing restlessness, agitation, and anxiety
24. _____ a division of the autonomic nervous system that controls the slowing of arousal and energy conservation
25. _____ index cases: people who have a disorder and then their relatives are examined to see if they also have the disorder
26. _____ a division of the autonomic nervous system that is associated with increased arousal and expenditure of energy
27. _____ experience is not random, but is related to one's genes
28. _____ chainlike structures in the nucleus of all cells

MATCHING VI

Answers are found at the end of this chapter. Match these terms and concepts with the definitions that follow:

1.	Affiliation	6.	Emotions
2.	Attachments	7.	Temperament
3.	Ethology	8.	Autosomal gene
4.	Imprinting	9.	Dominant/recessive inheritance
5.	Dominance	10.	Evolutionary psychology

11.   Personality
12.   Natural selection
13.   Sexual selection
14.   Modeling
15.   Insecure attachment
16.   Attributions
17.   Identity
18.   Authoritative
19.   Self-esteem
20.   Self-control
21.   Socialization

22.   Developmental stage
23.   Developmental transition
24.   Social roles
25.   Labeling theory
26.   Self-fulfilling prophecy
27.   Social support
28.   Gender roles
29.   Relational
30.   Instrumental
31.   Androgyny

a.   _____   internal rules for guiding appropriate behavior
b.   _____   internal feeling states
c.   _____   the view that abnormal behavior is created by social expectations or roles
d.   _____   learning through imitation of others
e.   _____   oriented toward others
f.   _____   the study of animal behavior
g.   _____   the special and selective bonds that infants form with their caregivers early in life
h.   _____   styles of behavior according to the expectations of the social situation
i.   _____   possessing both female and male gender-role characteristics
j.   _____   the emotional and practical assistance received from others
k.   _____   uncertain parent-child relationships resulting from inconsistent or unresponsive parenting, particularly in the first year of life
l.   _____   the hierarchical ordering of a social group into more and less powerful members
m.   _____   roles associated with social expectations about gendered behavior
n.   _____   people's actions conforming to the expectations created by a label given to them
o.   _____   an inflexible process of forming selective bonds in the first hours of life which occurs in some species
p.   _____   people's beliefs about cause and effect relationships
q.   _____   characteristic styles of relating to the world that are very stable
r.   _____   definition of self
s.   _____   the process whereby parents, teachers, and peers use discipline, praise, and example to teach children prosocial behavior and set limits on antisocial behavior
t.   _____   the idea that stressful and important changes occur during times of rapid biological, psychological, or social development
u.   _____   oriented toward action and achievement
v.   _____   periods of time delineated by age or social task during which people face common social and emotional challenges
w.   _____   a trait caused by one gene that has only one locus and two alleles: two possible phenotypes and three possible genotypes
x.   _____   a single gene
y.   _____   the essential traits that describe human behavior
z.   _____   the application of the principles of evolution to our understanding of the human and animal mind
aa.   _____   successful inherited adaptations to environmental problems become more common in successive generations
bb.   _____   better reproductive success due to mate selection

cc. _____ relationships between different members of the same species
dd. _____ a parenting style that is both warmly responsive and firm in discipline
ee. _____ valuing one's abilities

MATCHING VII

Answers are found at the end of this chapter. Match these names with the descriptions of their contributions to the study of abnormal psychology.

a.	Sigmund Freud	e.	Erik Erikson
b.	B. F. Skinner	f.	John B. Watson
c.	Rene Descartes	g.	Gregor Mendel
d.	John Bowlby	h.	Ivan Pavlov

1. _____ attempted to balance religious teachings with emerging scientific reasoning by proposing dualism
2. _____ founded behaviorism and applied learning theory to the study of abnormal behavior
3. _____ developed attachment theory, based in part on ethology
4. _____ developed psychoanalytic theory; focused on the importance of early childhood experiences and unconscious conflicts
5. _____ conducted a series of studies on classical conditioning
6. _____ discovered genetic inheritance; made the distinction between genotypes and phenotypes
7. _____ his stage theory of development through the lifespan stressed the importance of social factors
8. _____ conducted a series of studies on operant conditioning

CONCEPT REVIEW

Answers are found at the end of this chapter. After you have read and reviewed the material, test your comprehension by filling in the blanks or circling the correct answer.

1. The cause of abnormal behavior has been discovered: **true**   **false**

2. In the twentieth century, the four different paradigms proposed to explain abnormal behavior were

_____, _____, _____, and

_____; now most researchers advocate a/an _____ approach

using the _____ model.

3. What three major events encouraged advances in the scientific understanding of the etiology of

psychopathology in the nineteenth and twentieth centuries? _____,

_____, and _____

4. The development of a _____ for general paresis inspired a search for its cause, which took 100

years of investigation.

5. General paresis was eliminated with the advent of _____.

6. The elimination of general paresis encouraged researchers to adopt what paradigm in their research on

etiology of mental disorders? _____

7. Freud thought that abnormal behavior was caused by _____ mental conflicts.

8. What approach did Wundt use in studying psychological phenomena? _____

9. Cognitive behaviorists are primarily concerned with the _____ of mental disorders rather than understanding their causes.

10. Behaviorists focus on _____ and not on _____ and _____ because they cannot be measured objectively.

11. _____ psychology was a reaction against the determinism of biomedical, psychoanalytic, and behavioral theories of abnormal behavior.

12. Humanistic psychologists tend to blame dysfunctional, abnormal, or aggressive behavior on:

    the individual   society

13. The textbook example of the Martian scientists trying to figure out what causes automobiles to move points out the importance of the _____ that a research approach uses.

14. A predisposition toward developing a disorder is called a: **stress   diathesis**

15. Psychological problems usually have: **one cause   a group of causes operating together**

16. The density and sensitivity of _____ on neurons has been implicated in some types of abnormal behavior.

17. All psychological experience has a representation in the biochemistry of the

    _____.

18. A _____ is caused by blood vessels in the brain rupturing and cutting off the supply of oxygen to parts of the brain, thereby killing surrounding brain tissue.

19. Psychophysiological **overarousal   underarousal** has been hypothesized to be responsible for excessive anxiety, while psychophysiological   **overarousal   underarousal** has been linked with antisocial behavior.

20. The simple mode of dominant/recessive inheritance has been linked with forms of which of the following kinds of abnormal behavior?   **schizophrenia   mental retardation**

    depression

21. The genetic contributions to most disorders are hypothesized to be caused by:

22. If a disorder is purely genetic, the concordance for MZ twins would be _____ percent and the concordance for DZ twins would be _____ percent.

23. If the concordance rates for MZ and DZ twins are the same, then what type of factors are responsible for the disorder?   **genetic   environmental**

24. Family incidence studies ask whether diseases_____.

25. If a disorder is shown to be genetic, then nothing can change it: **true   false**

26. According to attachment theorists, displays of distress by human infants serve to keep caregivers in _____, making infants more likely to survive.

27. Evolutionary theory asserts that two types of selection, _____ and _____, have affected the evolution of human psychology.

28. The most effective parents are those who provide both high levels of _____ and _____.

29. Two prominent stage theories are those proposed by which theorists? _____and_____

30. There is a correlation between marital status of parents and emotional _____ of children.

31. A close relationship with an adult outside the family can protect children from the effects of troubled family circumstances: **true   false**

32. Some theorists have suggested that _____ are responsible for the much higher rates of depression among women.

33. One study found that 12 percent of school-aged children had seen a _____ in the streets outside their homes in a Washington neighborhood.

MULTIPLE CHOICE

Answers are found at the end of this chapter. These multiple choice questions will test your understanding of the material presented in the chapter. Read each question and circle the letter representing the best answer.

1. Which of the following views psychopathology as resulting from physical factors that form a predisposition when combined with a threatening or challenging experience?
   a.   medical model
   b.   diathesis-stress model
   c.   threshold model
   d.   biopsychosocial model

2. The assumption that biological explanations are more useful than psychological explanations because they deal with smaller units is called
   a.   biological perspective.
   b.   genetic predisposition.
   c.   biological reductionism.
   d.   medical model.

3. Which regulates the function of various organs, such as the heart and stomach?
   a.   somatic nervous system
   b.   autonomic nervous system
   c.   sympathetic nervous system
   d.   parasympathetic nervous system

4. According to Freud, this is the part of the personality that attempts to fulfill id impulses while at the same time dealing with the realities of the world.
   - a.   ego
   - b.   id
   - c.   superego
   - d.   libido

5. All but which of the following are methods of learning?
   - a.   classical conditioning
   - b.   operant conditioning
   - c.   introjection
   - d.   modeling

6. Developmental theory suggests that children whose parents are _____ and _____ are better adjusted than those whose parents are inadequate on one or both of these dimensions.
   - a.   loving; firm in their discipline
   - b.   authoritative; hold high expectations of their child
   - c.   demanding; promote individuality
   - d.   congenial; encourage separation and independence

7. Freud was trained by this neurologist, who successfully used hypnosis to treat hysteria.
   - a.   Skinner
   - b.   Bertalanffy
   - c.   Perls
   - d.   Charcot

8. While watching her daughter play kickball in the street of their neighborhood, Mrs. Jones sees her daughter being hit by a car. Soon thereafter, Mrs. Jones loses her vision. After visits to numerous doctors, there is no known organic impairment to cause the blindness. What might her diagnosis be?
   - a. depression
   - b. conversion disorder
   - c. hysteria
   - d. hypochondriasis

9. Which of the following could be considered an uncertain or ambivalent parent-child relationship that is a consequence of inconsistent and unresponsive parenting, particularly during the first year of life?
   - a.   anxious attachment
   - b.   neurotic attachment
   - c.   oppositional attachment
   - d.   apathetic attachment

10. In the famous experiments on which classical conditioning was based, the bell was the _____ and the meat powder was the _____.
   - a. conditioned response; unconditioned response
   - b. unconditioned response; conditioned response
   - c. conditioned stimulus; unconditioned stimulus
   - d. unconditioned stimulus; conditioned stimulus

11. The enigma written by Lord Byron and presented in this chapter illustrates that
    a. paradigms are unscientific and should not be used in evaluating situations.
    b. the hidden meanings in life are sometimes difficult to comprehend; however, the use of a paradigm can aid in this process.
    c. we should use our paradigm to reveal the meaning from certain situations.
    d. assumptions made by a paradigm can at times act as blinders and lead an investigator to overlook what otherwise might be obvious.

12. Brad's mother took away his privilege to use the computer for two days because he hit his sister. This is an example of
    a. punishment.
    b. response cost.
    c. extinction.
    d. negative reinforcement.

13. _____ are chainlike structures found in the nucleus of cells.
    a. Neurotransmitters
    b. Genes
    c. Chromosomes
    d. Lobes

14. Which is a pattern of behavior that precedes the onset of the disorder?
    a. prognosis
    b. premorbid history
    c. determinism
    d. self-fulfilling prophecy

15. Advances in the scientific understanding of the etiology of psychopathology did not appear until the nineteenth and early twentieth centuries, when all of the following major events occurred except
    a. the number of people diagnosed with some form of psychopathology rapidly increased.
    b. the cause of general paresis was discovered.
    c. the emergence of Sigmund Freud.
    d. the creation of a new academic discipline called psychology.

16. According to Freud's theory of psychosexual development, a son's forbidden sexual desire for his mother is called a/an
    a. defense mechanism.
    b. neurotic anxiety.
    c. Electra complex.
    d. Oedipal conflict.

17. As described by the bipolar dimensions of personality, this domain is characterized by trusting and kind versus hostile and selfish:
    a. conscientiousness
    b. agreeable
    c. neuroticism
    d. extraversion

18. According to the psychodynamic paradigm, the cause of abnormality is
    a. early childhood experiences.
    b. social learning.
    c. frustrations of society.
    d. genes, infection, or other physical damage.

19. The cornerstone of humanistic psychology is _____, the assumption that human behavior is not determined, but is a product of how people choose to act.
    a. holism
    b. self-fulfilling prophecy
    c. individuation
    d. free will

20. This nervous system is responsible for controlling activities associated with increased arousal and energy expenditure:
    a. sympathetic nervous system
    b. parasympathetic nervous system
    c. autonomic nervous system
    d. somatic nervous system

21. Freud can be credited with all of the following, with the exception of
    a. offering specific, empirically-derived hypotheses about his theory.
    b. calling attention to unconscious processes.
    c. formulating a stage theory of child development.
    d. identifying numerous intra-psychic defenses.

22. Which of the following are characteristic ways of behaving according to the expectations of the social situation?
    a. prescribed roles
    b. social roles
    c. gender roles
    d. transitional roles

23. All of the following statements are true from a systems perspective regarding the etiology of psychopathology, except
    a. there may be biopsychosocial contributions to psychopathology, but clear hypotheses must still be supported by empirical evidence.
    b. social domains of behavior are the most significant contribution to the causes of abnormal behavior.
    c. different types of abnormal behavior have very different causes.
    d. causes of almost all forms of abnormal behavior are unknown at present.

24. Which of the following is a defense mechanism that includes the insistence that an experience, memory, or internal need did not occur or does not exist?
    a. sublimation
    b. reaction formation
    c. denial
    d. repression

25. This occurs when a conditioned stimulus is no longer presented together with an unconditioned stimulus.
    a. extinction
    b. punishment
    c. negative reinforcement
    d. response cost

26. A _____ is an individual's actual genetic structure.
    a. locus
    b. genotype
    c. negative reinforcement
    d. phenotype

27. The concept that one particular event can lead to different outcomes is known as
    a. reciprocal causality.
    b. equifinality.
    c. linear causality.
    d. multifinality.

28. Genetic influences on mental disorders
    a. are the only important causal influences.
    b. operate independently and separately from environmental influences.
    c. are not ás important as environmental influences.
    d. interact with environmental influence.

SHORT ANSWER
Answer the following short answer questions. Compare your work to the material presented in the text.

1. Compare and contrast the following behavior genetics investigations: twin, adoption, and family incidence studies. In what ways are these findings helpful? In what ways could these findings possibly be misinterpreted?

2. Discuss Bowlby's attachment theory. Does this theory have empirical support? Explain.

3. Compare and contrast Freud's and Erikson's theories of development. Which theory makes the most sense to you and your personal experience? Why?

4. Discuss why it is not enough to focus on one subsystem or level of analysis when viewing psychopathology.

5. Why is it important not to infer causation from correlation?

ANSWER KEY

MATCHING I

1.	f	7.	r	13.	o	19.	d
2.	a	8.	e	14.	t	20.	l
3.	p	9.	n	15.	c	21.	u
4.	m	10.	h	16.	q	22.	v
5.	s	11.	k	17.	i		
6.	g	12.	b	18.	j		

MATCHING II

a.	5	h.	20	o.	4	v.	1
b.	16	i.	17	p.	22		9
c.	25	j.	2	q.	13	w.	1
d.	9	k.	24	r.	8		1
e.	23	l.	10	s.	7	x.	1
f.	12	m.	3	t.	18		4
g.	1	n.	15	u.	21	y.	6

MATCHING III

1.	h	8.	e	15.	a	22.	c
2.	q	9.	o	16.	g	23.	z
3.	l	10.	j	17.	u	24.	y
4.	v	11.	p	18.	m	25.	d
5.	f	12.	w	19.	i	26.	aa
6.	t	13.	b	20.	r	27.	s
7.	n	14.	k	21.	x		

MATCHING IV

a.	6	i.	19	q.	11	y.	2
b.	13	j.	17	r.	12		6
c.	1	k.	8	s.	16	z.	2
d.	20	l.	18	t.	3		5
e.	22	m.	9	u.	10		
f.	7	n.	23	v.	24		
g.	2	o.	21	w.	15		
h.	14	p.	5	x.	4		

MATCHING V

1. a	8. w	15. m	22. aa
2. n	9. q	16. b	23. d
3. t	10. e	17. h	24. j
4. g	11. bb	18. s	25. x
5. y	12. k	19. o	26. i
6. v	13. r	20. u	27. z
7. f	14. c	21. p	28. l

MATCHING VI

a. 20	i. 31	q. 7	y. 11
b. 6	j. 27	r. 17	z. 10
c. 25	k. 15	s. 21	aa. 12
d. 14	l. 5	t. 23	bb. 13
e. 29	m. 28	u. 30	cc. 1
f. 3	n. 26	v. 22	dd. 18
g. 2	o. 4	w. 9	ee. 19
h. 24	p. 16	x. 8	

MATCHING VII

1. c	3. d	5. h	7. e
2. f	4. a	6. g	8. b

CONCEPT REVIEW

1. false
2. biological; psychodynamic; cognitive behavioral; humanistic; integrated; biopsychosocial
3. discovery of the cause of general paresis; Freud; birth of psychology
4. diagnostic category
5. Penicillin
6. Biological
7. unconscious
8. the scientific method
9. treatment
10. behaviors; thoughts; feelings
11. Humanistic
12. society
13. level of analysis
14. diathesis
15. a group of causes operating together
16. receptors
17. brain
18. stroke
19. overarousal; underarousal
20. mental retardation
21. multiple genes
22. 100; 50
23. environmental
24. runs in families
25. false
26. proximity
27. natural; sexual
28. love; discipline
29. Freud; Erikson
30. problems
31. true
32. gender roles
33. dead body

MULTIPLE CHOICE

1. b	8. b	15. a	22. b
2. c	9. a	16. d	23. b
3. b	10. c	17. b	24. c
4. a	11. d	18. a	25. a
5. c	12. b	19. d	26. a
6. a	13. c	20. a	27. d
7. d	14. b	21. a	28. d

CHAPTER THREE

TREATMENT OF PSYCHOLOGICAL DISORDERS

CHAPTER OUTLINE

OBJECTIVES

You should be able to:
1.   Distinguish between the biological, psychodynamic, cognitive, behavioral, and humanistic approaches to treatment.
2.   Describe electroconvulsive therapy and psychosurgery and their current applications.

3.   Discuss the effectiveness of psychopharmacology in the treatment of mental illness.
4.   Describe the basic goals and primary techniques involved in psychoanalysis.
5.   Discuss the theory underlying ego analysis and distinguish between psychoanalysis and psychodynamic psychotherapy.
6.   Discuss the ways in which classical conditioning principles are utilized in treatment.
7.   Describe contingency management and social skills training programs.
8.   Discuss the principles of attribution retraining therapy, self-instruction training, cognitive therapy, and rational-emotive therapy.
9.   Discuss how client-centered therapy reflects the underlying principles of humanistic psychology.
10.   Describe the findings of psychotherapy outcome studies.
11.   Define psychotherapy process research and describe some of its basic findings.
12.   Discuss the goals, techniques, and outcomes of couples therapy, family therapy, and group therapy.

MATCHING I

Answers are found at the end of this chapter. Match these terms and concepts with the definitions that follow:

a.	Psychotherapy	o.	Electroconvulsive therapy (ECT)
b.	Outcome	p.	Bilateral ECT
c.	Process	q.	Unilateral ECT
d.	Eclectic	r.	Psychosurgery
e.	Ethnic identity	s.	Prefrontal lobotomy
f.	Psychodynamic psychotherapies	t.	Cingulotomy
g.	Psychotropic medications	u.	Psychopharmacology
h.	Acculturation	v.	Allegiance effect
i.	Humanistic psychotherapies	w.	Couples therapy
j.	Retrograde amnesia	x.	Family therapy
k.	Homework	y.	Parent management training
l.	Meta-analysis	z.	Group therapy
m.	Trephining	aa.	Evidence-based
n.	Symptom alleviation		

1.   ____ what makes therapy work
2.   ____ an ancient form of surgery to treat mental disorders consisting of chipping a hole in the patient's skull
3.   ____ treatments based on Freud's writings and later related theorists: focus on exploring the patient's past and unconscious to promote insight
4.   ____ electroconvulsive therapy through both brain hemispheres
5.   ____ an ethnic minority member's understanding of self in terms of his or her own culture
6.   ____ a procedure in which the frontal lobes of the brain are surgically destroyed
7.   ____ a statistical procedure that combines the results of many studies
8.   ____ treatments focusing on present feelings that encourage the client to take responsibility for his or her actions
9.   ____ taking on the majority group's cultural patterns
10. ____ surgical destruction of specific regions of the brain
11. ____ treatment for mental illness involving the induction of a seizure by passing electricity through the brain
12. ____ electroconvulsive therapy through one brain hemisphere

13. _____ the loss of memory of past events: a side effect of ECT
14. _____ research supports the effectiveness of a treatment
15. _____ a form of limited psychosurgery that may be effective for very severe cases of obsessive-compulsive disorder
16. _____ the study of the use of medications to treat psychological disturbances
17. _____ the use of psychological techniques to try to produce change in the context of a special, helping relationship
18. _____ activities assigned to the client designed to continue treatment outside the therapy session
19. _____ an approach of picking different treatments according to the needs of individual disorders and individual clients
20. _____ chemical substances that affect psychological state
21. _____ reducing the dysfunctional symptoms of a disorder but not eliminating its root cause
22. _____ treating several people at the same time in one session
23. _____ treating more than one family member with the goal of improving family relationships
24. _____ the tendency for researchers to find that their favorite treatment is most effective
25. _____ treating intimate partners in psychotherapy
26. _____ teaching parents new parenting skills to help raise their children more effectively
27. _____ how well a treatment works

MATCHING II

Answers are found at the end of this chapter. Match these terms and concepts with the definitions that follow:

1. Therapeutic alliance
2. Free association
3. Psychoanalysis
4. Insight
5. Interpretation
6. Therapeutic neutrality
7. Transference
8. Countertransference
9. Clinically significant
10. Ego analysis
11. Short term psychodynamic psychotherapy
12. Behaviorism
13. Experimental method

14. Hypothesis
15. Independent variable
16. Experimental group
17. Control group
18. Random assignment
19. Dependent variable
20. Statistically significant
21. Confounded
22. Internal validity
23. External validity
24. Tertiary prevention
25. Primary prevention
26. Secondary prevention

a. _____ bringing formerly unconscious material into conscious awareness
b. _____ a form of treatment involving active focus on a particular emotional issue rather than free association: usually completed in about twenty-five sessions
c. _____ subjects who receive an active treatment
d. _____ an analyst's suggestion to the patient of the hidden meaning of his or her symptoms, dreams, or verbalizations
e. _____ the outcome that is hypothesized to vary according to the manipulations of the independent variable
f. _____ the bond between therapist and client
g. _____ the belief that observable behaviors rather than cognitive or emotional states are the appropriate focus of psychological study
h. _____ subjects who receive no treatment or a placebo

i. _____ a purposefully distant and uninvolved stance the therapist takes to minimize his or her influence on free association

j. _____ changes in the dependent variable can be accurately attributed to changes in the independent variable

k. _____ a therapeutic technique wherein patients report without censorship whatever thoughts cross their minds, no matter how trivial

l. _____ a type of scientific investigation that can establish cause and effect

m. _____ the factor that is controlled and manipulated by the experimenter

n. _____ revisions of psychoanalysis wherein the therapist is more engaged and directive and treatment is often briefer

o. _____ the independent variable is unknowingly related to some other unmeasured factor which is not evenly distributed among the treatment groups

p. _____ the form of psychological therapy developed by Freud

q. _____ the experimenter's specific prediction about cause and effect

r. _____ the probability that the observed difference between the groups occurred by chance alone rather than the effect of the independent variable is less than 5 percent

s. _____ the process whereby patients transfer their feelings about key people in their lives onto their therapists

t. _____ ensuring that each subject has a statistically equal chance of receiving different levels of the independent variable

u. _____ the process whereby therapists' feelings and reactions toward their patients affects their responses to them

v. _____ findings of an experiment can be validly generalized to other circumstances

w. _____ innovations in psychoanalytic theory giving more importance to the ego and the role of society and culture

x. _____ improving the environment to prevent new cases of a mental disorder from developing

y. _____ catching mental disorders early so that they can be resolved before they become severe

z. _____ treating identified mental disorders and their consequences

MATCHING III

Answers are found at the end of this chapter. Match these terms and concepts with the definitions that follow:

a.	Internalization	p.	Self-instruction training
b.	Systematic desensitization	q.	Cognitive therapy
c.	Progressive muscle relaxation	r.	Rational-emotive therapy (RET)
d.	Hierarchy of fears	s.	Emotional awareness
e.	*In vivo* desensitization	t.	Client-centered therapy
f.	Flooding	u.	Empathy
g.	Aversion therapy	v.	Self-disclosure
h.	Contingency management	w.	Unconditional positive regard
i.	Token economy	x.	Spontaneous remission
j.	Social skills training	y.	Double-blind study
k.	Assertiveness training	z.	Placebo effect
l.	Role playing	aa.	Dialectical behavior therapy
m.	Social problem solving	bb.	Awareness and commitment
n.	Cognitive behavior therapy		therapy
o.	Attribution retraining		

1. _____ the therapist's description of his or her own feelings and reactions
2. _____ a technique for challenging negative distortions in thinking whereby the therapist gently confronts the client's fallacies
3. _____ teaching clients new, desirable ways of behaving that are likely to be rewarded in the everyday world
4. _____ a third-wave CBT approach for borderline personality disorder that increases mindfulness (the person's awareness of his or her thoughts and feelings)
5. _____ a treatment for impulsive children wherein an adult first models an appropriate behavior while saying the self-instruction aloud, then the child does so, and gradually shifts from saying the self-instruction aloud to saying it silently to him- or herself
6. _____ non-judgmentally valuing clients for who they are regardless of their behavior
7. _____ gradually being exposed to the feared stimulus in real life while simultaneously maintaining a state of relaxation
8. _____ neither patient nor physician knows whether the patient's pill is placebo or medication
9. _____ a humanistic therapy that follows the client's lead: the therapist offers warmth, empathy, and genuineness, but the client solves his or her own problems
10. _____ an improvisational acting technique that allows clients to rehearse new social skills
11. _____ emotional understanding of others' unique feelings and perspectives
12. _____ exposure at full intensity to the feared stimulus with prevention of avoidance of the stimuli until the fear response is eliminated through extinction
13. _____ a problem-solving technique wherein the problem is first assessed in detail, alternative solutions are brainstormed, the different options are evaluated, one alternative is implemented, and its success is evaluated objectively
14. _____ a formalized contingency management system adopted in an institutional setting
15. _____ teaching clients to be direct about their feelings and wishes
16. _____ a cognitive behavior therapy technique designed to directly challenge irrational beliefs about oneself and the world
17. _____ a method of inducing a calm state through the contraction and subsequent relaxation of all the major muscle groups
18. _____ trying to change how a person ascribes causes to various events in his or her life by abandoning intuitive strategies for more scientific methods
19. _____ a third-wave CBT approach that focuses on values and self-awareness
20. _____ a treatment for overcoming fears involving systematic exposure to imagined, feared events while simultaneously maintaining relaxation
21. _____ helping children develop internal controls over their behavior
22. _____ pairing an unpleasant response with the stimuli that was previously sought: used for helping people stop smoking cigarettes and drinking alcohol
23. _____ recognizing and experiencing true feelings
24. _____ the application of behavior therapy into the cognitive realm
25. _____ focuses on directly changing the rewards and punishments for various behaviors, rewarding the desired behavior and punishing the undesirable behavior
26. _____ improvement by inert treatments
27. _____ ordering fears ranging from very mild to very frightening
28. _____ improvement in the absence of treatment

MATCHING IV

Answers are found at the end of this chapter. Match these names with the descriptions of their contributions to the study of abnormal psychology:

a.	Egas Moniz	h.	John B. Watson
b.	Joseph Breuer	i.	Joseph Wolpe
c.	Sigmund Freud	j.	Aaron Beck
d.	Harry Stack Sullivan	k.	Albert Ellis
e.	Erik Erikson	l.	Carl Rogers
f.	Karen Horney	m.	Hans Eysenck
g.	John Bowlby	n.	Jerome Frank

1. _____ proposed a theory that people have conflicting ego needs to move toward, against, and away from others
2. _____ developed attachment theory
3. _____ developed client-centered therapy
4. _____ abandoned the cathartic method for free association
5. _____ an ego analyst who focused on interpersonal relationships rather than intrapsychic dynamics
6. _____ developed rational-emotive therapy
7. _____ pioneered the cathartic method
8. _____ investigated the common factors of different psychotherapies
9. _____ developed behaviorism
10. _____ won a Nobel Prize for discovering prefrontal lobotomy
11. _____ developed a cognitive behavior therapy for depression
12. _____ a researcher who concluded that psychotherapy was completely ineffective
13. _____ developed systematic desensitization
14. _____ developed a psychosocial stage theory of development

CONCEPT REVIEW

Answers are found at the end of this chapter. After you have read and reviewed the material, test your comprehension by filling in the blanks or circling the correct answer.

1. About **7 percent**   **47 percent**   **87 percent**   of people with a diagnosable mental illness have not had any treatment for their disorder in the past year.

2. The surgical removal of sexual organs was one biological treatment used for emotional problems in the past: **true   false**

3. The development of ECT originated in attempts to treat schizophrenia that were based on the incorrect conclusion that schizophrenia was rare among people who had _____.

4. Which type of ECT produces less memory loss: **unilateral   bilateral**

5. Which type of ECT is more effective: **unilateral   bilateral**

6. Research has shown electroconvulsive therapy to be quite effective in treating what type of mental illness?

_____

7. Psychosurgery is a reversible treatment: **true   false**

8. Antipsychotic medications that relieve symptoms in schizophrenics have what effect on other people?

_____

9. What was the number-one selling prescription medicine for any type of ailment in the 1990s? _____

10. Psychotropic medications: **cure mental disorders**   **alleviate symptoms**

11. According to psychoanalysis, uncovering unconscious material and sharing the _____

view of their intra-psychic life is necessary for treatment.

12. Why do psychoanalysts maintain a distant and neutral stance in relation to their patients?

_____

13. Psychoanalysis is thought to be more effective for what types of disorders?

_____

14. Sullivan hypothesized that there are two basic dimensions of interpersonal relationships:

_____ and _____.

15. Horney stressed the need for a person to have _____among the three

styles in which they relate to others.

16. Research shows that systematic desensitization is an effective form of treatment for fears and phobias:

true   **false**

17. Research shows that aversion therapy is effective in the long-term alleviation of substance use:

true   **false**

18. What is the shortcoming in using token economies? _____

19. Attribution retraining involves teaching clients to give up intuitive strategies in favor of _____.

20. One of the main strengths of the behavior therapy approach is its focus on demonstrating its effectiveness

through _____.

21. Humanistic psychotherapists are very active in directing therapy: **true   false**

22. In addition to the problem of wasting time and money on bogus "alternative" therapies, the problem with

sham treatments is that _____.

23. There is no research evidence that psychotherapy works: **true   false**

24. Research has documented that psychotherapy is more effective in treating mental disorders than

chemotherapy is in treating breast cancer: **true   false**

25. What proportion of people improve without any treatment: **one quarter   one third   two thirds**

26. The quickest improvements in therapy occur in the first several months of therapy: **true   false**

27. What does YAVIS stand for? _____

28. One key component of persuasion in psychotherapy that is curative may be that psychotherapy instills

_____.

29. In the classic study by Sloane and colleagues comparing behavior therapy and psychodynamic psychotherapy, both forms of therapy were more effective than no treatment, but were not significantly different from each other: **true   false**

30. In that same study, the single most important aspect of both types of therapy for the client was his or her _____.

31. The "file drawer problem" refers to the scientist hesitating before _____ findings that contradict his or her expectations.

32. Potent placebo effects have been demonstrated in cancer treatment and in surgery: **true   false**

33. All forms of therapy emphasize the importance of _____ in the therapist-client relationship.

34. According to family systems therapists, a well-functioning family is one where the primary alliance is between _____.

35. Self-help groups are different from other forms of group therapy because if they have a leader, the leader not a _____.

MULTIPLE CHOICE
Answers are found at the end of this chapter. The multiple choice questions will test your understanding of the material presented in the chapter. Read each question and circle the letter representing the best answer.

1. The type of prevention that involves changing the environment so mental disorders do not develop at all is called
   a. tertiary prevention.
   b. primary prevention.
   c. secondary prevention.
   d. allegiance effect.

2. Treatment outcome researchers widely accept the finding that approximately _____ of clients improve as a result of psychotherapy.
   a. one third
   b. two thirds
   c. one quarter
   d. one half

3. Empathy involves
   a. trying to put yourself in someone else's shoes in order to understand his or her feelings and perspectives.
   b. trying to understand the etiology of someone else's behavior.
   c. feeling sorry for someone because of their life situation.
   d. all of the above.

4. The "placebo effect" is treatment

    a. in which the client has a dialogue with an imagined part of himself or herself.

    b. in which the client is taught relaxation skills for the condition being evaluated.

    c. that contains no "special ingredient" for treating the condition being evaluated.

    d. which involves full intensity exposure to feared stimuli.

5. Which of the following would most likely ask a patient to do homework?

    a.   a biological therapist

    b.   a psychodynamic psychotherapist

    c.   a humanistic therapist

    d.   a cognitive behavior therapist

6. All of the following are examples of cognitive behavior therapy, with the exception of

    a.   flooding.

    b.   social skills training.

    c.   aversion therapy.

    d.   ego analysis.

7. One complicating issue for electroconvulsive therapy is

    a.   that it is typically used instead of less invasive procedures that should be tried first, like medication.

    b.   that there is a controversy raging among researchers about whether or not it ever works.

    c.   that it is mostly used for people who have committed crimes to control their behavior.

    d.   that the most effective voltages and forms of the therapy are also the riskiest.

8. Every day that Sally completes all of her chores at home, her mother gives her a star. After Sally has accumulated fifteen stars, her mother will take her out for ice cream. Her mother is most likely using which of the following to get Sally to do her chores?

    a.   token economy

    b.   counterconditioning

    c.   *in vivo* desensitization

    d.   classical conditioning

9. An experiment has internal validity if

    a. the findings can be generalized to other circumstances.

    b. changes in the dependent variable can be accurately attributed to changes in the independent variable.

    c. the researcher can control all aspects of the experimental environment.

    d. the researcher is able to control and manipulate the dependent variable.

10. This type of therapy is primarily used to treat substance abuse disorders such as alcoholism and cigarette smoking:

    a.   cognitive therapy

    b.   psychodynamic therapy

    c.   aversion therapy

    d.   contingency therapy

11. Sam is a first-year college student who is extremely afraid of heights. He entered therapy after failing his first semester chemistry course because it was located on the fifth floor of a building and Sam was too afraid to go the fifth floor to attend class. Sam's therapist gradually exposes Sam to increasing heights while having Sam simultaneously maintain a state of relaxation. Sam's therapist is using which technique to help Sam alleviate his fear of heights?
    a. *in vivo* desensitization
    b. systematic desensitization
    c. flooding
    d. counterconditioning

12. Albert Ellis is to _____ as Aaron Beck is to _____.
    a. client-centered therapy; ego analysis
    b. ego analysis; client-centered therapy
    c. rational-emotive therapy; cognitive therapy
    d. cognitive therapy; rational-emotive therapy

13. According to Freud, all of the following are ways to reveal aspects of the unconscious mind except for
    a. slips of the tongue.
    b. countertransference.
    c. dreams.
    d. free association.

14. One major difference in technique between humanistic and cognitive behavior therapists is that
    a. humanistic psychotherapists view the nature of the therapist-client relationship differently than do behavior therapists.
    b. humanistic psychotherapists focus on the patients' past and present interpersonal relationships.
    c. humanistic psychotherapists focus on treatment irrespective of its causes.
    d. none of the above

15. All of the following have caused a decline in the practice of classical psychoanalysis except
    a. the substantial amount of time required.
    b. the accessibility of treatment only by those who are relatively financially secure.
    c. that research has proven classical Freudian psychoanalysis to be ineffective.
    d. the limited data available on the outcome of treatment.

16. In the 1990s, this medication had outsold every prescription medication, including all medications used to treat physical ailments:
    a. Valium
    b. Prozac
    c. Ritalin
    d. Lithium

17. All of the following can be viewed as goals of psychoanalysis except
    a. to rid the patient of his or her defenses.
    b. to increase self-understanding.
    c. to bring unconscious material into conscious awareness.
    d. to release pent-up emotions and unexpressed feelings.

18. Pavlov is to _____ as Skinner is to _____.
    a. *in vivo* desensitization; systematic desensitization
    b. systematic desensitization; *in vivo* desensitization
    c. operant conditioning; classical conditioning
    d. classical conditioning; operant conditioning

19. Psychotherapy outcome research indicates that
    a. clients who are young, attractive, verbal, intelligent, and successful tend to improve more in psychotherapy.
    b. if psychotherapy is going to be effective, it will be effective rather quickly.
    c. psychotherapy is generally effective when compared with no treatment at all.
    d. all of the above

20. Aversion therapy is a/an _____technique.
    a. classical conditioning
    b. operant conditioning
    c. cognitive-behavioral
    d. social skills training

21. _____ is one of the earliest examples of a spiritual or religious tradition of healing.
    a. Taboo death
    b. Exorcism
    c. Trephining
    d. Stoning

22. Research indicates that _____is the most effective approach to treating psychological disorders.
    a. humanistic psychotherapy
    b. psychodynamic psychotherapy
    c. cognitive behavior therapy
    d. research generally reveals few differences among approaches

23. The term "unconditional positive regard" refers to
    a. valuing clients for who they are and refraining from judging them.
    b. making positive comments to a client and never devaluing him or her as a person.
    c. the relationship between the client and therapist.
    d. none of the above

24. _____ has been the most promising avenue of biological treatment.
    a. Psychosurgery
    b. Classical conditioning
    c. Operant conditioning
    d. Psychopharmacology

25. In order for a finding to be statistically significant, it would need to occur by chance alone in less than
    a. one out of every five experiments.
    b. one out of every ten experiments.
    c. one out of every fifteen experiments.
    d. one out of every twenty experiments.

26. This method became the cornerstone of Freud's psychoanalysis.
    a. free association
    b. hypnosis
    c. catharsis
    d. interpretation

SHORT ANSWER

Answer the following short answer questions. Compare your work to the material presented in the text.

1. Compare and contrast the biological, psychodynamic, cognitive behavioral, and humanistic approaches to treating psychological disorders. In what ways might they be similar in working with a patient with depression? In what ways might they be different?

2. Discuss how the ideas of ego analysts differ from the original ideas of Freud. In what ways are they still similar?

3. Discuss some of the issues addressed by psychotherapy researchers.

4. Outline the design of the experimental method. Provide one example.

ANSWER KEY

MATCHING I

1. c	8. i	15. t	22. z
2. m	9. h	16. u	23. x
3. f	10. r	17. a	24. v
4. p	11. o	18. k	25. w
5. e	12. q	19. d	26. y
6. s	13. j	20. g	27. b
7. l	14. aa	21. n	

MATCHING II

a. 4	h. 17	o. 21	v. 23
b. 11	i. 6	p. 3	w. 10
c. 16	j. 22	q. 14	x. 25
d. 5	k. 2	r. 20	y. 26
e. 19	l. 13	s. 7	z. 24
f. 1	m. 15	t. 18	
g. 12	n. 9	u. 8	

MATCHING III

1. v	8. y	15. k	22. g
2. q	9. t	16. r	23. s
3. j	10. l	17. c	24. n
4. aa	11. u	18. o	25. h
5. p	12. f	19. bb	26. z
6. w	13. m	20. b	27. d
7. e	14. i	21. a	28. x

MATCHING IV

1. f	5. d	9. h	13. i
2. g	6. k	10. a	14. e
3. l	7. b	11. j	
4. c	8. n	12. m	

CONCEPT REVIEW

1. 87 percent
2. true
3. epilepsy
4. unilateral
5. bilateral
6. severe depression
7. false
8. makes them sleepy and disoriented
9. Prozac
10. alleviate symptoms
11. analyst's
12. to minimize their influence on free association
13. milder forms of depression and anxiety
14. power and closeness
15. balance
16. true
17. false
18. they do not generalize to uncontrolled environments
19. objective or scientific strategies
20. research
21. false
22. the patient might miss out on legitimate treatment
23. false
24. true
25. one third
26. true
27. young, attractive, verbal, intelligent, and successful
28. hope
29. true
30. relationship with the therapist
31. publishing
32. true
33. warmth
34. the parents
35. professional

MULTIPLE CHOICE

1. b	5. d	9. b	13. b	17. a	21. c	25. d
2. b	6. d	10. c	14. a	18. d	22. d	26. a
3. a	7. d	11. a	15. c	19. d	23. a	
4. c	8. a	12. c	16. b	20. a	24. d	

CHAPTER FOUR

CLASSIFICATION AND ASSESSMENT OF ABNORMAL BEHAVIOR

CHAPTER OUTLINE

OBJECTIVES

You should be able to:
1. Define classification system, assessment, and diagnosis.
2. Distinguish between categorical and dimensional approaches to classification.
3. Explain why the DSM-III represented a turning point in the diagnosis of psychiatric disorders.
4. Describe the axes utilized in the DSM-IV-TR.
5. Discuss the meaning and implications of reliability and validity in diagnosis and classification.
6. Discuss the advantages and limitations of interview data for assessment.
7. Discuss several observational procedures used in assessment.
8. Describe the strengths and weaknesses of the MMPI-2.

9. List several advantages and limitations of utilizing projective tests for assessment and diagnosis.
10. Describe the applications of psychophysiological assessment procedures and discuss the limitations of this approach.
11. Distinguish between static and dynamic brain imaging techniques.

MATCHING I

Answers are found at the end of this chapter. Match these terms and concepts with the definitions that follow:

a.	Assessment	p.	Reliability
b.	Diagnosis	q.	Rating scales
c.	Classification system	r.	Validity
d.	Categorical approach	s.	Kappa
e.	Dimensional approach	t.	Etiological validity
f.	Stigma	u.	Concurrent validity
g.	Culture-bound syndrome	v.	Predictive validity
h.	*Ataques de nervios*	w.	Behavioral coding systems
i.	Barnum effect	x.	Reactivity
j.	*Diagnostic and Statistical Manual of Mental Disorders* (DSM)	y.	Personality inventories
		z.	Actuarial interpretation
k.	*International Classification of Diseases* (ICD)	aa.	Projective tests
		bb.	Magnetic resonance imaging (MRI)
l.	Labeling theory	cc.	Positron emission tomography
m.	Multiaxial classification	dd.	Comorbidity
n.	Functional magnetic resonance imaging (fMRI)	ee.	*Minnesota Multiphasic Personality Inventory*
o.	Structured interviews		

1. _____ loss of control over emotions and behavior unique to Caribbean individuals triggered by changes in their social world
2. _____ a system for grouping together objects or organisms that share certain properties
3. _____ a system in which the person is rated with regard to several separate aspects of behavior or adjustment
4. _____ the process of gathering and organizing information about a person's behavior
5. _____ looks at the social context in which abnormal behavior occurs: sees mental disorders as maladaptive social roles
6. _____ assumes that distinctions between members of different categories are qualitative
7. _____ concerned with factors that contribute to the onset of the disorder
8. _____ the diagnostic system for mental disorders published by the World Health Organization
9. _____ describes the objects of classification in terms of continuous dimensions
10. _____ concerned with the present time and with correlations between the disorder and other symptoms, circumstances, and test procedures
11. _____ focus on the frequency of specific behavioral events, requiring fewer inferences on the part of the observer
12. _____ saying things about a specific person that are true of most people
13. _____ the diagnostic system for mental disorders published by the American Psychiatric Association

14. _____ a quick series of brain images that reflect second-to-second differences in blood flow to brain areas while engaged in cognitive tasks

15. _____ the identification or recognition of a disorder on the basis of its characteristic symptoms

16. _____ patterns of unusual thinking or behavior unique to a particular society that express distress

17. _____ an assessment interview that follows a specific question-and-answer format

18. _____ a statistic of reliability that reflects the proportion of agreement that occurred above and beyond what would have occurred by chance alone

19. _____ the meaning or systematic importance of a construct or measurement

20. _____ the most extensively used personality inventory

21. _____ a label that sets the person apart from others in a negative way

22. _____ concerned with the future and with the stability of the problem over time

23. _____ an assessment device wherein the observer makes judgments that place the person along a dimension

24. _____ objective tests consisting of a series of straightforward statements that the person uses to indicate how true or false they are in relation to him- or herself

25. _____ the consistency of measurements

26. _____ analysis of test results based on an explicit set of rules derived from empirical research

27. _____ a dynamic brain imaging technique using special radioactive elements to produce relatively detailed images of the brain, which can reflect changes in brain activity as a person performs various tasks

28. _____ personality tests in which the person is asked to interpret a series of ambiguous stimuli

29. _____ a brain imaging technique that passes electromagnetic phenomena through brain tissue to provide a static image of brain structures

30. _____ the simultaneous appearance of two or more disorders in the same person

31. _____ people altering their behavior, either intentionally or unintentionally, when they know that they are being observed

MATCHING II

Answers are found at the end of this chapter. Match these names with the descriptions of their contributions to the study of abnormal psychology:

 a. Stark Hathaway b. Hermann Rorschach

1. _____ developed the best-known projective test, the inkblot test
2. _____ developed the MMPI

CONCEPT REVIEW

Answers are found at the end of this chapter. After you have read and reviewed the material, test your comprehension by filling in the blanks or circling the correct answer.

1. In the field of psychopathology, assigning a diagnosis implies the etiology of the person's problem:

 true **false**

2. Classification systems can be based on descriptive or _____ similarities.

3. Which type of emphasis typically comes first in the development of scientific classification systems?

 etiological factors description

4. What were three criticisms of psychiatric classification systems during the 1950s and 1960s?

_____, _____, and _____

5. The major change that occurred in the third edition of the DSM was a focus on clinical description

rather than on

_____.

6. Labeling theory views symptoms of mental disorders as violations of unwritten social

_____.

7. Labeling theory predicts that people from lower status groups, like the impoverished, are

more   **less**   likely to receive a diagnosis.

8. The authors of your text conclude that labeling theory provides a good account for abnormal behavior:

true   **false**

9. How many diagnostic axes are there in the DSM-IV-TR? _____

10. The presence of general medical conditions are coded on one of the axes of a DSM-IV-TR diagnosis:

true false

11. The DSM-IV-TR   **encourages**   **discourages**   the consideration of cultural factors when

making a diagnosis.

12. Clinicians have been more willing to drop old categories in revisions of the DSM than to include new

categories: **true**   **false**

13. Comorbidity rates among mental disorders as defined in the DSM system are very low:

true   **false**

14. What are the three primary goals that guide most assessment procedures?

_____

15. The meaning or importance of an assessment procedure is known as its: **reliability**

validity

16. There are only a few select assessment procedures available to clinicians today: **true**   **false**

17. Clinical interviews provide clinicians with the opportunity to assess a person's appearance and

nonverbal behavior: **true**   **false**

18. Clinical interviews are either structured or _____.

19. One advantage of structured interviews is that anybody can conduct them, saving the expense of a

clinician's time: **true**   **false**

20. Clinical interviews are of limited use with young children: **true**   **false**

21. Observations can provide a more realistic view of behavior than do people's recollections of their

actions and feelings: **true**   **false**

22. One problem with observational procedures is that they can be time-consuming and expensive:

    true   **false**

23. The MMPI is the most extensively used personality inventory: **true**   **false**

24. One advantage of the MMPI is that it allows the clinician to use his or her intuition in coming up with scores on the clinical scales: **true**   **false**

25. A unique feature of the MMPI is the   **clinical**   **validity**   scales.

26. On the MMPI, interpretation of the high-point _____ is conducted.

27. The Rorschach test was based on which theory of personality?

    psychoanalytic   **cognitive behavioral**

28. One strength of the original Rorschach scoring system was its high reliability: **true**   **false**

29. Projective tests are more likely to be used by a therapist with which type of theoretical orientation?

    psychodynamic   **behavioral**

30. Brain imaging techniques are used to rule out _____ as a cause of behavioral or cognitive deficits.

MULTIPLE CHOICE

Answers are found at the end of this chapter. These multiple choice questions will test your understanding of the material presented in the chapter. Read each question and circle the letter representing the best answer.

1. A characteristic of all projective tests is
    a. a true-false response format.
    b. the use of a list of open-ended sentences that the individual must answer.
    c. the use of items describing various thoughts, feelings, and behaviors that the individual must rate.
    d. the use of ambiguous stimuli.

2. Which approach to classification is based on an ordered sequence or on quantitative measurements rather than qualitative judgments?
    a. dimensional approach
    b. categorical approach
    c. diagnostic approach
    d. interview approach

3. Which of the following is not coded on an axis of the DSM-IV-TR?
    a. global rating of adaptive functioning
    b. psychosocial and environmental problems
    c. general medical conditions that may be relevant to the patient's current behaviors or may affect treatment
    d. familial communication style

4. Which would not be considered a limitation of a clinical interview?

    a. The information gathered is subjective and may be influenced or distorted by errors in memory or perception.

    b. The person may be reluctant to directly share with the interviewer experiences that are embarrassing or socially undesirable.

    c. Interviews are expensive and time-consuming.

    d. People may not give a rational account of their problems due to limited verbal skills or psychosis.

5. Analyzing a test on the basis of an explicit set of rules based on empirical research is referred to as what type of procedure?

    a. actuarial

    b. self-report

    c. diagnostic

    d. cookbook

6. Which of the following does not reflect a rationale for classifying abnormal behavior?

    a. A diagnostic system can be used to help clinicians more effectively communicate with one another.

    b. A diagnostic system can be used to organize information that may be helpful for research purposes.

    c. A diagnostic system can be used to label people who are socially deviant.

    d. A diagnostic system can be used in making management and treatment decisions.

7. A criticism of psychiatric diagnosis in the 1950s and 1960s was that

    a. the system in use was too detailed and included too many categories.

    b. the system was too descriptive and did not make assumptions about etiology.

    c. once labeled with a diagnosis, individuals did not receive the appropriate treatment.

    d. once labeled with a diagnosis, an individual might be motivated to continue to act in a manner expected from someone who is mentally ill.

8. When an observer is asked to make judgments about some aspect of an individual's behavior along a dimension, the observer would be using

    a. a projective instrument.

    b. a rating scale.

    c. a self-report inventory.

    d. a structured interview.

9. Interpretation of a person's responses to the MMPI-2 is based upon

    a. reviewing the clinical scale for which the person received the highest score.

    b. reading through all of the inventory items and noting how the person answered each one.

    c. reviewing the clinical scale for which the person received the lowest score.

    d. examining the pattern of scale scores, paying particular attention to those scales that have elevated scores.

10. An example of a type of observational procedure would be

    a. the Rorschach test.

    b. the MMPI-2.

    c. a behavioral coding system.

    d. dynamic brain imaging.

11. Which would not be considered a primary goal of assessment?
    a. making predictions
    b. reconstructing people's developmental history
    c. planning interventions
    d. evaluating interventions

12. An advantage of the MMPI-2 is that
    a. it provides information about the individual's test-taking attitude.
    b. it assesses a wide range of problems that would take several hours to review in an interview.
    c. it is scored objectively and is not influenced by the clinician's personal opinion about the individual.
    d. all of the above

13. How many axes are included in the DSM-IV-TR?
    a. three
    b. four
    c. five
    d. six

14. The most commonly used procedure in psychological assessment is
    a. self-report inventories.
    b. projective testing.
    c. clinical interview.
    d. behavioral observation.
    e.

15. Projective techniques place considerable emphasis upon which of the following?
    a. the importance of unconscious motivations such as conflicts and impulses
    b. the importance of familial values that may influence the person's behavior
    c. the presence of symptoms which suggest that the person has lost contact with reality and is presently psychotic
    d. the importance of the person's cultural background in understanding his or her personality

16. Which type of study could be used to validate a clinical syndrome?
    a. a follow-up study that demonstrated a distinctive course or outcome
    b. a family study supporting that the syndrome "breeds true"
    c. a study demonstrating an association between the clinical syndrome and an underlying biochemical abnormality
    d. all of the above

17. An advantage of psychophysiological assessment is that
    a. these types of procedures do not depend on self-report and may be less likely to be under the person's control.
    b. physiological reactivity and stability are very consistent across populations.
    c. physiological assessment is less expensive and less time-consuming than the use of personality inventories.
    d. physiological procedures are frequently used in clinical settings.

18. What would be considered an advantage of a structured clinical interview compared to a regular clinical interview?
    a. It provides the interviewer with a series of systematic questions that allow for the collection of important diagnostic information.
    b. It allows for the establishment of a better therapeutic rapport with the client.
    c. It allows the interviewer flexibility in gathering information.
    d. all of the above

19. A limitation of brain-imaging procedures is that
    a. brain-imaging procedures can be used only with certain populations.
    b. although useful for research, brain-imaging procedures cannot be used for diagnostic purposes because norms have not yet been established.
    c. brain-imaging procedures tend to give imprecise information.
    d. the results of brain-imaging procedures tend to be overly responsive to outside factors such as whether the person is presently medicated.

20. Which of the following problems could not be assessed through the use of an observational measure?
    a. hand-washing
    b. crying
    c. low self-esteem
    d. hitting, punching, or spitting in school

21. A limitation of the use of projective tests is that
    a. information obtained from projective tests tends to duplicate what can already be obtained from a clinical interview.
    b. projective tests cannot be used with children.
    c. projective tests cannot be used with psychotic individuals.
    d. the reliability of scoring and interpretation appears to be low.

22. Which type of study could be used to demonstrate the reliability of a set of diagnostic criteria?
    a. a study demonstrating that clinicians using the same set of criteria arrived at the same diagnosis for the same set of individuals
    b. a study supporting that individuals with the same diagnosis responded to the same kind of treatment
    c. a study supporting that the set of diagnostic criteria could be meaningful to other cultures when properly translated
    d. all of the above

23. The L (Lie) Scale of the MMPI-2 is an example of which type of scale?
    a. reactivity
    b. clinical
    c. projective
    d. validity

24. The first two axes of the DSM-IV-TR primarily focus on
    a. symptomatic behaviors.
    b. family functioning.
    c. medical history.
    d. intrapsychic functioning.

25. Which would not be considered a drawback of using a physiological assessment measure?
    a. The equipment used may be intimidating to certain people.
    b. Physiological responses can be influenced by many outside factors such as age and medication.
    c. Physiological response measures have not demonstrated adequate validity.
    d. The stability of physiological response systems varies from person to person.

SHORT ANSWER
Answer the following short answer questions. Compare your work to the material presented in the text.

1. Review examples of both scientific and nonscientific factors that affect the development of diagnostic systems. When do you believe nonscientific factors play an important role in this process?

2. Describe the major purposes of clinical assessment. What are the major assumptions regarding the nature of human behavior upon which the assessment process is based?

3. Assume the role of a clinician who has just received a call from a potential client. The problem for which the client is seeking treatment is depression. What assessment procedures reviewed in your chapter could you use to determine whether or not the client is depressed? What type of information would you expect to obtain from each method?

ANSWER KEY

MATCHING I

1.	h	12.	i	23.	q
2.	c	13.	j	24.	y
3.	m	14.	n	25.	p
4.	a	15.	b	26.	z
5.	l	16.	g	27.	cc
6.	d	17.	o	28.	aa
7.	t	18.	s	29.	bb
8.	k	19.	r	30.	dd
9.	e	20.	ee	31.	x
10.	u	21.	f		
11.	w	22.	v		

MATCHING II

1.	b	2.	a

CONCEPT REVIEW

1.	false	9.	five
2.	structural	10.	true
3.	description	11.	encourages
4.	lack of consistency in diagnoses among clinicians; diagnoses are problems in living, not medical disorders; labels might increase maladaptive behavior	12.	false
		13.	false
		14.	making predictions, planning interventions, and evaluating interventions
5.	theories of psychopathology	15.	validity
6.	rules	16.	false
7.	more	17.	true
8.	false	18.	nondirective
19.	false	25.	validity
20.	true	26.	MMPI
21.	true	27.	psychodynamic
22.	true	28.	false
23.	true	29.	psychodynamic
24.	false	30.	brain tumors

MULTIPLE CHOICE

1. d	6. c	11. b	16. d	21. d
2. a	7. d	12. d	17. a	22. a
3. d	8. b	13. c	18. a	23. d
4. c	9. d	14. c	19. b	24. a
5. a	10. c	15. a	20. c	25. c

CHAPTER FIVE

MOOD DISORDERS AND SUICIDE

CHAPTER OUTLINE

OBJECTIVES

You should be able to:
1. Distinguish between major depressive disorder and dysthymic disorder.
2. Define emotion, affect, mood, depression, and mania.
3. Identify the major emotional, cognitive, and somatic symptoms involved in depression.
4. Describe the features of bipolar disorder and cyclothymic disorder and distinguish between them.
5. Discuss the etiology of depression.
6. Discuss several perspectives related to the etiology and treatment of mood disorders.
7. Discuss the interaction between social, psychological, and biological factors in the development and maintenance of mood disorders.
8. Discuss the effectiveness of several treatment approaches for depression and bipolar disorders.
9. Discuss Durkheim's theory of suicide.
10. Discuss the incidence of suicide and theoretical perspectives on its causes.
11. Discuss suicide prevention efforts.

MATCHING I

Answers are found at the end of this chapter. Match these terms and concepts with the definitions that follow:

a.	Emotion		m.	Euphoria
b.	Affect		n.	Somatic symptoms
c.	Mood		o.	Psychomotor retardation
d.	Depression		p.	Dementia praecox
e.	Depressed mood		q.	Dysthymia
f.	Clinical depression		r.	Hypomania
g.	Mania		s.	Cyclothymia
h.	Mood disorders		t.	Melancholia
i.	Unipolar mood disorder		u.	Seasonal affective disorder
j.	Bipolar mood disorder		v.	Rapid cycling
k.	Manic-depressive disorder		w.	Bipolar II disorder
l.	Dysphoria/dysphoric mood		x.	Psychotic features

1. _____ a mood disorder with onset of episodes associated with changes in the seasons
2. _____ a state of incredible well-being and elation
3. _____ a term for a mood or a clinical syndrome that involves sadness, despair, and disappointment
4. _____ at least four episodes of mood disturbance in a year
5. _____ chronic, mild depression lasting for at least two years
6. _____ observable behaviors associated with a person's feelings
7. _____ a former term for schizophrenia
8. _____ a disturbance in mood that can include elation, decreased need for sleep, pressured speech, and inflated self-esteem
9. _____ symptoms related to bodily functions, like sleep and appetite disturbance
10. _____ an especially severe form of depression
11. _____ subjective states of feeling, often accompanied by physiological changes

12. ____ a category of mental disorders involving episodes of disturbance of mood, characterized either by clinical depression or mania

13. ____ chronic, mild form of bipolar disorder with episodes of hypomania and depression lasting at least two years

14. ____ a pervasive, long-standing emotional response that affects a person's perception of the world

15. ____ a classification of mood disorder involving periods of depression only

16. ____ a classification of mood disorder involving periods of depression and mania, or sometimes mania alone

17. ____ a mood state involving sadness and despair that is not a psychiatric syndrome

18. ____ the former term for bipolar disorder

19. ____ a psychiatric syndrome involving sadness and despair as well as fatigue, sleep disturbance, loss of energy, or changes in appetite

20. ____ a state of depression, despondency, or sadness

21. ____ an episode of increased energy that is not as extreme as mania

22. ____ significant slowing of movements or speech

23. ____ hallucinations or delusions

24. ____ at least one major depressive episode, at least one hypomanic episode, and no manic episodes

MATCHING II

Answers are found at the end of this chapter. Match these terms and concepts with the definitions that follow:

1. Remission
2. Relapse
3. Depressive triad
4. Schema
5. Causal attributions
6. Hopelessness
7. Ruminative style
8. Distracting style
9. HPA axis
10. DST
11. Analogue studies
12. Tricyclics
13. MAO-inhibitors
14. SSRIs
15. Lithium carbonate
16. Electroconvulsive therapy
17. Suicidal ideation

a. ____ studies that focus on behaviors that are similar to mental disorders, or features of mental disorders: often animal models of psychopathology

b. ____ focusing one's attention on an unpleasant mood

c. ____ a category of antidepressant medication which must not be taken with certain foods, especially cheese and chocolate

d. ____ a theory that depression may be related to a person's expectation that good things will not happen and bad things will, regardless of his or her actions

e. ____ a lasting and highly organized cognitive structure that influences how people perceive and interpret events in their environment

f. ____ a period of recovery from a mental disorder

g. ____ thoughts of suicide

h. ____ a medication often used to treat bipolar disorder

i. ____ diverting one's attention from an unpleasant mood

j. ____ a pathway in the endocrine system that regulates hormone secretions by the adrenal glands: may be involved in the etiology of depression

k. ____ a series of treatments in which electric current is run through the patient's brain: effective in the treatment of severe depression
l. ____ the return of active symptoms in a person who had recovered from a previous episode
m. ____ used to study endocrine dysfunction in people with mood disorders: half of depressed patients show an abnormal response to this test
n. ____ a new class of antidepressants which have fewer side effects than older medications
o. ____ an older class of antidepressants that benefit many depressed people
p. ____ a person's beliefs relating to explanations of an event
q. ____ negative, demeaning views of the self, the world, and the future

MATCHING III
Answers are found at the end of this chapter. Match these names with the descriptions of their contributions to the study of abnormal psychology:

a. Aaron Beck   b. Emil Kraeplin   c. Emile Durkheim

1. ____ conceptualized depression as cognitive in origin, arising from distortions, errors, and biases common in the thinking of depressed people
2. ____ identified four types of suicide based on the type of society in which the person lives
3. ____ proposed the first classification system for mental disorders, dividing disorders into dementia praecox and manic-depressive psychosis

CONCEPT REVIEW
Answers are found at the end of this chapter. After you have read and reviewed the material, test your comprehension by filling in the blanks or circling the correct answer.

1. Major depression is the leading cause of disability worldwide: **true   false**

2. Many depressed and manic patients are irritable: **true   false**

3. People who are depressed often have trouble with their thinking. They have trouble

_____, and can't make _____.

4. The depressive triad is typical of depressed patients. They focus on the negative aspects of

_____, _____, and _____.

5. People with _____ can be easily distracted, incoherent, and grandiose.

6. People with _____ may be preoccupied with thoughts of suicide.

7. Sometimes depressed people have difficulty falling asleep and wake up throughout the night or very early in the morning. However, it is more common for a depressed person to sleep much more than usual: **true   false**

8. Depressed people typically eat more than usual: **true   false**

9. People with _____ are less likely to initiate sexual activity.

10. List three types of disorders that have high comorbidity with mood disorders (and are also found in higher rates than expected among relatives of people with mood disorders):

    _____, _____, and

    _____.

11. Some people with mood disorders experience psychotic symptoms during their episodes of depression or mania: **true   false**

12. Most people with unipolar disorder experience only a single, isolated episode during their lifetimes:

    true   false

13. People with Bipolar I Disorder have clear-cut _____ episodes, while people with Bipolar II Disorder do not.

14. Rapid cycling bipolar patients typically do not respond as well to treatment as other bipolar patients:

    true   false

15. People with seasonal depression are more likely to gain weight and sleep more than people with non-seasonal depression patterns: **true   false**

16. The average age of onset of a first episode of unipolar disorder is:

    adolescence (15–25)   young adulthood (25–35)   middle age (40–50)

17. The average number of lifetime depressive episodes of people with unipolar disorder is _____.

18. A person's risk of _____ of depression goes down the longer they are in remission.

19. The average age of onset of a first episode of bipolar disorder is:

    adolescence (15–25)   young adulthood (25–35)   middle age (40–50)

20. People with bipolar disorder tend to have more episodes than those with unipolar disorder:

    true   false

21. Lifetime risk for major depressive disorder is _____ percent; for dysthymia is _____ percent; and for bipolar disorder is _____ percent.

22. Most people with mood disorders do not seek treatment: **true   false**

23. Which sex is more likely to experience major depression and dysthymia? _____

24. There are no significant gender differences in rates of _____.

25. Some studies indicate similar frequencies of mood disorders in different countries and cultures, but differences in specific symptoms. For example, depressed people in Europe and North America are more likely to exhibit _____, while depressed people in non-Western countries, like China, are more likely to exhibit _____.

26. Mood disorders are less common among the elderly than among young and middle-aged adults:

    true   **false**

27. The frequency of depression has decreased in recent years: **true**   **false**

28. Prospective research design has demonstrated that which one, depression or stressful events, comes first? _____

29. Research has shown that the _____ of an important person or role precipitates depression.

30. When severe events were linked to feelings of _____ or _____, women were particularly at risk for depression.

31. Bipolar patients who leave the hospital to live with hostile, critical family members are more likely to experience _____.

32. Research indicates that communities with the highest rates of severe events have the highest prevalence of _____.

33. Beck described several types of cognitive distortions he thought were related to depression. Research has shown that these distortions are present during an episode of depression, but not before or after an episode: **true**   **false**

34. A depressogenic attributional style is characterized by a tendency to explain negative events, like failing an exam, in which of the following terms: **external/internal**

stable/unstable specific/global

35. College students who had negative cognitive styles at the beginning of freshman year were much more likely to develop _____.

36. Research has shown that depressed people actually do have smaller and less supportive social networks, and that it is not just their perceptions but the actual situation that is negative:

true   false

37. People with a ruminative style have **more   less**   depression that people with a distracting style. Men are   **more   less**   likely to have a ruminative style than women.

38. Among relatives of people with unipolar disorder, there   **is   is not**   an increased risk for unipolar disorder, and there   **is   is not**   an increased risk for bipolar disorder.

39. Which disorder—major depressive disorder, bipolar disorder, or dysthymia—shows the highest rate of twin concordance (genetic heritability)? _____ Which shows the lowest?

    _____

40. Researchers think that the genetic influence on mood disorders is due to: **a single gene**

multiple genes

41. Stressful life events combined with a genetic predisposition to depression may lead to a mood disorder through abnormalities in the regulation of _____.

42. Current research on the role of neurotransmitters in the etiology of depression suggests that the early theories were too complex: **true   false**

43. There are approximately   **three   fifty   one hundred**   different kinds of neurotransmitters in the central nervous system.

44. Brain imaging studies have failed to find any differences in brain function related to mood:

   true   false

45. Rats exposed to stressful events in the laboratory develop symptoms similar to those of depressed people. Antidepressant drugs given to these animals can reverse or prevent these symptoms: **true   false**

46. In treating depressed people, _____ therapy focuses on changing the client's negative schemas and irrational beliefs, and _____ therapy focuses on changing current relationships.

47. Antidepressants typically are effective within twenty-four hours if they are going to be helpful at all:

   true   false

48. Antidepressant medication is far more effective in treating depression than either cognitive or interpersonal therapy: **true   false**

49. Among patients with seasonal affective disorder, it is difficult to evaluate whether exposure to broad-spectrum light is effective in reducing depression because of difficulty creating a convincing placebo condition: **true   false**

50. ECT almost always interferes with memory: **true   false**

51. What percentage of people with mood disorders will eventually commit suicide?

   1–3 percent   15–20 percent 50–55 percent

52. The rate of suicide has been increasing among adolescents in recent decades: **true   false**

53. There are gender differences in rates of suicide; more   **males   females**   make suicide attempts, and more **males   females**   actually complete a suicide.

54. Which group has the highest rate of suicide?

   young black men   middle-aged white women   older white men

55. Suicide runs in families: **true   false**

56. Media coverage of a suicide increases the rate of suicides committed: **true   false**

57. Suicide hotlines decrease suicide rates: **true   false**

MULTIPLE CHOICE

Answers are found at the end of this chapter. These multiple choice questions will test your understanding of the material presented in the chapter. Read each question and circle the letter representing the best answer.

1. Which of the following is not a general area describing the signs and symptoms representative of mood disorders?
   a. emotional symptoms
   b. psychological symptoms
   c. somatic symptoms
   d. cognitive symptoms

2. A promising form of treatment for seasonal affective disorder is
   a. light therapy.
   b. lithium.
   c. nutritional therapy.
   d. meditation.

3. What is the percent of completed suicides that occur as a result of a primary mood disorder?
   a. under 15 percent
   b. under 30 percent
   c. over 50 percent
   d. over 78 percent

4. Which is an example of a somatic symptom?
   a. suicidal ideation
   b. loss of interest
   c. sleep disturbance
   d. low self-esteem

5. An advantage of an analogue study is that
   a. experimental procedures may be employed.
   b. it is easy to generalize the results beyond the laboratory.
   c. human subjects are not used.
   d. it is easy to reproduce a clinical disorder in the laboratory.

6. Which symptom would not be characteristic of clinical depression?
   a. racing thoughts
   b. loss of energy
   c. feelings of worthlessness
   d. difficulty concentrating

7. Why might it be more difficult to diagnose depression in the elderly?
   a. Cognitive impairment or other problems common in the elderly may mask the symptoms of depression.
   b. The elderly are more reluctant to seek treatment for depression.
   c. The symptoms and features of depression change as age increases.
   d. The elderly are less likely to report somatic symptoms associated with depression.

8. Which of the following is NOT a common theme in suicide?
    a. feelings of unbearable psychological pain
    b. feelings of helplessness or hopelessness
    c. need for escape
    d. feeling needed by too many people

9. Which age group has experienced increased rates of suicide since the 1960s?
    a. adolescents
    b. people who are in their thirties
    c. people between the ages of forty-five and fifty-five years
    d. people over sixty-five

10. When two loci occupy positions close together on the same chromosome, they are
    a. polygenic.
    b. matched.
    c. homogenous.
    d. linked.

11. Which is a social factor which may contribute to the onset of depression?
    a. the belief that one cannot control events in one's life
    b. cognitive distortions
    c. stressful life events
    d. neuroendocrine disturbances

12. Which disorder is often comorbid with a mood disorder?
    a. schizophrenia
    b. dissociative disorder
    c. paranoid personality disorder
    d. alcoholism

13. What age would a person most likely have a first episode of bipolar disorder?
    a. 18–23 years
    b. 28–33 years
    c. 38–43 years
    d. 48–53 years

14. Which of the following is a common element of suicide?
    a. The common goal of suicide is cessation of consciousness.
    b. The common emotion in suicide is anger.
    c. The common purpose of suicide is to get revenge.
    d. The common stressor in suicide is financial difficulties.

15. Decreased need for sleep, pressure to keep talking, grandiosity, and distractibility are common symptoms of which disorder?
    a. mania
    b. dysthymia
    c. major depression
    d. cyclothymia

16. Advantages of selective serotonin reuptake inhibitors include all of the following except
    a. fewer side effects.
    b. decreased likelihood of multiple episodes of depression.
    c. they are less dangerous in the case of an overdose.
    d. ease of ingestion.

17. Which is an example of a depressogenic premise?
    a. "I find time in my day to relax."
    b. "I should be at the top of my performance at all times."
    c. "I congratulate myself when I finish a hard day at work."
    d. "I try to forgive myself when I screw things up."

18. Research on electroconvulsive therapy supports the idea that
    a. memory impairment may be permanent.
    b. only bipolar depressed patients respond to ECT.
    c. ECT is as effective as a placebo.
    d. some depressed patients may respond to ECT more than to antidepressants.

19. Which statement is not true about unipolar depression?
    a. Episodes of unipolar depression tend to be longer in duration compared to episodes of depression in bipolar disorder.
    b. At least half of unipolar patients will experience more than one episode.
    c. Female patients tend to relapse more quickly than male patients.
    d. Unipolar patients have their first episode at a much younger age than do bipolar patients.

20. Some depressed people exhibit a depressogenic attributional style that is characterized by the tendency to explain negative events in terms of
    a. internal, stable, global factors.
    b. internal, unstable, specific factors.
    c. external, unstable, specific factors.
    d. external, stable, specific factors.

21. A standard part of cognitive treatment for depression would be
    a. gaining insight into suppressed anger in close relationships.
    b. developing a better understanding of family relationships.
    c. substituting more flexible self-statements for rigid and absolute ones.
    d. nondirect discussions of unexpressed emotions.

22. An important assumption of the hopelessness theory of depression is
    a. loss of a parent early in life increases risk for depression.
    b. desirable events will not occur regardless of what the person does.
    c. depressed people are more likely to feel in control of the events in their lives.
    d. depressed people have a positive impact on other people's moods.

23. Which type of coping behavior is associated with longer and more severely depressed moods?
    a. processing style
    b. ruminative style
    c. intellectual style
    d. distracting style

24. Studies investigating genetic transmission of mood disorders indicate that
   a. genetic factors are more influential in bipolar disorders than major depressive disorder.
   b. the concordance rate for mood disorders is higher for DZ than MZ twins.
   c. there is no increased risk of bipolar disorder for relatives of bipolar patients.
   d. genetic factors account for about 90 percent of the variance for dysthymia.

25. How do depressed people often respond to a test dose of dexamethasone?
   a. They show a suppression of cortisol secretion.
   b. They show a failure of suppression of cortisol secretion.
   c. They show a dramatic increase of cortisol secretion.
   d. They show an abnormal fluctuation of cortisol secretion.

26. An example of a DSM-IV-TR subtype of depression is
   a. retarded.
   b. dysphoric.
   c. narcissistic.
   d. melancholic.

27. Which of the following areas of the brain have not been found to show changes in activity when mood is disturbed?
   a. cerebellum
   b. amygdala
   c. hypothalamus
   d. limbic system

SHORT ANSWER
Answer the following short answer questions. Compare your work to the material presented in the text.

1. Discuss the controversy regarding the definition of mood disorders. What issues are involved? Would you advocate the use of sub-typing? Why?

2. Discuss the methodological problems in studying mood disorder across cultures. How have cross-cultural investigations assisted our understanding of mood disorders?

3. Describe the treatments for depression that employ cognitive and interpersonal factors.

4. Discuss analogue studies. What are their advantages and limitations?

5. Discuss the biological factors in the etiology of mood disorders.

ANSWER KEY

MATCHING I

1. u	7. p	13. s	19. f
2. m	8. g	14. c	20. l
3. d	9. n	15. i	21. r
4. v	10. t	16. j	22. o
5. q	11. a	17. e	23. x
6. b	12. h	18. k	24. w

MATCHING II

a. 11	f. 1	k. 16	p. 5
b. 7	g. 17	l. 2	q. 3
c. 13	h. 15	m. 10	
d. 6	i. 8	n. 14	
e. 4	j. 9	o. 12	

MATCHING III

1. a   2. c   3. b

CONCEPT REVIEW

1. true
2. true
3. concentrating, decisions
4. themselves, their environment, the future
5. mania
6. depression
7. false
8. false
9. depression
10. alcoholism, eating disorders, anxiety disorders
11. true
12. false
13. manic
14. true
15. true
16. middle age (40–50)
17. 5 or 6
18. relapse
19. young adulthood (25–35)
20. true
21. 5; 3; 1
22. true

23. females
24. bipolar disorder
25. guilt and suicidal feelings; somatic feelings
26. true
27. false
28. stressful event
29. loss
30. humiliation; entrapment
31. relapse
32. depression
33. false
34. internal, stable, global
35. major depressive disorder
36. true
37. more; less
38. is; is not
39. bipolar disorder; dysthymia
40. multiple genes
41. hormones
42. false
43. one hundred

44. false
45. true
46. cognitive, interpersonal
47. false
48. false
49. false
50. true

51. 15–20 percent
52. true
53. females, males
54. older white men
55. true
56. true
57. false

MULTIPLE CHOICE

1. b	8. d	15. a	22. b
2. a	9. a	16. b	23. b
3. c	10. d	17. b	24. a
4. c	11. c	18. d	25. a
5. a	12. d	19. d	26. d
6. a	13. b	20. a	27. a
7. a	14. a	21. c	

CHAPTER SIX

ANXIETY DISORDERS

CHAPTER OUTLINE

Overview
Symptoms
    Anxiety
    Excessive Worry
    Panic Attacks
    Phobias
    Obsessions and Compulsions
Diagnosis
    Brief Historical Perspective
    Contemporary Classification
    "Lumpers" and "Splitters"
    Course and Outcome
Frequency
    Prevalence
    Comorbidity
    Gender Differences
    Anxiety across the Lifespan
    Cross-Cultural Comparisons
Causes
    Adaptive and Maladaptive Fears
    Social Factors
    Psychological Factors
    Biological Factors
Treatment
    Psychological Interventions
    Biological Interventions
Summary

OBJECTIVES

You should be able to:
1. Define anxiety and describe its symptoms and associated features.
2. Define and describe panic disorder. Distinguish panic attacks from other types of anxiety.
3. Compare specific phobias with generalized anxiety disorder.
4. Define obsessions and compulsions.
5. Describe the historical connection between anxiety and neurosis.
6. Discuss the manner in which DSM-IV-TR classifies panic disorder, specific phobia, social phobia, generalized anxiety disorder, obsessive-compulsive disorder, and agoraphobia.
7. Discuss the prevalence of anxiety disorders.
8. Understand the role of preparedness in anxiety and anxiety disorders.
9. Recognize the role of social factors in the development of anxiety disorders.

10. Describe several causal hypotheses regarding anxiety disorders.
11. Recognize the role of neurochemistry in anxiety disorders.
12. Describe the various treatment approaches for anxiety disorders.

MATCHING I

Answers are found at the end of this chapter. Match these terms and concepts with the definitions that follow:

a.	Fear	l.	Panic disorder
b.	Anxiety	m.	Obsessions
c.	Worry	n.	Compulsions
d.	Panic Attack	o.	Generalized anxiety disorder
e.	Phobia	p.	Catastrophic misinterpretation
f.	Agoraphobia	q.	Situational exposure
g.	Social phobia	r.	Interoceptive exposure
h.	Specific phobia	s.	Thought suppression
i.	Preparedness model	t.	Pharmacological challenge procedures
j.	Anxious apprehension	u.	Decatastrophisizing
k.	Neurosis	v.	Breathing retraining

1. _____ a psychoanalytic term describing persistent emotional disturbances, such as anxiety or depression, in which anxiety is a major component
2. _____ a sudden, overwhelming experience of focused terror
3. _____ an emotion experienced in the face of real, immediate danger
4. _____ phobia of public spaces, or being in situations where escape might be difficult
5. _____ phobia cued by doing something, such as speaking or eating, in front of other people who might scrutinize the performance
6. _____ an emotional reaction out of proportion to threats from the environment
7. _____ a phobia cued by the presence of a specific object or situation
8. _____ persistent, irrational fears associated with a specific object or situation that lead the person to avoid the feared stimulus
9. _____ organisms are biologically predisposed, on the basis of neural pathways, to learn certain types of associations more quickly
10. _____ a more or less uncontrollable sequence of negative, emotional thoughts and images concerned with possible future danger
11. _____ a mental disorder consisting of recurring panic attacks
12. _____ maladaptive anxiety characterized by intense, generalized negative emotion, uncontrollability, and self-preoccupation
13. _____ exploring the client's worst-case scenarios to show that they worry about a greatly exaggerated outcome that is illogical
14. _____ repetitive, unwanted, intrusive thoughts, images, or impulses
15. _____ an active attempt to stop thinking about something that often leads to the paradoxical effect of an increase in strong emotions associated with unpleasant thoughts
16. _____ repetitive, ritualistic behavior aimed at reducing anxiety: the person perceives it as irrational and tries to resist performing it but cannot
17. _____ a disorder characterized by excessive and uncontrollable worry about a number of events or activities and associated symptoms of arousal
18. _____ perceiving bodily sensations as a signal of an impending disastrous event, such as a heart attack

19. _____ a research procedure where a particular brain mechanism is stressed by the artificial administration of chemicals, which, if it leads to a panic attack, may implicate that brain mechanism in the etiology of panic attack

20. _____ a treatment for agoraphobia that involves repeatedly confronting the situation that has previously been avoided

21. _____ learning to take slow deep breaths

22. _____ a treatment for panic disorder which involves standardized exercises that produce sensations often felt during a panic attack

MATCHING II

Answers are found at the end of this chapter. Match these names with the descriptions of their contributions to the study of abnormal psychology:

1. David Clark   4. John Bowlby
2. Sigmund Freud   5. Kenneth Kendler
3. Thomas Borkovec

a. _____ studied the influence of genes and environment on anxiety disorders; found that their influences are fairly disorder-specific

b. _____ developed a theory of anxiety based on work with many patients; saw anxiety as warning the person that he or she is about to do or think something that is unacceptable and triggering ego defenses to prevent the thought or action

c. _____ saw anxiety as an innate response to separation or threat of separation from caregiver

d. _____ conducted research on catastrophic misinterpretation

e. _____ researched uncontrollable worry; conceptualized it as a verbal rather than visual event

CONCEPT REVIEW

Answers are found at the end of this chapter. After you have read and reviewed the material, test your comprehension by filling in the blanks or circling the correct answer.

1. There is considerable overlap between anxiety disorders and depression: **true   false**

2. Maladaptive anxiety, or anxious apprehension, consists of:_____,

_____, and _____.

3. Panic attacks have what type of onset: **gradual   sudden**

4. Panic attacks can happen when the person is in bed: **true   false**

5. Agoraphobia is different from other phobias in that agoraphobics are often afraid they will lose

_____ in public.

6. List two ways that obsessions are different from worry. Obsessions

_____ and _____.

7. People without a mental illness seldom experience obsessions: **true   false**

8. Which is a common compulsion: **scratching   coughing   cleaning**

9. People with anxiety disorders typically require hospitalization: **true   false**

10. The Freudian perspective of obsessive-compulsive disorder proposes that obsessive or compulsive behaviors serve to keep _____ impulses unconscious.

11. Experts who classify mental disorders may be described as "lumpers" or "splitters." Earlier classification systems used the   **lumping   splitting**   approach, and contemporary systems use the   **lumping   splitting**   approach.

12. Intrusive thoughts about real problems are one form of obsession: **true   false**

13. Panic disorder almost always goes away without treatment: **true   false**

14. Many patients with obsessive-compulsive disorder show improved levels of functioning over time, although they may continue to have some symptoms: **true   false**

15. Anxiety disorders are the most common form of mental disorder: **true   false**

16. What percentage of people who meet the criteria for one anxiety disorder also meet the criteria for another anxiety disorder?   **5 percent   20 percent   50 percent**

17. Depressive disorders and anxiety disorders show high comorbidity; another disorder with high comorbidity with anxiety disorders is _____.

18. Which are more likely to experience specific phobias: **men   women**

19. Which anxiety disorder occurs equally as often among men and women?

    _____

20. Men are more likely to relapse from an anxiety disorder than women: **true   false**

21. What age group has the lowest prevalence of anxiety disorders?

    _____

22. Anxiety disorders are almost entirely specific to people in Western societies; very few people in nonindustrialized countries experience them: **true   false**

23. An evolutionary perspective on anxiety disorders suggests that each type of disorder may be a _____ of a mechanism evolved to protect from a particular danger.

24. Stressful life events have been linked to both depressive disorders and anxiety disorders. People who experience an event involving _____ are more likely to experience depression and those who experience an event involving _____ are more likely to experience anxiety.

25. What type of anxiety disorder is often preceded by interpersonal conflict?

    _____

26. Children who experience adversity such as prenatal maternal stress, multiple maternal partner changes, parental indifference or neglect, or physical abuse are   **more   less**   likely to develop anxiety disorders as adults.

27. People who have anxiety disorders were more likely to have had an _____ attachment to their parents as toddlers.

28. Some psychologists argue that the mind has a _____ relating to fears that makes it easy to develop certain fears as they would have given a selective advantage.

29. Monitoring one's heart rate when aroused minimizes the fear response: **true   false**

30. People who believe they are able to control their environment are   **more   less**   likely to show symptoms of anxiety than people who believe they are helpless.

31. One example of the limitation of the catastrophic misinterpretation model of panic attacks is that they can occur while a person is _____.

32. Worry has the result of   **avoiding   increasing**   bodily feelings of anxiety.

33. In contrast to a depressed person, who is convinced that failure will occur, an anxious person is _____ that failure will occur.

34. Thought suppression has been found to be quite effective in reducing worrying and intrusive thoughts: **true   false**

35. Genetic factors account for   **0–5 percent   20–30 percent   80–90 percent**   of the variance in the transmission of generalized anxiety disorder.

36. When levels of the neurotransmitters serotonin and GABA are reduced, people report   **reduced   increased**   levels of anxiety.

37. Exposure to the feared object or situation is an effective treatment for anxiety disorders: **true   false**

38. The best form of behavior therapy for OCD is _____.

39. Cognitive therapy for anxiety disorders often involves analyzing errors in the patient's _____ as well as the process of _____.

40. Anti-anxiety medications are particularly effective in reducing a person's worry and problems with rumination: **true   false**

41. Benzodiazepines are more effective in the treatment of _____ and _____, and less effective in the treatment of _____ and _____.

42. Benzodiazepines are addictive: **true   false**

43. Antidepressants are effective in treating some anxiety disorders: **true   false**

MULTIPLE CHOICE

Answers are found at the end of this chapter. These multiple choice questions will test your understanding of the material presented in the chapter. Read each question and circle the letter representing the best answer.

1. The most frequently used types of minor tranquilizers for the treatment of anxiety disorders are
   a. tricyclics.
   b. benzodiazepines.
   c. serotonin.
   d. GABA inhibitors.

2. Which of the following is least likely to be present in an anxiety disorder?
   a. lack of insight
   b. social impairment
   c. significant personal distress
   d. negative emotional response

3. Which of the following is an example of a potential unconditioned stimulus which could contribute to the development of a phobia?
   a. loss of a relationship
   b. chronic occupational difficulties
   c. a painfully loud and unexpected noise
   d. a sad song

4. _____ is experienced in the face of real, immediate danger; _____ is a diffuse reaction that is out of proportion to threats from the environment.
   a. Anxiety; fear
   b. Worry; anxiety
   c. Fear; anxiety
   d. Worry; fear

5. Results of genetic research investigating transmission of anxiety disorders suggest that
   a. there appears to be no genetic component to OCD.
   b. all the different types of anxiety disorders are linked to just one genetic factor.
   c. both genetic and environmental factors are important in the development of anxiety disorders.
   d. almost all of the risk for anxiety disorders appears to be due to genetic factors.

6. The two most common types of compulsions are
   a. counting and repeating.
   b. cleaning and checking.
   c. sorting and counting.
   d. checking and writing.

7. A junior in college, Jimmy is acutely distressed at the thought of having to write in front of others. He is afraid that he will drop his pen, lose control of his writing, or somehow embarrass himself while other people are watching. This fear has impaired his ability to take notes in class. His diagnosis may be
   a. specific phobia.
   b. agoraphobia.
   c. generalized anxiety disorder.
   d. social phobia.

8. Which is true regarding the relationship between anxiety and other disorders?
   a. Substance dependence is rarely associated with anxiety disorders.
   b. Anxiety disorders overlap considerably with other anxiety disorders.
   c. Anxiety disorders usually overlap with psychotic disorders.
   d. Anxiety disorders do not appear to be associated with depressive disorders.

9. "Free-floating" anxiety would be most characteristic of which anxiety disorder?
   a. social phobia
   b. panic disorder
   c. obsessive-compulsive disorder
   d. generalized anxiety disorder

10. Which of the following is the most common type of abnormal behavior?
   a. anxiety disorders
   b. major depression
   c. generalized anxiety disorder
   d. dysthymia

11. Treatment for panic disorder that involves purposefully inducing dizziness, lightheadedness, or other physical sensations that are similar to those experienced during a panic attack is called
   a. psychopharmacology.
   b. relaxation and breathing retraining.
   c. systematic desensitization.
   d. interoceptive exposure.

12. Specific phobias may be best understood in terms of learning experiences. The association between the object and intense fear can develop through all but which of the following?
   a. direct experience
   b. observational learning
   c. exposure to fear—irrelevant stimuli
   d. exposure to warnings about dangerous situations

13. Which of the following is not consistent with Freud's model of anxiety?
   a. Repression is the product of anxiety.
   b. Anxiety is the result of a harsh superego in conflict with the defense mechanisms that are employed by the ego.
   c. The specific form of overt symptoms is determined by the defense mechanisms that are employed by the ego.
   d. Different types of anxiety disorders can be distinguished by many factors within the analytic framework: for example, the developmental stage at which the person experiences problems.

14. Anxiety disorder categories did not emerge in psychiatric classifications during the last century primarily because
    a. the prevalence of anxiety disorders was much lower during the last century.
    b. they were considered to be neurological disorders.
    c. very few cases of anxiety disorders required institutionalization.
    d. physicians were not trained to recognize the symptoms of anxiety disorders.

15. Which of the following is not a symptom of a panic attack?
    a. feeling of choking
    b. trembling
    c. nausea
    d. headache

16. Research into the relationship between stressful life events and anxiety disorders suggests that
    a. the onset of agoraphobia may be associated with interpersonal conflict.
    b. marital distress is associated with the onset of simple phobia.
    c. the onset of agoraphobia may be associated with the experience of a conditioning event, such as a sudden painful injury.
    d. severe loss is associated with the onset of an anxiety disorder.

17. Which cognitive factor shares an important relationship with panic attacks?
    a. perception of control over events in one's environment
    b. thought suppression
    c. cognitive minimization of traumatic events
    d. all-or-none thinking about future events

18. Which is not included in the DSM-IV-TR's classification of anxiety disorders?
    a. panic disorder
    b. agoraphobia
    c. cyclothymia
    d. obsessive-compulsive disorder

19. If a panic attack only occurs in the presence of a particular stimulus, it is said to be
    a. a situationally cued attack.
    b. an anticipated attack.
    c. a below-threshold attack.
    d. a cognitively processed attack.

20. Karen has consistent worries that she is going to lose her job, that something is going to happen to her husband, and that her health may take a turn for the worse. She knows that her worries are causing friction in her marriage, but she feels she cannot control them. Although she has always been a "worrier," the intensity and frequency of her worries has worsened in the past year. Her diagnosis may be
    a. agoraphobia.
    b. panic disorder.
    c. generalized anxiety disorder.
    d. simple phobia.

21. The most serious adverse side effect of benzodiazepines is
    a. heart palpitations.
    b. significant weight gain.
    c. necessary dietary restrictions.
    d. their potential for addiction.

22. The types of symptoms most characteristic of a panic attack are
    a. interpersonal difficulties.
    b. physical symptoms.
    c. emotional reactions.
    d. cognitive reactions.

23. Cross-cultural research on anxiety disorders suggests that
    a. anxiety disorders are not experienced in certain cultures.
    b. phobic avoidance is the most commonly reported symptom across cultures.
    c. the focus of typical anxiety complaints can vary dramatically across cultures.
    d. anxiety disorders are more common in preliterate cultures.

24. An important consideration in diagnosing panic disorder is that the person must
    a. experience recurrent, situationally cued panic attacks.
    b. experience recurrent panic attacks in anticipation of a feared event.
    c. report the experience of feeling out of control.
    d. experience recurrent unexpected panic attacks.

25. Which of the following is not included in the DSM-IV-TR as a criterion to establish the boundary
    between normal behavior and compulsive rituals?
    a. The rituals cause marked distress.
    b. The rituals can be observed by other people.
    c. The rituals interfere with normal occupational and social functioning.
    d. The rituals take more than one hour per day to perform.
26. Which of the following would be a typical situation that would cause problems for an agoraphobic?
    a. traveling on the subway
    b. speaking to a friend on the phone
    c. cleaning the house
    d. encountering a snake

27. According to recent research, what percentage of the people who qualify for an anxiety disorder
    diagnosis actually seek treatment for their disorder?
    a. 15 percent
    b. 25 percent
    c. 40 percent
    d. 50 percent

28. What is an important difference between compulsions and some addictive behaviors such as
gambling?
    a. Addictive behaviors reduce anxiety more effectively than compulsions.
    b. Compulsions are more resistant to treatment.
    c. Addictive behaviors are not repetitive in nature.
    d. Compulsions reduce anxiety but they do not produce pleasure.

29. Women are about twice as likely as men to experience all but which of the following anxiety disorders?
   a. OCD
   b. agoraphobia
   c. GAD
   d. panic disorder

SHORT ANSWER

Answer the following short answer questions. Compare your work to the material presented in the text.

1. Learning processes have been associated with the etiology of phobias, while cognitive factors have been used to explain the development of panic attacks. Review several learning and cognitive theories that account for each type of disorder. Do differences in etiological processes imply that these disorders are unrelated? Why or why not?

2. Discuss the relationship between anxiety and depression. Do you believe anxiety and depression are separate types of disorders, or do you think they represent different manifestations of the same problem? What evidence supports your position?

3. Consider the following psychological interventions used for the treatment of anxiety disorders: desensitization, situational and interoceptive exposure, prolonged exposure and response prevention, and cognitive therapy. Select an anxiety disorder and discuss how you would approach the treatment of this disorder. Which intervention technique(s) would you choose? Why?

ANSWER KEY

MATCHING I

1. k	7. h	13. u	19. t
2. d	8. e	14. m	20. q
3. a	9. i	15. s	21. v
4. f	10. c	16. n	22. r
5. g	11. l	17. o	
6. b	12. j	18. p	

MATCHING II

a. 4	c. 5	e. 1
b. 2	d. 3	

CONCEPT REVIEW

1. true
2. high levels of negative emotion, a sense of lack of control, and self preoccupation
3. sudden
4. true
5. control
6. are out of the blue, and involve socially unacceptable and horrific themes
7. false
8. cleaning
9. false
10. forbidden aggressive or sexual
11. lumping; splitting
12. false
13. false
14. true
15. true
16. 50 percent
17. alcoholism
18. women
19. OCD
20. false
21. the elderly

22. false
23. dysfunction
24. loss; danger
25. agoraphobia
26. more
27. insecure-anxious
28. module
29. false
30. less
31. asleep
32. avoiding
33. not sure
34. false
35. 20–30 percent
36. increased
37. true
38. prolonged exposure with response prevention
39. thinking; decatastrophizing
40. false
41. GAD; social phobia; specific phobia; OCD
42. true
43. true

MULTIPLE CHOICE

1. b	6. b	11. d	16. a	21. d	26. a
2. a	7. d	12. c	17. a	22. b	27. b
3. c	8. b	13. b	18. c	23. c	28. d
4. c	9. d	14. c	19. a	24. d	29. a
5. c	10. a	15. d	20. c	25. b	

ACUTE AND POSTTRAUMATIC STRESS DISORDERS, DISSOCIATIVE DISORDERS, AND SOMATOFORM DISORDERS

CHAPTER OUTLINE

OBJECTIVES

You should be able to:

1.   Describe the features of posttraumatic stress disorder.
2.   Distinguish between posttraumatic stress disorder and acute stress disorder.
3.   Describe several treatment approaches for posttraumatic stress disorder.
4.   Distinguish between dissociative and somatoform disorders.
5.   Describe several perspectives of hysteria. Compare these perspectives with current views.
6.   Define dissociation and psychogenic amnesia.
7.   Discuss the connection between psychological trauma and fugue, amnesia, and dissociative identity disorder.
8.   Define selective amnesia.
9.   Identify the DSM-IV-TR criteria for depersonalization disorder and dissociative identity disorder.

10.   Define prosopagnosia and explain the significance of this disorder from the biological perspective.
11.   Discuss the psychological view of dissociative disorders.
12.   Describe the goals of therapy for dissociative identity disorder.
13.   Discuss the DSM-IV-TR criteria for body dysmorphic disorder, hypochondriasis, somatization disorder, pain disorder, and conversion disorder.
14.   Discuss the danger in misdiagnosing somatoform disorders.
15.   Discuss Freud's theory of primary and secondary gain as these relate to somatoform symptoms.
16.   Describe the behavioral approach in treating chronic pain.
17.   Outline the manner in which physicians should treat patients who present multiple physical concerns that are not physiologically based.

MATCHING I

Answers are found at the end of this chapter. Match these terms and concepts with the definitions that follow:

a.	Traumatic stress	o.	Multiple personality disorder
b.	Acute stress disorder (ASD)	p.	Hypnosis
c.	Posttraumatic stress disorder (PTSD)	q.	Hardiness
		r.	Retrospective reports
d.	Dissociative disorders	s.	State-dependent learning
e.	Somatoform disorders	t.	Iatrogenesis
f.	Malingering	u.	Critical incident stress debriefing
g.	Factitious disorder	v.	Dissociation
h.	Flashbacks	w.	Exaggerated startle response
i.	Depersonalization	x.	Meaning making
j.	Derealization	y.	Posttraumatic growth
k.	Dissociative amnesia	z.	Emotional processing
l.	Selective amnesia	aa.	Prolonged exposure
m.	Depersonalization disorder	bb.	Imagery rehearsal therapy
n.	Dissociative identity disorder	cc.	*Hwa-byung*

1.   _____   a disorder characterized by the sudden inability to recall extensive and important personal information
2.   _____   a sense of feeling cut off from oneself or one's environment
3.   _____   a personal sense of commitment, control, and challenge in facing stress
4.   _____   characterized by persistent, maladaptive disruptions in the integration of memory, consciousness, or identity
5.   _____   a marked sense of unreality about oneself or one's environment
6.   _____   recollections about the past that have questionable reliability and validity
7.   _____   an altered state of consciousness during which people are especially susceptible to suggestion
8.   _____   occurs within four weeks of exposure to a trauma: characterized by dissociative symptoms, re-experiencing of the event, avoidance of reminders of the event, and anxiety or arousal
9.   _____   lasts over a month after exposure to a trauma, or has a delayed onset (six or more months after trauma): characterized by dissociative symptoms, reexperiencing of the event, avoidance of reminders of the event, and anxiety or arousal
10.   _____   disruption of the typically integrated mental processes of memory, consciousness, identity, or perception

11. _____ exposure to some event that involves actual or threatened death or serious injury to self or others
12. _____ one-time group meeting to prevent trauma complications
13. _____ a dissociative disorder characterized by the existence of two or more distinct personalities in a single individual, which repeatedly take over the person's behavior outside of their awareness
14. _____ the previous term for dissociative identity disorder
15. _____ sudden, intrusive, vivid memories during which a trauma is replayed in images or thoughts
16. _____ pretending to have a psychological disorder in order to achieve some external gain
17. _____ pretending to have a psychological disorder in order to assume the sick role
18. _____ a dissociative disorder characterized by severe and persistent feelings of being detached from oneself
19. _____ learning that occurs in one state of affect or consciousness is recalled most accurately while in that same state
20. _____ a form of amnesia in which people do not lose their memory completely but are unable to remember only certain personal events and information
21. _____ characterized by unusual physical symptoms that occur in the absence of a known physical illness
22. _____ creation of a disorder by attempts at treatment
23. _____ excessive fear reactions to unexpected stimuli
24. _____ fatigue, insomnia, and pain in response to unexpressed anger among Koreans
25. _____ facing fear, diminishing its intensity, and coming to a new understanding about a trauma
26. _____ a cognitive behavioral therapy which teaches rewriting of nightmares
27. _____ positive changes resulting from trauma
28. _____ reliving the trauma repeatedly in therapy
29. _____ finding a broad reason or value for enduring a trauma

MATCHING II

Answers are found at the end of this chapter. Match these terms and concepts with the definitions that follow:

1. Alexithymia
2. Two-factor theory
3. Munchausen syndrome
4. EMDR
5. Recovered memories
6. False memories
7. Dissociative fugue
8. Hysteria
9. Amnesia
10. Psychogenic amnesia
11. Conversion disorder
12. Somatization disorder
13. *La belle indifference*

14. Briquet's syndrome
15. Hypochondriasis
16. Pain disorder
17. Body dysmorphic disorder
18. Diagnosis by exclusion
19. Primary gain
20. Secondary gain
21. Prosopagnosia
22. Multisomatoform disorder
23. Explicit memory
24. Implicit memory
25. Imagery rehearsal therapy
26. Abreaction

a. _____ the emotional reliving of a past traumatic experience
b. _____ a somatoform disorder characterized by preoccupying fear or belief that one is suffering from a physical illness, even in the face of a clean bill of health by a physician
c. _____ a somatoform disorder characterized by physical symptoms that mimic those found in neurological diseases, but which often do not make sense anatomically

d. _____ amnesia that is psychologically caused, resulting from trauma or emotional distress

e. _____ a process of identifying somatoform disorders by ruling out physical causes that could account for the symptoms

f. _____ a new proposed diagnostic somatoform category requiring only three chronic physical symptoms

g. _____ a controversial treatment using rapid back-and-forth eye movements to induce relaxation while reliving a traumatic event

h. _____ a somatoform disorder characterized by constant preoccupation with some imagined or grossly exaggerated defect in physical appearance

i. _____ dramatic recollections of a long-forgotten traumatic experience

j. _____ partial or complete loss of recall for a particular event or time period

k. _____ an unintentionally invented memory of an event that did not actually occur

l. _____ a psychoanalytic term that a symptom protects the ego from an unacceptable thought by serving as a symbolic, disguised expression of that thought

m. _____ a somatoform disorder characterized by multiple, somatic complaints in the absence of organic impairment

n. _____ a rare disorder characterized by sudden, unplanned travel, the inability to remember details about the past, and identity confusion or assumption of a new identity

o. _____ a psychoanalytic term meaning that a symptom is rewarding because it allows a patient to avoid responsibility or elicit sympathy or attention from others

p. _____ a flippant lack of concern about the physical symptoms of a somatoform disorder

q. _____ a historic diagnostic category that included both dissociative and somatoform disorders: based on the ancient Greek idea that these symptoms were caused by a "dislodged, wandering uterus"

r. _____ a somatoform disorder characterized by preoccupation with pain in which psychological factors are involved

s. _____ explains the development of symptoms following trauma using a combination of classical and operant conditioning, whereby classical conditioning creates fears and operant conditioning maintains them

t. _____ a rare, repetitive form of factitious disorder where the patient repeatedly seeks treatment for invented or self-created symptoms to get attention from medical personnel

u. _____ impairment of face recognition

v. _____ a name sometimes used to refer to somatization disorder

w. _____ changes in memory but with no conscious recollection

x. _____ conscious recollection of a past event

y. _____ reliving recurring nightmares while awake and rewriting the outcome

z. _____ difficulty recognizing and expressing one's emotions

MATCHING III

Answers are found at the end of this chapter. Match these names with the descriptions of their contributions to the study of abnormal psychology:

a. Pierre Janet   d. Jean Charcot
b. Edna Foa   e. Sigmund Freud
c. Nicholas Spanos

1. _____ argued that multiple personalities are caused by role playing

2. _____ viewed dissociation as a normal process, similar to repression, whereby the ego defends itself against unacceptable thoughts

3. _____ used hypnosis to treat hysteria
4. _____ viewed dissociation as an abnormal process indicative of psychopathology
5. _____ explained PTSD symptoms using the two-factor theory

CONCEPT REVIEW

Answers are found at the end of this chapter. After you have read and reviewed the material, test your comprehension by filling in the blanks or circling the correct answer.

1. PTSD is characterized by these three symptoms: _____, _____, and _____.

2. ASD is characterized by the above three symptoms and _____.

3. Sometimes the re-experiencing of PTSD and ASD occurs as a(n) _____ state, which is usually brief.

4. In PTSD, avoidance may manifest as _____, where feelings seem dampened or nonexistent.

5. Many people with PTSD and ASD are jumpy and nervous, showing an "exaggerated _____ response."

6. The development of ASD as a diagnostic category was, in part, an attempt to _____ the development of PTSD by providing early treatment.

7. What was wrong with earlier definitions of trauma? _____

8. What are five types of experience that often lead to the development of PTSD? _____, _____, _____, _____, and _____

9. A woman cannot become pregnant as the result of a sexual assault: **true   false**

10. What three disorders commonly co-occur with PTSD? _____, _____, and _____

11. It is thought that about _____ percent of women and _____ percent of men will develop PTSD at some point in their lives.

12. People who experience what type of trauma develop PTSD in the highest proportions? _____

13. People with a history of being anxious are   **more   less**   likely to experience trauma and are **more   less**   likely to develop PTSD.

14. There is evidence to suggest that some patients with PTSD dissociate; they report low anxiety, but tests show they have _____ arousal.

15. The   **majority   minority**   of WWII prisoners of war with PTSD were fully recovered forty years later.

16. Monozygotic (MZ) twins had a   **higher   lower**   concordance rate than dizygotic (DZ) twins for experiencing trauma in the form of exposure to combat and for developing PTSD symptoms in a study of Vietnam veterans.

17. According to the two-factor theory, **classical** **operant** conditioning creates the fear response to trauma and **classical** **operant** conditioning maintains it through avoidance.

18. Research has suggested that an increase in the production of the neurotransmitter _____ in response to trauma causes the increased arousal seen in PTSD.

19. After September 11, New Yorkers spent **more** **less** than the government set aside for psychotherapy.

20. People cope **better** **worse** with trauma when they anticipate its onset.

21. What three characteristics of an attack increase the chance that victims of sexual assault will develop PTSD? _____, _____, and _____

22. What three types of experiences among Vietnam veterans increase the risk of PTSD? _____, _____, and _____

23. Social support **increases** **decreases** the risk for PTSD.

24. Research **supports** **does not support** the idea that immediate, emergency psychological treatment is effective in preventing PTSD.

25. **Antidepressant** **Antianxiety** medication is effective in the treatment of PTSD.

26. Although painful and difficult, _____ is the essential component of effective treatment for PTSD.

27. EMDR is a highly effective treatment method: **true** **false**

28. There is a debate over whether repression of memories of traumatic events occurs: **true** **false**

29. It is very difficult to establish whether a recovered memory is accurate: **true** **false**

30. Contemporary scientists view the unconscious mind as: **dumb** **smart**

31. Dissociative identity disorders are **rarely** **usually** diagnosed outside of the United States and Canada.

32. What traumatic experience is hypothesized to play a role in the etiology of many dissociative disorders?

_____

33. Only two hundred case histories of _____ disorder appeared in the entire world literature before 1980.

34. Some professionals question the existence of dissociative identity disorder, arguing that it is created by the power of _____.

35. Dissociative identity disorder may be the result of role _____.

36. Patients with prosopagnosia demonstrate the normal preference for viewing faces that are familiar. This finding implies a dissociation between _____ and _____ cognitive processes.

37. Research using **retrospective** **prospective** methods is more accurate, but **retrospective** **prospective** research is more expensive.

38. A twin study found _____ genetic contribution to dissociative symptoms.

39. Some psychologists argue that dissociative identity disorder is produced by iatrogenesis; in other words, who causes the disorder? _____

40. The goal of treatment for dissociative identity disorder is _____.

41. What kind of professional do people with somatoform disorders typically see? _____

42. Multisomatoform disorder has been proposed and requires _____ physical symptoms.

43. In one study, 27 percent of women undergoing what type of surgery actually suffered from somatization disorder? _____

44. Somatization disorder must have its onset in: **young adulthood   middle age**

45. Conversion disorders are   **more   less**   common now than in the past, possibly because of poor differential diagnosis.

46. Somatization disorder is more common in which of each of the following:

    women or men   blacks or whites   the less educated or the more educated

47. Somatoform disorders show high comorbidity with _____.

48. People with somatization disorder are more likely to have male relatives with _____ disorder.

49. In one study, what percentage of patients diagnosed with conversion disorders were eventually found to have a neurological disease? _____

50. Somatoform disorders are not more frequent in non-industrialized countries: **true   false**

MULTIPLE CHOICE
Answers are found at the end of this chapter. These multiple choice questions will test your understanding of the material presented in the chapter. Read each question and circle the letter representing the best answer.

1. Many people who suffer from PTSD also meet the diagnostic criteria for another mental disorder, particularly _____ and _____.
   a. depression; substance abuse
   b. hypomania; antisocial personality disorder
   c. depression; adjustment disorder
   d. hypomania; paranoid personality disorder

2. All of the following are cultural myths of sexual assault with the exception of
   a. women who are raped provoke it.
   b. women who are raped seldom sustain physical injuries.
   c. women who are raped often enjoy it.
   d. many women who are raped are raped by an acquaintance.

3. Surveys have found that approximately _____ of U.S. women have been raped.
   a. 2 percent
   b. 10 percent
   c. 30 percent
   d. 40 percent

4. The most common cause of PTSD among men is
    a. observing domestic violence in the home as a child.
    b. being a victim of physical abuse as a child.
    c. participation in the Vietnam War.
    d. witnessing a friend or relative die from a traumatic event.

5. Jack, a Vietnam veteran, runs for cover every time he hears an airplane pass by overhead. Jack's reaction can best be described as a
    a. flashback.
    b. dissociative state.
    c. brief psychotic reaction.
    d. hallucination.

6. All of the following are factors that increase the risk for PTSD, with the exception of
    a. having a history of emotional problems.
    b. being a minority group member.
    c. being female.
    d. being wealthy.

7. As many as _____ of all stranger rapes are not reported to authorities.
    a. one third
    b. two thirds
    c. one quarter
    d. one half

8. What is the problem with the earlier version of the DSM that defined trauma as an event outside the range of usual human experience?
    a. Trauma is common.
    b. Trauma has to occur more than once to qualify.
    c. It is a process, not an event.
    d. That definition only applies to men.

9. Studies indicate that _____ is the most effective treatment for PTSD.
    a. hypnotherapy
    b. supportive therapy
    c. relaxation training
    d. cognitive behavior therapy

10. _____ is the help and understanding received from friends and family as well as from professionals.
    a. A personal network
    b. Social support
    c. Psychotherapy
    d. None of the above

11. Which of the following is not typically a symptom of PTSD?
    a. difficulty falling or staying asleep
    b. irritability or outbursts of anger
    c. paranoid thoughts or ideas
    d. difficulty concentrating

12. A disorder that develops after a horrifying experience and involves general increases in anxiety and arousal, avoidance of emotionally charged situations, and the frequent reliving of the traumatic event is called
    a. posttraumatic stress disorder.
    b. victimization.
    c. acute stress disorder.
    d. generalized anxiety disorder.

13. Sudden, unplanned travel, the inability to remember certain past details, and confusion about one's identity are primary features of
    a. general amnesia.
    b. Briquet's syndrome.
    c. body dysmorphic disorder.
    d. dissociative fugue.

14. Abnormal fears of having a serious medical disorder, even after a thorough medical evaluation reveals nothing wrong, are characteristic of
    a. hypochondriasis.
    b. depersonalization disorder.
    c. somatization disorder.
    d. conversion disorder.

15. This term is used to describe people who habitually and deliberately pretend to have a physical illness:
    a. hypochondriasis.
    b. psychosis.
    c. factitious disorder.
    d. adjustment disorder.

16. An unfortunate consequence of having a somatoform disorder is
    a. the patient does not attend to the medical aspects of the disorder, resulting in underutilization of health care.
    b. the psychological nature of the patient's problems go unnoticed, and unnecessary medical procedures are performed.
    c. the seriousness of the physical complaints are overlooked, and necessary medical treatments are refused.
    d. mental health professionals are consulted instead of physicians, resulting in poor physical health care.

17. Which disorder does not appear to overlap with somatoform disorders?
    a. anxiety disorders
    b. depression
    c. antisocial personality disorder
    d. multiple personality disorder

18. Freud believed that both dissociative and somatoform disorders were
    a. expressions of unresolved anger.
    b. reactions of the superego toward repressed impulses.
    c. expressions of unconscious conflict.
    d. conscious reactions to traumatic situations.

19. Whenever Tom looks into the mirror, the first thing he notices is his large and somewhat pointed ears. Although friends have reassured him otherwise, he is convinced that his ears are the first thing others notice about him, too. In fact, he wonders whether some people may call him Mr. Spock behind his back. He has consulted with several plastic surgeons and his first surgery has just been scheduled. Tom displays symptoms of
    a. somatization disorder.
    b. Briquet's syndrome.
    c. conversion disorder.
    d. body dysmorphic disorder.

20. "*La belle indifference*" is occasionally exhibited by patients with
    a. multiple personality disorder.
    b. pain disorder.
    c. psychogenic amnesia.
    d. somatization disorder.

21. Sally is depressed about her relationship with her boyfriend as she studies for her spring chemistry final. The next fall, she takes another chemistry course and easily remembers the material from her spring course while studying for her first quiz. She is also depressed now due to a fight with her roommate. This is
    a. state-dependent learning.
    b. abreaction.
    c. hypnotic recall.
    d. recovered memory.

22. How might antianxiety, antipsychotic, or antidepressant medications be helpful in the treatment of dissociative disorders?
    a. They facilitate reintegration of the dissociated states.
    b. They reduce the level of the patient's emotional distress.
    c. They increase the likelihood of having one personality become dominant over other personalities.
    d. They are not recommended treatment for dissociative disorders.

23. A critical consideration in the diagnosis of a somatoform disorder is that the person
    a. may be aware of the psychological factors producing the disorder.
    b. may minimize physical complaints, resulting in health professionals not detecting the disorder.
    c. may also have coexisting multiple personalities.
    d. may actually have a real but as yet undetected physical illness.

24. Which disorder is not a type of somatoform disorder?
    a. depersonalization disorder
    b. body dysmorphic disorder
    c. conversion disorder
    d. pain disorder

25. A distinguishing feature of somatization disorder is
    a. the physical complaints involve multiple somatic systems.
    b. the physical complaints are limited to only one somatic system.
    c. the patient appears very serious, obsessive, and emotionally withdrawn.
    d. the onset of the disorder rarely occurs before age thirty.

26. The onset of a dissociative episode
    a. is typically abrupt and precipitated by a traumatic event.
    b. is slow and insidious in nature.
    c. can be traced to certain metabolic deficiencies.
    d. typically happens following a severe head injury.

27. When is the diagnosis of a dissociative disorder not appropriate?
    a. when the patient has a history of child sexual abuse
    b. when the dissociative process is abrupt in onset
    c. when the patient additionally reports feeling depressed
    d. when the dissociation occurs in the presence of substance abuse or organic pathology

28. Which of the following is the best definition of a conversion symptom?
    a. a physical symptom in one part of the body that is actually referred pain or trauma from another part of the body
    b. a symptom produced by psychological conflict that mimics a symptom found in a neurological disease
    c. a symptom produced by injury that is exacerbated by psychological conflict
    d. an emotional symptom such as depressed mood produced by physical trauma

29. Joe, a house painter, reports to his family doctor that he has not been able to work for six months because of pain in his legs. He can barely walk to the kitchen from his bedroom because of the pain. No injury has occurred that would explain the situation. His wife has been taking care of him, but is very concerned by the financial strain this is causing. His doctor orders a thorough examination. If nothing is found, what diagnosis should his doctor consider?
    a. conversion disorder
    b. hypochondriasis
    c. pain disorder
    d. somatoform disorder

30. The separation of mental processes such as memory or consciousness that are usually integrated is referred to as
    a. abreaction.
    b. dissociation.
    c. repression.
    d. *déjà vu.*

31. The effect of a conversion symptom getting the patient out of unpleasant duties is referred to as
    a. *la belle indifference.*
    b. secondary gain.
    c. diagnosis by exclusion.
    d. hypochondriasis.

32. While both disorders involve memory loss, a major difference between dissociative amnesia and dissociative fugue is that
    a. dissociative fugue is characterized by sudden and unexpected travel away from home.
    b. the memory loss in dissociative amnesia has a physical basis.
    c. dissociative amnesia is characterized by the emergence of at least one additional personality.
    d. dissociative fugue additionally includes persistent feelings of being detached from oneself.

33. Research on the prevalence of somatoform disorders suggests that they
    a. appear to be more common than depression in the general population.
    b. appear to be less common during war time.
    c. appear to be rare in the general population.
    d. have increased in prevalence since Freud's time.

34. Why are people with somatoform disorders likely to reject a referral to a psychologist from their doctors?
    a. People may have difficulty accepting the possibility of the psychological basis for their physical symptoms.
    b. People may feel that their physician is belittling their problems.
    c. People may feel that their physician is not being empathetic.
    d. all of the above

35. A person with which of the following would be at risk for developing a dissociative disorder?
    a. a family history of depression
    b. a history of child sexual abuse
    c. a history of violent behavior
    d. all of the above

36. The sociocultural view of the etiology of somatoform disorders suggests that
    a. people with education and financial security have greater access to physicians who will listen to their somatic complaints.
    b. people in nonindustrialized societies have a greater sense of community and are more likely to describe their inner distress to others in their social network.
    c. people in industrialized societies have less opportunity to develop a more sophisticated vocabulary for their physical symptoms.
    d. people with less education are less likely to describe their inner turmoil in psychological terms.

37. Which statement is not correct about somatization disorder?
    a. It is more common among higher socioeconomic groups.
    b. It is more common among women.
    c. It is more common among African Americans than whites.
    d. It is less common in men.

38. Every Friday, Sarah's fifth grade class has a spelling test. Every Friday morning, she complains of a stomachache to her mother. This may be an example of
    a. expressing an emotional concern that has a genuine emotional basis.
    b. expressing an emotional concern in terms of a physical complaint.
    c. expressing a physical complaint that has been reinforced by the environment.
    d. expressing a psychological symptom that has an organic basis.

39. Somatoform disorders are characterized by
    a. physical complaints that can be traced to organic impairment.
    b. patients who deliberately lie about the presence of physical symptoms.
    c. physical symptoms that cannot be explained on the basis of underlying physical illness.
    d. physical symptoms which are consciously linked to psychological difficulties.

40. In contrast to Freud, contemporary cognitive scientists
   a. do not recognize the existence of unconscious processes.
   b. believe that unconscious processes are much less influential than conscious processes in shaping both normal and abnormal behavior.
   c. believe that unconscious processes are more influential than conscious processes in shaping both normal and abnormal behavior.
   d. have a much less restricted view of unconscious processes and their role in shaping behavior.

41. The analogue experiments by Spanos on the symptoms of dissociative identity disorder suggest that
   a. hypnosis had no relationship to the presence of symptoms of this disorder.
   b. they disappeared under hypnosis.
   c. they can be induced through role-playing and hypnosis.
   d. experimental hypnosis increases risk for dissociative identity disorder.

42. An example of a sociological theory of the cause of dissociative identity disorder is that
   a. it is caused by disturbances in the temporal lobe of the brain.
   b. it is caused by a perceptual disturbance that impairs the ability to recognize faces.
   c. it is produced by iatrogenesis, specifically through the leading questions of therapists.
   d. it is produced by recovered memories of the loss of a parent.

SHORT ANSWER
Answer the following short answer questions. Compare your work to the material presented in the text.

1. Briefly describe Posttraumatic Stress Disorder (PTSD). Provide an example of an experience that may result in PTSD, and identify the various symptoms that may accompany this disorder.

2. While some professionals believe that multiple personalities are real and more common than previously thought, others believe that the condition is no more than role-playing. Discuss this controversy, citing the research and clinical evidence that support both points of view.

3. Are recovered memories examples of dissociation, or are they produced through the power of suggestion? Defend your position.

4. Review the methodological concerns surrounding the use of retrospective reports. What questions have been raised regarding their reliability and validity? What are the implications of these concerns?

5. If you are a primary care physician with a patient who has a number of vague and inconsistent physical complaints, but an extensive medical evaluation reveals no organic pathology, what types of questions would you consider? How would you approach the treatment of this patient if a diagnosis of somatization disorder was assigned?

ANSWER KEY

MATCHING I

1. k	9. c	17. g	25. z
2. i	10. v	18. m	26. bb
3. q	11. a	19. s	27. y
4. d	12. u	20. l	28. aa
5. j	13. n	21. e	29. x
6. r	14. o	22. t	
7. p	15. h	23. w	
8. b	16. f	24. cc	

MATCHING II

a. 26	h. 17	o. 20	v. 14
b. 15	i. 5	p. 13	w. 24
c. 11	j. 9	q. 8	x. 23
d. 10	k. 6	r. 16	y. 25
e. 18	l. 19	s. 2	z. 1
f. 22	m. 12	t. 3	
g. 4	n. 7	u. 21	

MATCHING III

1. c	3. d	5. b
2. e	4. a	

CONCEPT REVIEW

1. re-experiencing, avoidance, and arousal or anxiety
2. dissociative symptoms
3. dissociative
4. numbing of responsiveness
5. startle
6. prevent
7. they defined trauma as outside usual experience but trauma is not that rare
8. war, rape, child sexual abuse, spouse abuse, witnessing disasters
9. false
10. depression, anxiety disorders, substance abuse
11. 10; 5
12. rape
13. more; more
14. high
15. minority
16. higher
17. classical; operant
18. norepinephrine
19. less
20. better
21. rape is completed; if they were physically injured; if their life was threatened
22. being wounded; being involved in death of civilians; witnessing atrocities
23. decreases
24. supports
25. antidepressants
26. facing distressing emotions
27. false
28. true
29. true
30. dumb

31. rarely
32. child sexual abuse
33. dissociative identity
34. suggestion
35. playing
36. conscious; unconscious
37. prospective; prospective
38. no
39. a therapist
40. to reintegrate the personalities into one

41. physician
42. fewer
43. hysterectomy
44. young adulthood
45. less
46. women; blacks; less educated
47. depression and anxiety
48. antisocial personality
49. 25 percent
50. true

MULTIPLE CHOICE

1. a	7. b	13. d	19. d	25. a	31. b	37. a
2. d	8. a	14. a	20. d	26. a	32. a	38. b
3. b	9. d	15. c	21. a	27. d	33. c	39. c
4. c	10. b	16. b	22. b	28. b	34. d	40. b
5. b	11. c	17. d	23. d	29. c	35. b	41. c
6. d	12. a	18. c	24. a	30. b	36. d	42. c

CHAPTER EIGHT

STRESS AND PHYSICAL HEALTH

CHAPTER OUTLINE

OBJECTIVES

You should be able to:

1. Explain the significance of stress factors in health and illness.
2. Describe the stages of the general adaptation syndrome.
3. Distinguish between several theories of stress and its impact on illness.
4. Define resilience and positive psychology.
5. Describe the emotional, cognitive, and behavioral responses to stress.
6. Understand how stress is used in diagnostic classification.
7. Understand the role of psychological factors in cancer, AIDS, and pain.
8. Distinguish between primary and secondary hypertension.
9. Describe the major causes of primary hypertension.
10. Discuss the impact of low-control, high-demand job strain.
11. Discuss the relationship between depression, anxiety, and CHD.
12. Describe the major characteristics of Type A personality and its impact on health.
13. Describe the primary, secondary, and tertiary preventive treatment approaches to CVD.

MATCHING I

Answers are found at the end of this chapter. Match these terms and concepts with the definitions that follow:

a.	Stress	n.	Carcinogens
b.	Traumatic stress	o.	Cardiovascular disease (CVD)
c.	Corticotrophin-releasing factor	p.	Hypertension
d.	Behavioral medicine	q.	Coronary heart disease (CHD)
e.	Health psychologists	r.	Myocardial infarction (MI)
f.	General adaptation syndrome	s.	Systolic blood pressure
g.	Primary appraisal	t.	Epinephrine
h.	Secondary appraisal	u.	Cortisol
i.	Optimism	v.	Homeostasis
j.	Fight or flight response	w.	Social support
k.	Sleep terror disorder	x.	Resilience
l.	Sleepwalking disorder	y.	Positive psychology
m.	Coping	z.	Tend and befriend

1. _____ a person's cognitive evaluation of the challenge, threat, or harm posed by a particular event

2. _____ a challenging event that requires physiological, cognitive, or behavioral adaptation

3. _____ a disorder involving abrupt awakening and intense autonomic arousal but little memory of a dream and a quick return to sleep

4. _____ a group of diseases of the heart

5. _____ an individual's assessment of his or her abilities and resources for coping with a difficult event

6. _____ a general cognitive style of taking a positive attitude

7. _____ a three-stage model of reaction to stress involving alarm, resistance, and exhaustion

8. _____ a heart attack, the most deadly form of CHD, caused by oxygen deprivation and death of heart muscle tissue

9. _____ stress caused by exposure to a catastrophic event involving actual or threatened death to oneself or others

10. _____ high blood pressure

11. _____ a multidisciplinary field including medical and mental health professionals who investigate psychological factors in the symptoms, etiology, and treatment of physical illness

12. _____ practical and emotional assistance

13. _____ the highest blood pressure reading, it is the pressure that the blood exerts against the arteries when the heart is beating

14. _____ a response to threat in which psychophysiological reactions prepare the body to take action against danger

15. _____ a disorder involving rising during sleep and walking about in an unresponsive state with no later memory of the episode

16. _____ focuses on people's psychological strengths

17. _____ a group of disorders affecting the heart and circulatory system

18. _____ cancer-causing agents

19. _____ the "stress hormone" that functions to help the body make repairs when injured or infected

20. _____ secreted in response to stress: stimulates the activation of the sympathetic nervous system

21. _____ the tendency to return to a steady state of normal functioning

22. _____ the ability to cope successfully with the challenges of life
23. _____ also known as adrenaline
24. _____ a response to stress that involves caring for offspring and social affiliation
25. _____ responses to diminish the burden of stress
26. _____ psychologists who specialize in behavioral medicine

MATCHING II

Answers are found at the end of this chapter. Match these terms and concepts with the definitions that follow:

1.	Psychoneuroimmunology	12.	Sudden cardiac death
2.	Pain management	13.	Secondary hypertension
3.	T cells	14.	Essential hypertension
4.	Lymphocytes	15.	Myocardial ischemia
5.	Antigens	16.	Atherosclerosis
6.	Immunosuppression	17.	Coronary occlusion
7.	Lifestyle diseases	18.	Cardiovascular reactivity
8.	Problem-focused coping	19.	Type A behavior pattern
9.	Emotion-focused coping	20.	AIDS
10.	Diastolic blood pressure	21.	HIV
11.	Angina pectoris	22.	Job strain

a. _____ hypertension resulting from a known problem such as a diagnosed kidney or endocrine disorder

b. _____ the decreased production of immune agents, often a result of stress

c. _____ a competitive, hostile, urgent, impatient, achievement-striving style of responding to challenge

d. _____ sudden oxygen deprivation when arteries are completely blocked by fatty deposits or when blood clots make their way to the heart muscle

e. _____ internally oriented coping involving attempts to alter subjective distress

f. _____ a category of white blood cells that fight off antigens

g. _____ a form of high blood pressure in which the hypertension is the principal disorder

h. _____ externally oriented coping that involves attempts to change a stressor

i. _____ temporary oxygen deprivation that accompanies intermittent chest pains which causes no permanent damage

j. _____ diseases affected by stress and health behaviors

k. _____ death within twenty-four hours of a coronary episode

l. _____ a measure of the intensity of an individual's cardiovascular reactions to stress in the laboratory which predicts future cardiovascular disease

m. _____ a major form of coronary heart disease involving intermittent chest pains brought on by some form of exertion

n. _____ high psychological demand and low decisional control

o. _____ foreign substances like bacteria that invade the body

p. _____ the lowest blood pressure reading, it is the pressure that the blood exerts against the arteries between heartbeats

q. _____ research on the effects of stress on the functioning of the immune system

r. _____ one of the major types of white blood cells of the immune system

s. _____ the thickening of the coronary artery wall as a result of the accumulation of blood lipids with age

t. _____ the virus that causes AIDS

u. _____ an infectious disease that attacks the immune system

v. _____ helping people cope effectively with chronic pain that cannot be eliminated

MATCHING III

Answers are found at the end of this chapter. Match these terms and concepts with the definitions that follow:

a.	Health behavior	l.	Social ecology
b.	Primary sleep disorder	m.	Antihypertensives
c.	Dyssomnias	n.	Beta blockers
d.	Parasomnias	o.	Stress management
e.	Primary insomnia	p.	Biofeedback
f.	Narcolepsy	q.	Role playing
g.	Breathing-related sleep disorder	r.	Primary hypersomnia
h.	Circadian rhythm sleep disorder	s.	Sleep apnea
i.	Nightmare disorder	t.	Illness behavior
j.	Longitudinal study	u.	Heart-focused anxiety
k.	Cross-sectional study	v.	Prospective design

1. _____ activities essential to promoting good health such as healthy eating, exercise, and avoidance of unhealthy activities like drug use

2. _____ a disorder involving frequent awakening to alertness by terrifying dreams

3. _____ disorders characterized by abnormal events that occur during sleep, like nightmares

4. _____ the interrelations between the individual and the social world

5. _____ the disruption of sleep due to breathing problems such as sleep apnea, the temporary obstruction of the respiratory airway

6. _____ a treatment to teach more effective coping skills, reduce adverse reactions to stress, and improve health behavior

7. _____ medications effective in reducing high blood pressure

8. _____ a type of research design in which subjects are studied over time, allowing researchers to make inferences about causation

9. _____ drugs that reduce the risk of myocardial infarction or sudden coronary death

10. _____ irresistible attacks of refreshing sleep

11. _____ a mismatch between the patient's twenty-four hour sleeping patterns and their twenty-four hour life demands

12. _____ a condition in which sleeping disturbance is the primary complaint

13. _____ a technique used in therapy of improvisational play acting to teach patients how to respond to stressful interactions with less hostility

14. _____ problems in the amount, quality, or timing of sleep

15. _____ a treatment using equipment to monitor physiological processes and provide the patient with feedback about them in order to help the patient gain conscious control over them

16. _____ research design in which subjects are studied at one point in time

17. _____ excessive sleepiness characterized by prolonged or daytime sleep that interferes with functioning

18. _____ difficulties initiating or maintaining sleep, or poor quality of sleeping

19. _____ a sleep disorder caused by temporary obstruction of the airway

20. _____ a follow-forward study

21. _____ behaving as if you are sick

22. _____ preoccupation with heart and chest sensations

MATCHING IV
Answers are found at the end of this chapter. Match these names with the descriptions of their contributions to the study of abnormal psychology:

a. Richard Lazarus   b. Hans Selye   c. Walter Cannon

1. _____ defined stress in terms of the general adaptation syndrome; did research on animal analogue studies of the GAS

2. _____ argued that stress is not just a stimulus but also the individual's response to the stimulus, specifically their cognitive appraisal of the event as being potentially harmful and exceeding their coping resources

3. _____ one of the first researchers to conduct systematic studies of stress: interested in the fight or flight response

CONCEPT REVIEW
Answers are found at the end of this chapter. After you have read and reviewed the material, test your comprehension by filling in the blanks or circling the correct answer.

1. Stress can be produced by daily _____ as well as by traumatic events.

2. Scientists used to think that psychological factors were **important** **irrelevant** in most physical illnesses; today they think they are **important** **irrelevant**.

3. The *Diagnostic and Statistical Manual* no longer contains a list of psychosomatic disorders because _____.

4. Holmes and Rahe developed "The Social Readjustment Rating Scale," an attempt to measure the amount of _____ caused by various life events.

5. List three criticisms of "The Social Readjustment Rating Scale":
_____, _____, and
_____.

6. What are the three stages of the GAS? _____,
_____, and _____

7. One problem with Lazarus's approach to defining stress is that it runs the risk of being tautological, or _____.

8. The fight or flight response is _____ in the modern world.

9. Research indicates that optimism **is** **is not** linked to better health habits and less illness.

10. An analogy for **Cannon's** **Selye's** theory is a car in which the engine continues to race instead of idling down after running fast, and an analogy for **Cannon's** **Selye's** theory is a car that has run out of gas and is damaged because stress keeps turning the key, trying to restart the engine.

11. Another mechanism whereby stress may cause physical illness is the stress response sapping _____ away from routine bodily functions.

12. Stress weakens immune functioning: **true   false**

13. In one study with newly married couples, partners who were more _____ during discussions of marital problems showed greater immunosuppression during the next twenty-four hours.

14. From an evolutionary perspective, heightened immune functioning is **adaptive   maladaptive** in response to immediate threat.

15. Regular church attendance is correlated with **higher lower** risk of mortality.

16. People who repress their anxiety show fewer psychophysiological reactions to stress: **true   false**

17. Predictability of a stressor   **improves   impairs**   our ability to cope with it.

18. Rats who can stop a shock by pressing a bar experience a bigger stress response than rats who receive an identical shock but don't have to worry about stopping it: **true   false**

19. One pathway that may explain how stress and illness are linked is that stress can reduce people's _____ behaviors.

20. The more a stressed monkey can interact with other monkeys, the less immunosuppression it demonstrates: **true false**

21. Stress can cause illness, but illness can also cause _____.

22. Instead of _____ or _____, the female response to stress may be more often to tend and befriend.

23. Implicit support (focusing on valued social groups) buffers stress for **Asians & Asian Americans European Americans,**   while explicit support (seeking advice or reassurance) buffers stress for **Asians & Asian Americans   European Americans**.

24. Why does the DSM-IV-TR not include the rating system for severity of stressors that was included in DSM-III and DSM-III-R? _____

25. Cancer deaths have risen substantially over the past thirty years: **true   false**

26. Cancer is the leading cause of death today: **true   false**

27. Stress can directly affect the body's ability to fight cancer cells: **true   false**

28. Psychological treatments, such as structured self-help groups, have been shown in some but not all studies to be effective in reducing the death rate among cancer patients: **true   false**

29. The prevalence of HIV/AIDS is particularly high on which continent? _____.

30. Most new HIV infections in the United States are due to   **sexual IV drug**   transmission.

31. Disorders of sleep are considered in the DSM-IV-TR only as symptoms of other disorders like anxiety or depression: **true   false**

32. Programs to educate the public about the transmission of HIV are quite effective in changing risky behaviors related to transmission: **true   false**

33. A wide range of treatments, such as biofeedback, hypnosis, relaxation training, and cognitive therapy, are quite useful in eliminating chronic pain: **true   false**

34. Cardiovascular disease is the third leading cause of death in the United States: **true   false**

35. Why is hypertension called the "silent killer"?

_____

36. The rate of death due to CVD has decreased in the United States in recent years: **true   false**

37. Where has the rate of death due to CVD increased? _____

38. Which are more likely to suffer from CHD? **men   women**

39. Which are more likely to suffer from CHD? **whites blacks**

40. Which of the following is not among the risk factors for CHD?

   drinking   smoking   obesity a fatty diet   a high income

41. Hypertension is twice as common among blacks, but black men living in high-stress neighborhoods had four times the average risk for hypertension: **true   false**

42. Rats with a genetic predisposition to develop hypertension do so only when exposed to salty diets or environmental stress: **true   false**

43. The Los Angeles earthquake was linked to   **higher lower**   levels of cardiac deaths.

44. Job strain involves a situation with   **high   low**   psychological demand and   **high   low**   decisional control.

45. The number of _____ a woman has increases her risk for heart disease if she works but not if she is a homemaker.

46. The key feature of the Type A behavior pattern in predicting CHD is _____.

47. Depression **is   is not**   correlated with CHD.

48. People exposed to an experimental media campaign to improve knowledge and change behavior related to CHD risk factors changed their behaviors relating to

_____ but not

_____.

49. The only two treatment conditions that lowered blood pressure in a study comparing weight reduction, salt reduction, stress management, calcium supplement, magnesium supplement, potassium supplement, and fish oil supplement, were

_____.

MULTIPLE CHOICE
Answers are found at the end of this chapter. These multiple choice questions will test your understanding of the material presented in the chapter. Read each question and circle the letter representing the best answer.

1. All of the following are criticisms of the Holmes and Rahe "Social Readjustment Rating Scale" except
    a. the inclusion of both positive and negative events as stressors.
    b. failure to distinguish between transient and chronic life events.
    c. a given stressor does not always produce the same number of life change units for all individuals in all situations.
    d. All of the above are criticisms of this scale.

2. Generally, hypertension is defined by a systolic blood pressure of above _____ and a diastolic blood pressure of above _____.
    a. 110; 60
    b. 120; 70
    c. 130; 80
    d. 140; 90

3. According to Walter Cannon, _____ is the mobilization of the body in reaction to a perceived threat.
    a. stage of alarm
    b. generalized arousal
    c. emergency response
    d. physiological toughness

4. Which of the following is not a reaction of the body to sympathetic nervous system arousal?
    a. heart rate increases
    b. blood pressure rises
    c. blood sugar lowers
    d. respiration rate increases

5. _____ decreases negative responding to an actual stressor.
    a. Predictability
    b. Surprise
    c. Expressing your anger toward your spouse
    d. Pessimism

6. Which of the following is not considered a lifestyle disease?
    a. tuberculosis
    b. stroke
    c. cancer
    d. heart disease

7. Stress plays a role in
    a. all physical disorders.
    b. some physical disorders.
    c. only heart disease.
    d. no physical disorders.

8. _____ of all deaths from CHD occur within twenty-four hours of a coronary event.
    a. One quarter
    b. One half
    c. One third
    d. Two thirds

9. Who would have the greatest risk for suffering from high blood pressure?
    a. an African-American male who is homeless
    b. a white male who is a stock broker
    c. an African-American female who is an attorney
    d. a white female who is a homemaker

10. This uses laboratory equipment to monitor physiological processes that generally occur outside of conscious awareness to help individuals learn how to control their autonomic nervous system functions voluntarily.
    a. biofeedback
    b. stress management
    c. systematic desensitization
    d. flooding

11. Which intervention shows the most promise with cardiovascular disease?
    a. biofeedback
    b. role playing to reduce hostility
    c. educational pamphlets
    d. No treatment is needed; just having a heart attack is enough to scare the person into change.

12. According to "The Social Readjustment Rating Scale," _____ is the most significant life event and constitutes the greatest number of life change units.
    a. pregnancy
    b. divorce
    c. foreclosure of a mortgage or loan
    d. death of one's spouse

13. Psychoneuroimmunology refers to the study of
    a. decreased production of T cells and other immune agents.
    b. inhibition and destruction of various immune agents.
    c. the effects of stress on the functioning of the immune system.
    d. white blood cells that fight off foreign substances that invade the body.

14. Which of the following is not a sleep disorder?
    a. apnea
    b. narcolepsy
    c. angina pectoris
    d. circadian rhythm disorder

15. Which is not a method of transmitting HIV?
    a. donating blood
    b. sharing needles
    c. sexual intercourse
    d. mother to fetus

16. According to the Framingham Study, which was reviewed in your textbook, which of the following is most likely to suffer from heart disease?
    a. a woman who is a homemaker and has two children
    b. a woman who is a homemaker and has four children
    c. a woman who is a sales manager and has two children
    d. a woman who is a waitress and has four children

17. Which problem typically has no symptoms?
    a. angina pectoris
    b. myocardial infarction
    c. sleep apnea
    d. hypertension

18. All of the following are examples of cognitive responses to stress with the exception of
    a. optimism.
    b. repression.
    c. appraisal.
    d. predictability.

SHORT ANSWER
Answer the following short answer questions. Compare your work to the material presented in the text.

1. Discuss Holmes and Rahe's "Social Readjustment Rating Scale." What is a life change unit? What are the strengths of this scale? What are the criticisms of this scale? How would you change this scale to address some of these criticisms?

2. Discuss Selye's and Cannon's approaches to studying stress. In what ways are they similar? In what ways do they differ?

3. Discuss the implications of considering cardiovascular disease a lifestyle disease. How has health psychology addressed this issue?

4. Discuss the characteristics of a longitudinal research design. What are its advantages and disadvantages?

ANSWER KEY

MATCHING I

1. g	8. r	15. l	22. x
2. a	9. b	16. y	23. t
3. k	10. p	17. o	24. z
4. q	11. d	18. n	25. m
5. h	12. w	19. u	26. e
6. i	13. s	20. c	
7. f	14. j	21. v	

MATCHING II

a. 13	h. 8	o. 5	v. 2
b. 6	i. 15	p. 10	
c. 19	j. 7	q. 1	
d. 17	k. 12	r. 3	
e. 9	l. 18	s. 16	
f. 4	m. 11	t. 21	
g. 14	n. 22	u. 20	

MATCHING III

1. a	7. m	13. q	19. s
2. i	8. j	14. c	20. v
3. d	9. n	15. p	21. t
4. l	10. f	16. k	22. u
5. g	11. h	17. r	
6. o	12. b	18. e	

MATCHING IV

1. b	2. a	3. c

CONCEPT REVIEW

1. hassles
2. irrelevant; important
3. all illnesses are now seen as psychosomatic
4. stress
5. doesn't account for different ages and backgrounds; includes positive life changes; doesn't consider different meanings for different people
6. alarm, resistance, exhaustion
7. circular
8. maladaptive
9. is
10. Cannon's; Selye's
11. energy
12. true
13. hostile or negative
14. maladaptive
15. lower
16. false
17. improves
18. false
19. health
20. true
21. stress
22. fight; flight
23. Asians & Asian Americans; European

Americans
24. the ratings were unreliable
25. true
26. false
27. true
28. true
29. Africa
30. sexual
31. false
32. false
33. false
34. false
35. it has no symptoms
36. true
37. Eastern Europe
38. men
39. blacks
40. a high income
41. true
42. true
43. higher
44. high; low
45. children
46. hostility
47. is
48. diet; smoking
49. weight and salt reduction

MULTIPLE CHOICE

1. d	4. c	7. a	10. a	13. c	16. d
2. d	5. a	8. d	11. b	14. c	17. d
3. c	6. a	9. a	12. d	15. a	18. d

CHAPTER NINE

PERSONALITY DISORDERS

CHAPTER OUTLINE

OBJECTIVES

You should be able to:

1. Distinguish between ego-syntonic and ego-dystonic and the implications for the assessment of personality disorders.
2. Define temperament and personality. Explain the relevance of these concepts to the study of personality disorders.
3. Discuss the categorization of personality disorders.

4. Distinguish between avoidant and dependent personality disorders.
5. Discuss prevalence rates for several personality disorders.
6. Describe the clinical features of schizotypal personality disorder, borderline personality disorder, and antisocial personality disorder.
7. Discuss treatment options for personality disorders.

MATCHING I

Answers are found at the end of this chapter. Match these terms and concepts with the definitions that follow:

a.	Personality	h.	Schizophrenic spectrum disorders
b.	Temperament	i.	Splitting
c.	Narcissistic personality disorder	j.	Impulse control disorders
d.	Transference relationship	k.	Intermittent explosive disorder
e.	Dependent personality disorder	l.	Pyromania
f.	Ego-dystonic	m.	Kleptomania
g.	Ego-syntonic	n.	Schizophrenic phenotype

1. _____ characteristic styles of relating to the world: evident in first years of life
2. _____ enduring patterns of perceiving, relating to, and thinking about the environment and oneself: displayed in a wide range of important social and personal contexts
3. _____ the idea that the symptoms of schizotypal personality disorder are seen among people who possess the genotype that makes them vulnerable to schizophrenia
4. _____ out of proportion aggressive behaviors resulting in serious assault or destruction of property
5. _____ stealing objects even though they are not needed or beneficial
6. _____ the way the patient behaves toward the therapist, seen as mirroring the early childhood relationships they had with their caregivers
7. _____ symptoms the person is distressed by and uncomfortable with
8. _____ the tendency to see people and events alternatively as all good or all bad
9. _____ disorders characterized by failure to resist a temptation to perform some pleasurable or tension-relieving act that is harmful to self or others
10. _____ paranoid, schizoid, and schizotypal personality disorders
11. _____ a pervasive pattern of grandiosity, need for admiration, and inability to empathize with people
12. _____ deliberate and purposive fire setting accompanied by fascination with fire: not for personal gain
13. _____ symptoms that are comfortable and acceptable to the person
14. _____ an enduring pattern of dependent and submissive behavior

MATCHING II

Answers are found at the end of this chapter. Match these terms and concepts with the definitions that follow:

1.	Power	4.	Cross-cultural psychology
2.	Antisocial personality disorder	5.	Paranoid personality disorder
3.	Obsessive-compulsive personality disorder	6.	Schizoid personality disorder
		7.	Schizotypal personality disorder

8.   Borderline personality disorder
9.   Histrionic personality disorder
10. Avoidant personality disorder
11. Trichotillomania

12. Pathological gambling
13. Dialectical behavior therapy
14. Psychopathy
15. Affiliation

a. _____ an enduring pattern of thinking and behavior characterized by excessive emotionality and attention seeking

b. _____ the scientific study of ways that human behavior and mental processes are influenced by social and cultural factors

c. _____ an enduring pattern of thinking and behavior whose primary feature is a pervasive instability of mood, self-image, and interpersonal relationships

d. _____ another term for antisocial personality disorder

e. _____ a pervasive pattern of orderliness, perfectionism, and mental and interpersonal control rather than flexibility, openness, and efficiency

f. _____ desire for close relationships

g. _____ repeated maladaptive gambling despite repeated efforts to stop

h. _____ an enduring pattern of thinking and behavior characterized by a pervasive tendency to be inappropriately suspicious of motives and behaviors of others

i. _____ an enduring pattern of thinking and behaving characterized by pervasive social discomfort, fear of negative evaluation, and timidity

j. _____ pulling out one's hair, resulting in noticeable hair loss

k. _____ an approach to psychotherapy with borderline patients

l. _____ an enduring pattern of thinking and behavior characterized by pervasive indifference to interacting with others and a diminished range of emotional experience and expression

m. _____ desire for impact, prestige, or dominance

n. _____ a persistent pattern of antisocial behavior beginning in childhood or adolescence

o. _____ an enduring pattern of discomfort with other people coupled with peculiar thinking and behavior, which takes the form of perceptual and cognitive disturbances

MATCHING III

Answers are found at the end of this chapter. Match these names with the descriptions of their contributions to the study of abnormal psychology:

a. Hervey Cleckley
b. Otto Kernberg

c. John Gunderson
d. Marsha Linehan

e. Terrie Moffitt

1. _____ furthered the psychodynamic view of borderline personality disorder by developing reliable, descriptive terms to allow reliable diagnosis

2. _____ advocated a psychodynamic theory of borderline personality disorder focusing on the faulty development of ego structure

3. _____ proposed that there are two forms of antisocial behavior

4. _____ wrote early descriptions of psychopathy

5. _____ developed a treatment for borderline personality disorder called Dialectical Behavior Therapy

CONCEPT REVIEW

Answers are found at the end of this chapter. After you have read and reviewed the material, test your comprehension by filling in the blanks or circling the correct answer.

1. People with personality disorders are especially likely to seek psychological treatment: **true**

2. What are some reasons why personality disorders are considered controversial among professionals?

   _____

3. The personality disorders are listed on Axis _____ of DSM-IV-TR.

4. Personality disorders are usually ego- **syntonic** **dystonic**.

5. Why are self-report measures limited in assessing personality disorders?

   _____

6. Which of the following is not a dimension of temperament?

   irritability **wealth** **activity level** **fearfulness**

7. Under what circumstances could a difficult temperament be adaptive for an infant?

   _____

8. Cultures differ in displays of _____ and in how much they value

   individualism versus _____.

9. Typologies of personality are likely to be **limited to the culture in which they are developed** or

   applicable across many different cultures.

10. The behavior of people who fit Cluster _____ is typically anxious and fearful.

11. The behavior of people who fit Cluster _____ is typically odd, eccentric, or asocial.

12. The behavior of people who fit Cluster _____ is typically dramatic, emotional, or erratic.

13. Only criminals meet the diagnostic requirements for antisocial personality disorder: **true** **false**

14. There may be an etiological link between histrionic and _____ personality

   disorders; both reflect a common, underlying tendency toward lack of inhibition and both form

   shallow, intense relationships with others.

15. One of the advantages of a categorical system over a dimensional system of personality diagnosis is

   that it provides a more complete description of each person: **true** **false**

16. The DSM-IV-TR uses a **categorical** **dimensional** system with personality disorders.

17. The overall lifetime prevalence for having any type of personality disorder is:

   1–2 percent **10–14 percent** **25–30 percent** **46–50 percent**

18. Name one of the three personality disorders that are the most common:

   _____

19. Which personality disorder is the least common?

_____

20. Very few people who meet the criteria for one personality disorder also meet the criteria for another personality disorder: **true   false**

21. Which personality disorder is most likely to be represented in inpatient and outpatient treatment settings? _____

22. Borderline personality disorder is more common among   **men   women**;   antisocial personality disorder is more common among   **men   women**;   and dependent personality disorder is more common among   **men   women**.

23. Some critics argue that criteria for personality disorders are unfairly biased against traditionally **masculine feminine**   traits.

24. People diagnosed with borderline personality disorder as young adults are   **more   less**   likely to still qualify for the diagnosis in their fifties than people diagnosed with schizotypal or schizoid personality disorders.

25. Research indicates that schizotypal personality disorder is genetically related to schizophrenia: **true   false**

26. When people with personality disorders appear for psychological treatment, it is usually because

_____.

27. Research has shown that low doses of antipsychotic medications are effective in alleviating symptoms of schizotypal personality disorder: **true   false**

28. The difference between impulsive and compulsive behavior is that the original goal for impulsive behavior is to experience _____ while for compulsive behavior it is to avoid _____.

29. Borderline personality disorder is often comorbid with what Axis I disorder?

_____

30. Borderline personality disorder patients have often had problematic relationships with their

_____.

31. Patients in dialectical behavior therapy for borderline personality disorder are less likely to

_____.

32. There is no evidence that psychotropic medication is effective for borderline personality disorder: **true   false**

33. Which personality disorder has been studied the most?

_____

34. The DSM-IV-TR category of antisocial personality disorder does not include traits relating to

    _____ that the Cleckley description included.

35. The expression of an antisocial personality is likely to _____ as the person ages.

36. Research indicates that antisocial behavior is caused by both _____ and

    _____.

37. In one study of adoptees, being raised in an adverse home environment **did** **did not** increase

    the likelihood of antisocial behavior among children with antisocial biological parents; being raised in

    an adverse home environment **did** **did not** increase the likelihood of antisocial behavior

    among children with nonantisocial biological parents.

38. Children raised in families with inconsistent or absent _____ were more likely

    to be antisocial as adults.

39. Children with difficult temperaments due to genetic predisposition to antisocial behavior may induce

    their parents to _____ .

40. There is research evidence that antisocial people lack _____, an emotion that normal people

    have.

41. Some researchers argue that lack of _____ and pathological egocentricity are more

    important than low anxiety in understanding antisocial personality disorder.

42. Research shows that experiencing physical abuse in childhood increases the risk for

    _____ personality disorder in adulthood.

43. Research shows that experiencing sexual abuse in childhood increases the risk for

    _____ personality disorder in adulthood.

44. Several forms of treatment have been shown to be effective with antisocial personality disorder:

    true **false**

45. People with borderline personality disorder become enraged and manipulative and people with

    dependent personality disorder become clingy and submissive when threatened with

    _____ .

46. What type of parents are likely to foster dependency in their children?

    _____

MULTIPLE CHOICE
Answers are found at the end of this chapter. These multiple choice questions will test your understanding of the material presented in the chapter. Read each question and circle the letter representing the best answer.

1. John is always on the lookout for potential harm. He has difficulty trusting anyone, even family members, and is consistently suspicious of their motives. He is oversensitive to minor events, reading into them ulterior meanings. His manner of relating to people has caused him problems at work and home. What type of personality disorder does John likely have?
   a.   schizoid
   b.   obsessive-compulsive
   c.   antisocial
   d.   paranoid

2. The overall lifetime prevalence of personality disorders is approximately
   a.   5–9 percent.
   b.   10–14 percent.
   c.   15–19 percent.
   d.   20–24 percent.

3. Which is a criterion used in DSM-IV-TR to define personality disorders?
   a.   The person must be aware of how his or her behavior is maladaptive.
   b.   The person's behavior must be rigid and inflexible.
   c.   The person's behavior must cause legal problems.
   d.   The person's behavioral difficulties must have started in childhood.

4. The most common personality disorder in both inpatient and outpatient treatment settings is
   a.   dependent.
   b.   antisocial.
   c.   borderline.
   d.   paranoid.

5. The Axis I disorder most often diagnosed with borderline personality disorder is
   a.   depression.
   b.   substance abuse.
   c.   anxiety.
   d.   sexual dysfunction.

6. According to the DSM-IV-TR, an important characteristic of personality disorders is that
   a.   they are typically experienced as ego-syntonic.
   b.   the impairment associated with these disorders is more severe than is found in other forms of mental disorder.
   c.   there is considerable overlap across diagnostic categories.
   d.   obsessive-compulsive personality disorder demonstrates the greatest amount of overlap with other personality disorders.

7. Research focusing on relationships among personality disorders suggests that
    a. there is little diagnostic overlap across all personality disorder categories.
    b. histrionic personality disorder demonstrates the least amount of diagnostic overlap with other personality disorder categories.
    c. there is considerable overlap across diagnostic categories.
    d. obsessive-compulsive personality disorder demonstrates the greatest amount of overlap with other personality disorders.

8. Which of the following statements represents an approach that has been used to conceptualize personality disorders?
    a. They are types of personality styles that are closely associated with specific forms of adult psychopathology.
    b. They result from problems in childhood development as conceptualized by psychodynamic theories.
    c. They are manifestations of the presence of specific psychological deficits.
    d. all of the above

9. Which statement is correct regarding treatment of personality disorders?
    a. People with personality disorders benefit most from insight-oriented therapy.
    b. People with personality disorders who present for treatment often do so because they have another type of mental disorder such as depression.
    c. People with personality disorders benefit most from antipsychotic drugs.
    d. People with personality disorders who present for treatment usually remain in treatment until it is completed.

10. The Axis I disorder most often diagnosed along with antisocial personality disorder is
    a. dissociative fugue.
    b. depression.
    c. schizophrenia.
    d. substance abuse.

11. Which is considered the primary feature of borderline personality disorder?
    a. consistent instability in self-image, mood, and interpersonal relationships
    b. extreme social anxiety
    c. consistent disregard for authority figures
    d. extreme fear of rejection from others

12. What is the key way that narcissistic personality disorder differs from borderline personality disorder?
    a. Sense of self is inflated instead of deflated.
    b. Only people with narcissistic personality disorder have problems with anger if criticized.
    c. Only people with narcissistic personality disorder need special favors from others.
    d. Only people with narcissistic personality disorder have trouble empathizing with others.

13. Warren is definitely a loner. He has no close friends and appears to be indifferent to relationships. Others would describe Warren as distant and aloof. In addition, Warren reports that he does not feel strongly about anything. He can't think of anything that really makes him excited, but he doesn't get upset or distressed about anything either. Warren might qualify for which of the following personality disorders?
    a. borderline
    b. schizoid
    c. paranoid
    d. narcissistic

14. Which of the following has not been a proposed explanation for the etiology of borderline personality disorder?
    a. early substance abuse
    b. negative consequences resulting from parental loss during childhood
    c. a history of physical and sexual abuse
    d. problematic relationships with parents

15. Personality disorders are listed on which axis of DSM-IV-TR?
    a. I
    b. II
    c. III
    d. IV

16. Which statement regarding gender differences in personality disorders is correct?
    a. Antisocial personality disorder is more frequently diagnosed in women.
    b. Men seek treatment for their personality disorders more often than women.
    c. The overall prevalence of personality disorders is about equal in men and women.
    d. Histrionic personality disorder is more likely to be diagnosed in men.

17. Which of the following would not be considered a characteristic feature of antisocial personality disorder?
    a. emotional instability
    b. failure to conform to social norms
    c. deceitfulness
    d. irritability and aggressiveness

18. Mary reports that she feels lonely and isolated. Although she has good relations with family members, she is so afraid of negative criticism from others that she tends to distance herself from relationships. She desperately wants to make friends, but is afraid of being rejected. She constantly watches for even minimal signs of disapproval. Which personality disorder diagnosis is most appropriate for Mary?
    a. schizoid
    b. histrionic
    c. narcissistic
    d. avoidant

19. Larry has extreme difficulty making decisions on his own. He tends to cling to other people and continually asks them for assistance in making even minor decisions. In addition, he constantly asks for his friends' advice and wants to be reassured about everything, even his ability to be a friend. A possible diagnosis for Larry is
    a. dependent personality disorder.
    b. avoidant personality disorder.
    c. narcissistic personality disorder.
    d. borderline personality disorder.

20. Studies investigating the long-term course of antisocial personality disorder indicate that
    a. antisocial individuals tend to become more careless as they grow older, resulting in increasing numbers of arrests.
    b. antisocial individuals continue their criminal activity well into middle age.
    c. antisocial individuals reform their behavior after several incarcerations.
    d. people exhibiting antisocial behavior tend to "burn out" when they reach middle age.

21. According to the five-factor model of personality, the willingness to cooperate and empathize with other people is the trait referred to as
    a. conscientiousness.
    b. affiliation.
    c. agreeableness.
    d. cooperativeness.

22. An advantage of a dimensional system of classifying personality disorders is that
    a. it eliminates the need for diagnosis.
    b. personality disorders are more reliably assessed.
    c. it is more useful for those individuals whose symptoms and behaviors fall on the boundaries between different personality disorder diagnoses.
    d. it requires less time to arrive at a diagnosis.

23. Individual psychotherapy with borderline patients can be difficult because
    a. borderline patients frequently cannot afford the cost of such treatment.
    b. borderline patients are often so transient that it is difficult for them to remain in treatment for more than a brief period of time.
    c. maintaining the type of concentration necessary for individual therapy is particularly difficult for such patients.
    d. establishing and maintaining the type of close relationship necessary between therapist and patient is particularly difficult for borderlines.

24. The personality disorders listed in DSM-IV-TR are divided into how many clusters?
    a. 2
    b. 3
    c. 4
    d. 5

25. Research on the genetics of antisocial personality disorder suggests which of the following statements?
   a. Genetic and environmental factors combine to produce criminal behavior.
   b. The presence of any type of genetic factor in the production of antisocial behavior is dubious.
   c. Without the presence of genetic factors, environmental factors alone can never predict the development of criminal behavior.
   d. Environmental factors are much more important than genetic factors in the production of criminal behavior.

26. Which statement regarding treatment of antisocial personalities is correct?
   a. Treatment is usually successful if the individual does not have a history of legal difficulties.
   b. Currently, the best treatment available for this disorder is family therapy.
   c. Approximately two-thirds of individuals with this disorder show clinical improvement if treated with psychodynamic therapy.
   d. No treatment has documented effectiveness.

27. Sally takes pride in efficient performance and rational behavior. While others see her as rigid, perfectionistic, inflexible, and judgmental, Sally believes that others simply do not share the same standards and are not worthy of her high opinion. She does not show affection and finds 'mushy' feelings in others distasteful. Which personality disorder might Sally be diagnosed with?
   a. schizotypal
   b. antisocial
   c. obsessive-compulsive
   d. schizoid

SHORT ANSWER
Answer the following short answer questions. Compare your work to the material presented in the text.

1. Describe the five-factor model of personality. What are the five factors and their definitions? What would be characteristics of low and high scorers on these traits?

2. Discuss the problems associated with the treatment of individuals with personality disorders. Why is a poor prognosis for treatment associated with most of these disorders? What treatment approaches seem most promising to you?

3. Review the controversies that surround the issue of stability of personality. What methods have been used to demonstrate stable traits? What do you think are methodological limitations of these approaches?

4. Do you believe personality disorders should be classified using a dimensional or categorical approach? Why?

5. Discuss the importance of cross-cultural research. Provide an example.

ANSWER KEY

MATCHING I

1.	b	8.	i
2.	a	9.	j
3.	n	10.	h
4.	k	11.	c
5.	m	12.	l
6.	d	13.	g
7.	f	14.	e

MATCHING II

a.	9	i.	10
b.	4	j.	11
c.	8	k.	13
d.	14	l.	6
e.	3	m.	1
f.	15	n.	2
g.	12	o.	7
h.	5		

MATCHING III

1.	c	4.	a
2.	b	5.	d
3.	e		

CONCEPT REVIEW

1. false
2. difficult to diagnose reliably; etiology is poorly understood; little evidence they are treatable
3. II
4. syntonic
5. people with personality disorders have poor insight into their own behavior
6. wealth
7. during a famine, while being raised in an institution, in a busy daycare center
8. emotion, collectivism
9. limited to the culture in which they are developed
10. C
11. A
12. B
13. false
14. antisocial
15. false
16. categorical
17. 10–14 percent
18. obsessive-compulsive, antisocial, or avoidant personality disorder
19. narcissistic personality disorder
20. false
21. borderline
22. women; men; women
23. feminine
24. less
25. true
26. have another mental disorder
27. true
28. pleasure; anxiety
29. depression
30. parents

31.   leave treatment
32.   true
33.   antisocial
34.   emotions and interpersonal behavior
35.   change forms
36.   genes; environment
37.   did; did not
38.   discipline

39.   be inconsistent or give up in discipline
40.   fear or anxiety
41.   shame
42.   antisocial
43.   borderline
44.   false
45.   abandonment
46.   overprotective or authoritarian

MULTIPLE CHOICE

1. d	7. c	13. b	19. a	25. a
2. b	8. d	14. a	20. d	26. d
3. b	9. b	15. b	21. c	27. c
4. c	10. d	16. c	22. c	
5. a	11. a	17. a	23. d	
6. a	12. c	18. d	24. b	

CHAPTER TEN

EATING DISORDERS

CHAPTER OUTLINE

OBJECTIVES

You should be able to:
1. Discuss the characteristics of eating disorders, anorexia nervosa, and bulimia nervosa.
2. Describe several ways in which those with anorexia have distorted perceptions of self.

3. Identify several medical complications associated with anorexia nervosa and bulimia nervosa.
4. Describe the symptoms of bulimia nervosa and the compensatory behavior that typifies the disorder.
5. Identify the two subtypes of anorexia nervosa and bulimia nervosa.
6. Discuss the gender differences involved in eating disorders.
7. Discuss introceptive awareness and its role in eating disorders.
8. Identify several social, psychological, and biological factors responsible for the development of eating disorders.
9. Discuss the concept of set point.
10. Discuss the techniques utilized in the treatment of anorexia nervosa and bulimia nervosa.
11. Describe the course and outcome associated with eating disorders.

MATCHING I

Answers are found at the end of this chapter. Match these terms and concepts with the definitions that follow:

a.	Eating disorders	n.	Incidence
b.	Anorexia nervosa	o.	Cohort effects
c.	Bulimia nervosa	p.	Enmeshed families
d.	Body mass index	q.	Perfectionism
e.	Distorted body image	r.	Introceptive awareness
f.	Amenorrhea	s.	Dietary restraint
g.	Lanugo	t.	Weight set points
h.	Electrolyte imbalance	u.	Hypothalamus
i.	Binge eating	v.	Metabolic rate
j.	Purging	w.	Hyperlipogenesis
k.	Rumination	x.	Maudsley method
l.	Binge eating disorder	y.	Feminist therapy
m.	Obesity	z.	Dieting disorder

1. _____ a fine, downy hair on the face or trunk of the body
2. _____ a proposed term for eating disorders that reflects the central features of dread of weight gain and obsession with weight loss
3. _____ eating an amount of food in a fixed period of time that is clearly larger than most people would eat under similar circumstances
4. _____ the area of the brain that regulates routine biological functions like appetite
5. _____ absence of at least three consecutive menstrual cycles
6. _____ differences that distinguish one group, born during a particular time period, from another group born at a different time period
7. _____ a disturbance in the levels of potassium, sodium, calcium, and other vital elements found in bodily fluids that can lead to cardiac arrest or kidney failure
8. _____ families whose members are overly involved in one another's lives
9. _____ the endless pursuit of unrealistically high standards
10. _____ repeated episodes of binge eating followed by inappropriate compensatory behaviors with other symptoms related to eating and body image
11. _____ excess body fat: body weight over 20 percent above the expected weight
12. _____ an inaccuracy in how one perceives their body size and shape
13. _____ an intentional act designed to eliminate consumed food from the body

14. _____ severe disturbances in eating behavior that result from obsessive fear of gaining weight
15. _____ direct consequences of restricted eating

16. _____ a controversial diagnosis defined by repeated episodes of binge eating in the absence of compensatory behavior
17. _____ the body's preference for a fixed weight that may have biologically controlled homeostatic mechanisms
18. _____ refusal to maintain a minimally normal body weight along with other symptoms related to eating and body image
19. _____ the regurgitation and rechewing of food
20. _____ recognition of internal cues including emotional states as well as hunger
21. _____ a calculation derived from weight and height used to determine whether someone is significantly underweight
22. _____ encourages pursuing one's own values instead of adopting prescribed social roles
23. _____ the rate at which the body expends energy
24. _____ a type of family therapy for the treatment of anorexia nervosa in which parents take complete control of children's eating, gradually increasing their independence as they improve
25. _____ the storage of abnormally large amounts of fat in fat cells throughout the body
26. _____ number of new cases

MATCHING II
Answers are found at the end of this chapter. Match these names with the descriptions of their contributions to the study of abnormal psychology:

a. Hilde Bruch   b. Christopher Fairburn

1. _____ asserted that a struggle for control and perfectionism is the central psychological issue in the development of eating disorders
2. _____ developed a cognitive behavioral treatment for bulimia nervosa

CONCEPT REVIEW
Answers are found at the end of this chapter. After you have read and reviewed the material, test your comprehension by filling in the blanks or circling the correct answer.

1. People with anorexia nervosa suffer from a loss of appetite: **true   false**

2. Anorexia and bulimia are how much more common in women than in men:

　　　　twice as common   four times as common   ten times as common

3. Males in our society see themselves as thin when they weigh 105 percent of their expected weight,

　　while females see themselves as thin when they weight 90 percent of their expected weight:

　　true false

4. Female anorexics may be proud of their emaciation, while male anorexics are likely to be stigmatized

　　for it: **true   false**

5. Eating disorders are more common among men who are wrestlers and men who are gay:

   true   **false**

6. Often, eating disorders begin with a _____.

7. What percent of people with anorexia nervosa die of starvation, suicide, or medical complications?

   _____

8. A person with anorexia often becomes more and more afraid of fat the thinner they become:

   true   **false**

9. It is likely that amenorrhea and lack of interest in sex common among anorexics are a result rather than a predisposition of the weight loss: **true**   **false**

10. Although anorexia is a serious mental disorder, it seldom involves medical complications:

    true false

11. A person with anorexia can be seen as exceptionally successful in what area?

    _____

12. The study with World War II conscientious objectors found that obsessive-compulsive behaviors probably   **precede**   **follow**   the change in eating patterns.

13. Anorexia seldom co-occurs with symptoms of bulimia: **true**   **false**

14. Binge eating is often triggered by _____.

15. Lack of control is characteristic of _____, while excessive control is characteristic of _____.

16. Vomiting prevents the absorption of how many of the calories consumed during a binge?

    almost none   **about half**   **almost all**

17. The two subtypes of anorexia are the _____ type and the _____ type.

18. The two subtypes of bulimia are the _____ type and the_____ type.

19. Bulimia nervosa and anorexia nervosa each have two subtypes, which   **are**   **are not** found by research to be distinct and meaningful subtypes.

20. Research indicates that obesity is primarily caused by lack of willpower in eating habits:

    true   **false**

21. Eating disorders have become somewhat less common since the 1960s and 1970s: **true**   **false**

22. Which type of eating disorder is more common? _____

23. In Third World countries, weighing more is a status symbol: **true**   **false**

24. Young women working in which fields have higher rates of eating disorders?

    _____

25. People with which type of eating disorder are more likely to report that their families have high levels of conflict? _____

26. Clinicians note that enmeshed families are more characteristic of people with which type of eating disorder? _____

27. Hilde Bruch identified two characteristics in people with eating disorders: _____ and _____.

28. Negative evaluations of one's weight, shape, and appearance predict the subsequent development of eating disorders: **true   false**

29. People with anorexia nervosa: **insist that their weight is not a problem   admit that they are too thin, but cannot overcome the symptoms**

30. When food intake is reduced, there is an increase in the metabolic rate: **true   false**

31. There is strong evidence that eating disorders are genetic: **true   false**

32. There is evidence that family therapy is more effective than individual therapy in treating adolescents with anorexia: **true   false**

33. Current forms of treatment for anorexia are quite effective: **true   false**

34. Psychotherapy tends to be more effective than antidepressant medication in the treatment of bulimia: **true   false**

35. Interpersonal therapy was found to be as effective as cognitive behavior therapy in the treatment of bulimia: **true   false**

36. People with bulimia nervosa tend to: **keep their binges secret   binge in front of others, hoping someone will stop them**

37. Prevention programs for eating disorders are most effective when they: **prevent weight gain   focus on healthy eating and rejection of the thin ideal**

38. Bulimia is more likely to lead to death than anorexia: **true   false**

MULTIPLE CHOICE
Answers are found at the end of this chapter. These multiple choice questions will test your understanding of the material presented in the chapter. Read each question and circle the letter representing the best answer.

1. Both bulimia and anorexia nervosa are characterized by which of the following?
   a. struggle for control
   b. considerable shame
   c. obsessive-compulsive disorder
   d. the absence of menstruation

2. All of the following are compensatory behaviors of bulimia nervosa except
    a. misuse of laxatives.
    b. complete avoidance of food.
    c. intense exercise.
    d. misuse of enemas.

3. All of the following are symptoms of anorexia nervosa except
    a. an intense fear of gaining weight.
    b. refusal to maintain weight at or above minimally normal weight for age and height.
    c. acknowledgment of the seriousness of low body weight, but refusal to change eating behavior.
    d. amenorrhea.

4. Which of the following theories offers the most promising explanations for eating disorders?
    a. biological
    b. social
    c. psychological
    d. All of the above equally offer promising explanations of eating disorders.

5. All of the following are symptoms of bulimia nervosa except
    a. recurrent episodes of binge eating that involve large amounts of food.
    b. that it occurs solely during episodes of anorexia nervosa.
    c. recurrent inappropriate compensatory behavior, especially purging.
    d. undue influence of weight and body shape on self-evaluation.

6. Both bulimia and anorexia nervosa are approximately _____ times more common among women than among men.
    a. ten
    b. fifteen
    c. twenty
    d. twenty-five

7. Many professionals agree that anorexia is a source of which of the following to their patients?
    a. shame
    b. pride
    c. gratification
    d. resentment

8. Bulimia nervosa is most prevalent among which of the following groups?
    a. women born after 1960
    b. women born before 1960
    c. girls ages 10–15
    d. women born in the 1950s

9. Which of the following is not a finding that provides evidence that social factors are very important in eating disorders?
    a. Eating disorders have recently become much more common.
    b. Eating disorders are much more common among women working in fields that emphasize weight and appearance, such as modeling and ballet.
    c. Eating disorders are more common among middle- and upper-class whites.
    d. Eating disorders have a higher concordance rate in MZ rather than DZ twins.

10. Medical complications from anorexia can include all but
    a. growth of downy hair on the face.
    b. dry, cracked skin.
    c. hallucinations.
    d. kidney failure.

11. Women from which ethnic group have the lowest level of body dissatisfaction?
    a. European Americans
    b. African Americans
    c. Latinas
    d. They all have the same level.

12. The average person with anorexia
    a. gains about five pounds.
    b. does not change weight.
    c. loses about ten to fifteen pounds.
    d. loses 25–30 percent of normal body weight.

13. Which disorder is not frequently comorbid with bulimia nervosa?
    a. antisocial personality disorder
    b. depression
    c. substance abuse
    d. anxiety

14. Which is not one of the medical complications of bulimia nervosa?
    a. damage to the teeth
    b. starvation
    c. regurgitation and rechewing of food
    d. swollen face due to salivary gland enlargement

15. Which disorder may be culture-bound, and not appear in other cultures?
    a. anorexia nervosa
    b. binge eating disorder
    c. bulimia nervosa
    d. obesity

16. Exposure to which of the following has been shown to increase a girl's internalization of the ideal of thinness?
    a. *Seventeen* magazine
    b. competitive swimming
    c. other cultures
    d. campaigns promoting acceptance of a wider range of body types as beautiful

17. Introceptive awareness is
    a. awareness of one's physical appearance.
    b. awareness of one's caloric intake.
    c. awareness of one's emotional states.
    d. awareness of one's energy expenditure during exercise.

18. Genetics
    a. are not involved in the cause of eating disorders.
    b. may influence a personality characteristic that increases the risk for bulimia.
    c. are shown to be critically important in eating disorders by the dramatic increase in recent years in the rates of eating disorders.
    d. are mostly the cause of eating disorders.

19. Which treatment for bulimia resulted in patients continuing to improve in the year after treatment ended?
    a. antidepressant medication
    b. cognitive behavior therapy
    c. behavior therapy
    d. interpersonal therapy

20. What aspect of a prevention program for eating disorders is effective?
    a. content criticizing diets and purging
    b. content critical of the thin ideal
    c. content focusing on stress management
    d. content focusing on the dangers of eating disorders

SHORT ANSWER
Answer the following short answer questions. Compare your work to the material presented in the text.

1. Discuss the differences between anorexia nervosa and bulimia nervosa in terms of symptomatology, prevalence, etiology, and treatment.

2. Which social factors play a role in the etiology of eating disorders? Provide examples.

3. If you were a therapist and a young woman entered therapy for an eating disorder, what would your treatment plan entail? Would your treatment for a male patient differ from treatment for a female patient? Explain.

4. Discuss the role of placebo control groups in psychological research. What are the challenges in using such groups?

5. If you were going to plan a program to prevent eating disorders, what would you include and why?

ANSWER KEY

MATCHING I

1. g	8. p	15. s	22. y
2. z	9. q	16. l	23. v
3. i	10. c	17. t	24. x
4. u	11. m	18. b	25. w
5. f	12. e	19. k	26. n
6. o	13. j	20. r	
7. h	14. a	21. d	

MATCHING II

1. a	2. b

CONCEPT REVIEW

1.	false	21.	false
2.	ten times as common	22.	bulimia
3.	true	23.	true
4.	true	24.	modeling, ballet dancing, gymnastics
5.	true	25.	bulimia
6.	diet	26.	anorexia
7.	10 percent	27.	struggle for control; perfectionism
8.	true	28.	true
9.	true	29.	insist that their weight is not a problem
10.	false	30.	false
11.	self-control	31.	false
12.	follow	32.	true
13.	false	33.	false
14.	an unhappy mood	34.	true
15.	bulimia; anorexia	35.	true
16.	about half	36.	keep their binges a secret
17.	restricting; binge-eating/purging	37.	focus on healthy eating and rejection of the thin ideal
18.	purging; nonpurging	38.	false
19.	are not		
20.	false		

MULTIPLE CHOICE

1. a	4. b	7. b	10. c	13. a	16. a	19. d
2. b	5. b	8. a	11. b	14. b	17. c	20. b
3. c	6. a	9. d	12. d	15. c	18. b	

CHAPTER ELEVEN

SUBSTANCE USE DISORDERS

CHAPTER OUTLINE

OBJECTIVES

You should be able to:
1. Distinguish between substance abuse, substance dependence, and polysubstance abuse.
2. Define tolerance and withdrawal.
3. Discuss several short-term effects and consequences of prolonged abuse of alcohol.
4. Describe several properties, short-term effects, and consequences of abusing benzodiazepines, opiates, nicotine, amphetamines, cocaine, cannabis, and hallucinogens.

5. Discuss the classification system utilized to differentiate between substance abuse and dependence.
6. Describe the typical course and outcome of alcoholism.
7. Discuss the epidemiology of alcoholism.
8. Explain how social factors influence initial experimentation with drugs and alcohol.
9. Discuss several research findings regarding the genetics of alcoholism.
10. Explain the endorphin and dopamine reward pathway hypotheses.
11. Describe the role of cognitive expectations on perceived effects of alcohol consumption.
12. Discuss the integrated systems approach to substance use and abuse.
13. Describe the use of detoxification, self-help groups, controlled drinking training, and relapse prevention training in the treatment of alcoholism.

MATCHING I

Answers are found at the end of this chapter. Match these terms and concepts with the definitions that follow:

a.	Substance dependence		p.	Tranquilizers
b.	Substance abuse		q.	Barbiturates
c.	Polysubstance abuse		r.	Benzodiazepines
d.	Addiction		s.	Cocaine
e.	Drug of abuse		t.	Opiates
f.	Hypnotics		u.	Morphine
g.	Anxiolytics		v.	Codeine
h.	Narcotic analgesics		w.	Heroin
i.	Craving		x.	Sedatives
j.	Psychological dependence		y.	Psychomotor stimulants
k.	Physiological dependence		z.	Cannabinoids
l.	Tolerance		aa.	Pharmacodynamic tolerance
m.	Withdrawal		bb.	Metabolic tolerance
n.	Alcohol withdrawal delirium		cc.	Behavioral conditioning mechanisms
o.	Delirium tremens			

1. _____ CNS depressants that are used for relieving anxiety
2. _____ a less severe pattern of drug use defined in terms of interference with a person's ability to fulfill major role obligations, the recurrent use of a drug in dangerous situations, or the experience of legal problems associated with the drug use
3. _____ drugs with properties similar to opium, often used to relieve pain
4. _____ convulsions, hallucinations, and a sudden disturbance of consciousness with changes in cognitive processes during withdrawal from alcohol
5. _____ the process through which the nervous system becomes less sensitive to the effects of a substance with repeated exposure to that substance
6. _____ a synthetic opiate often injected, inhaled, or smoked
7. _____ physical symptoms related to drug use, including tolerance and withdrawal
8. _____ a class of drugs, discovered in the early twentieth century, used widely for many years to treat anxiety, prevent seizures, and relieve pain
9. _____ drugs that produce their effects by simulating the actions of certain neurotransmitters
10. _____ a chemical substance that alters mood, level of perception, or brain functioning
11. _____ drugs that calm people or reduce excitement
12. _____ used to decrease anxiety or agitation

13. _____ CNS depressants used to help people sleep
14. _____ the abuse of several types of drugs
15. _____ opiates that can be used clinically to decrease pain
16. _____ a forceful urge to use drugs
17. _____ symptoms experienced when a person stops using a drug
18. _____ a more severe pattern of repeated self-administration often resulting in tolerance, withdrawal, or compulsive drug-taking behavior
19. _____ one of the active ingredients of opium, very similar to heroin
20. _____ one of the active ingredients of opium, available in small quantities in Canada in over-the-counter medications
21. _____ an older term used to describe substance use problems such as alcoholism
22. _____ feeling compelled to use a drug to control one's feelings or to prepare for certain activities
23. _____ an older term for alcohol withdrawal delirium
24. _____ synthetic drugs whose therapeutic effects were discovered in the 1950s, which have largely replaced barbiturates in medical practice
25. _____ a naturally-occurring stimulant drug extracted from the leaf of a small tree that grows at high elevations
26. _____ cues associated with the administration of a drug function as a conditioned stimulus and elicit a conditioned response opposite the direction of the drug's effect
27. _____ drugs like marijuana that produce euphoria and an altered sense of time
28. _____ when brain receptors adapt to the continued presence of the drug: also called down regulation
29. _____ when repeated exposure to a drug causes the liver to produce more enzymes to break down the drug, so the person has to take more and more to sustain the same level in the body

MATCHING II

Answers are found at the end of this chapter. Match these terms and concepts with the definitions that follow:

1.	Amphetamines		16.	Phencyclidine (PCP)
2.	Naltrexone		17.	Acamprosate
3.	Discontinuance syndrome		18.	Flashbacks
4.	Cannabis		19.	Endorphins
5.	Marijuana		20.	Balanced placebo design
6.	Hashish		21.	High-risk research design
7.	Temporal disintegration		22.	Risk factors
8.	Reverse tolerance		23.	MDMA
9.	Hallucinogens		24.	Detoxification
10.	LSD		25.	Antabuse
11.	Psilocybin		26.	Abstinence violation effect
12.	Mescaline		27.	Speedball
13.	Peyote		28.	Nicotine
14.	Risk		29.	Psychoactive substance
15.	Mesolimbic dopamine pathway			

a. _____ the dried leaves and flowers of the hemp plant
b. _____ a medication used in Europe to treat alcoholism: not yet approved by the FDA

c. _____ a newly approved medication to treat alcoholism which has been demonstrated to be effective in reducing relapse rates

d. _____ synthetically produced psychomotor stimulants such as dexedrine or methamphetamine

e. _____ a procedure that allows the investigator to separate the direct, biological effects of the drug from the subjects' expectations about how the drug should affect their behavior

f. _____ drugs that cause people to experience hallucinations at relatively low doses

g. _____ a drug that can block the chemical breakdown of alcohol, which will make the person taking it violently ill if he or she consumes alcohol

h. _____ brief visual aftereffects that can occur at unpredictable intervals long after a hallucinogen has cleared the body

i. _____ a technique where subjects are selected from the general population based on some identified risk factor that has a fairly high risk ratio

j. _____ symptoms from abruptly stopping high-dosage use of benzodiazepines, including the return of anxiety

k. _____ variables associated with a higher likelihood of developing a disorder

l. _____ a hallucinogen found in certain mushrooms which bears a chemical resemblance to serotonin

m. _____ a synthetic hallucinogen which bears a strong chemical resemblance to serotonin

n. _____ a condition often accompanying cannabis intoxication in which people have trouble retaining and organizing information

o. _____ becoming more sensitive to a drug with prolonged use: reported by users but not yet documented in laboratory studies

p. _____ a synthetic drug that can induce psychotic behavior at high doses

q. _____ the probability that a certain outcome will occur

r. _____ the brain reward pathway

s. _____ the guilt and perceived loss of control that a person feels whenever he or she slips and takes a drug after an extended period of abstinence

t. _____ the removal of a drug on which a person has become dependent

u. _____ a drug with the active ingredient called THC, derived from the hemp plant

v. _____ a type of hallucinogen that resembles norepinephrine

w. _____ the dried resin from the top of the female hemp plant

x. _____ also called Ecstasy: a synthetic amphetamine derivative

y. _____ a cactus that contains mescaline

z. _____ endogenous opioids that are naturally synthesized in the brain and are closely related to morphine

aa. _____ another term for drug of abuse

bb. _____ a mixture of cocaine and opiates

cc. _____ the active ingredient in tobacco

MATCHING III

Answers are found at the end of this chapter. Match these names with the descriptions of their contributions to the study of abnormal psychology:

a. George Vaillant   c. Robert Cloninger
b. Alan Marlatt

1. _____ proposed that there were two types of alcoholism: Type I, which has a later onset, psychological dependence, and the absence of antisocial personality traits, and Type II, which is seen predominantly among men, has an earlier onset, and co-occurs with antisocial behaviors

2. ____ conducted a longitudinal study of alcoholism among inner-city adolescents and college students

3. ____ developed a cognitive behavioral view of the relapse process and a relapse prevention mode for treatment of substance use

CONCEPT REVIEW

Answers are found at the end of this chapter. After you have read and reviewed the material, test your comprehension by filling in the blanks or circling the correct answer.

1. Most researchers have moved toward a view of substance abuse that emphasizes common causes,

   behaviors, and consequences of using the substance rather than a focus on the particular drug used:

   true   false

2. One of the best indices for defining alcoholism is the amount of alcohol a person consumes:

   true   false

3. A crucial feature of alcoholism is diminished _____.

4. The most substantial tolerance effects are found among people who use which drugs?

   _____

5. What drugs have not been shown to have tolerance effects? _____

6. _____ is the most widely used psychoactive substance in the world.

7. What organ metabolizes alcohol? _____

8. Blood alcohol levels are only weakly correlated with intoxicating effects: **true   false**

9. When blood alcohol levels go too high, the person will become unconscious and can always sleep off

   the effects of the alcohol with no acute dangers: **true   false**

10. There is a strong correlation between violent behavior and alcohol: **true   false**

11. The abuse of alcohol has more negative health consequences over an extended period of time than any

    other drug except nicotine: **true   false**

12. Sedatives and hypnotics can lead to a state of arousal similar to that of cocaine: **true   false**

13. When used to reduce anxiety, barbiturates and benzodiazepines produce a calm, relaxed feeling:

    true   false

14. Barbiturates may not be helpful because a return in symptoms occurs when a person stops taking   them: **true**

15. Opiates produce _____.

16. Heroin addicts suffer from few health problems and are not more likely to die than non-addicts:

    true   false

17. Nicotine may mimic the effects of _____ drugs.

18. Nicotine produces CNS   **arousal   depression.**

19. The FDA decided to regulate cigarettes as a   **drug   medical device**.

20. At what age does addiction to nicotine almost always begin? _____

21. From a psychological point of view, withdrawal from nicotine is just as difficult as withdrawal from

    _____.

22. Cocaine and amphetamines activate the sympathetic nervous system: **true   false**

23. Psychosis from amphetamine use is a permanent condition: **true   false**

24. The most common reaction to discontinuing stimulant drugs is

    _____.

25. Marijuana and hashish show strong tolerance effects: **true   false**

26. Hallucinogens may trigger persistent psychosis in people vulnerable to that type of disorder:

    true   false

27. A typical American during colonial times never consumed alcohol: **true   false**

28. Most alcoholics go through repeated periods of _____.

29. In Vaillant's study, relapse to alcohol abuse was unlikely if the period of abstinence was how many

    years? _____

30. What three types of disorders are commonly associated with substance abuse?

    _____, _____, and _____

31. Cannabis is used almost exclusively in North America: **true   false**

32. Among all men and women who have ever used alcohol, about _____ percent will develop serious

    problems with drinking sometime during their lives.

33. Men outnumber women in chronic abuse of alcohol by a ratio of about:

    2 to 1   5 to 1   10 to 1

34. Women who drink experience more social _____ than men.

35. Women metabolize alcohol differently than men, even when differences in body weight are

    controlled, so they have higher peak blood alcohol levels: **true   false**

36. The lifetime prevalence for addiction to nicotine is: **4 percent   14 percent   24 percent**

37. The lifetime prevalence for addiction to drugs (illegal and prescription) other than nicotine or alcohol

    is: **4.5 percent   7.5 percent   10.3 percent**

38. The elderly are more likely to be addicted to alcohol than are younger people: **true   false**

39. How do some researchers explain lower rates of alcohol abuse among Jews

    _____.

40. Adolescents with alcoholic parents are less likely to drink than those whose parents are not alcoholic:

    true   false

41. A flushing response to even a small amount of alcohol, including flushed skin, nausea, and an abnormal heartbeat, occurs in 30 to 50 percent of people of what ethnic ancestry?

_____

42. There is an elevated risk for alcoholism among first-degree relatives of alcoholics: **true   false**

43. Adoption studies indicate that genetic factors play some role in the increased risk for alcoholism among relatives of alcoholics: **true   false**

44. The Indians of South America who produce coca leaves to sell typically have severe dependence problems: **true   false**

45. Rates of cigarette smoking among young adults declined over the 1990s: **true   false**

46. There is evidence that alcohol triggers the reward pathways in the brain that typically respond to food and sex and involve which neurotransmitter? _____

47. The tension-reduction hypothesis suggests that people drink alcohol in an effort to reduce the impact of a _____ environment.

48. In one study, people who believed they consumed alcohol, but really did not, showed increased _____ and _____ arousal.

49. _____ expectancies about effects of alcohol predict drinking problems.

50. Detoxification from alcohol is typically accomplished by abruptly discontinuing consumption of alcohol: **true   false**

51. Many patients using Antabuse have poor compliance with treatment, that is, they stop taking the Antabuse: **true   false**

52. There is no research evidence that Alcoholics Anonymous is an effective form of treatment:
true   false

53. The heritability estimates for men and women in risk for alcoholism due to genetic factors are about:
1 in 10   2 in 3   9 in 10

54. The relapse prevention model of treatment teaches patients to interpret slips in abstinence as

_____.

55. Research suggests that a person's coping skills, social support, and stress are **better   worse** predictors of successfully stopping drinking than the particular type of treatment received.

56. The medication _____works by making a person feel sick if they drink, and the medication _____works by reducing the rewarding effects of alcohol.

57. Motivational interviewing takes a   **confrontational   nonconfrontational**   approach.

MULTIPLE CHOICE

Answers are found at the end of this chapter. These multiple choice questions will test your understanding of the material presented in the chapter. Read each question and circle the letter representing the best answer.

1. Because alcoholism is associated with many diverse problems, distinguishing between people who are dependent on alcohol and those who are not is often determined by which of the following?
   a. the presence of legal problems (e.g. driving under the influence)
   b. whether or not the person reports tolerance to alcohol
   c. the number of problems that the person experiences
   d. the presence of medical problems

2. Although disulfiram (Antabuse) can effectively block the chemical breakdown of alcohol, people discontinue using this drug because
   a. it is an extremely expensive drug to administer.
   b. the effect of the drug is very short-lived; it reduces alcohol intake for only a few hours after its ingestion.
   c. individuals who use this drug have to monitor their dietary intake.
   d. they want to start drinking again.

3. The two terms included in the DSM-IV-TR to describe substance use disorders are
   a. substance dependence and substance abuse.
   b. substance abuse and addiction.
   c. tolerance and addiction.
   d. substance abuse and polysubstance abuse.

4. Research on the long-term course of alcohol suggests that
   a. the typical individual is able to successfully stop drinking only after hospitalization.
   b. the typical individual cycles through periods of alcohol consumption, cessation, and relapse.
   c. the typical individual rarely experiences relapse after making the decision to stop drinking.
   d. the typical individual spends approximately ten years in the alcohol consumption period before making the decision to quit.

5. Which of the following is an example of a CNS stimulant?
   a. alcohol
   b. cocaine
   c. morphine
   d. hashish

6. Results from adoption studies focusing on the genetic transmission of alcohol indicate that
   a. the familial nature of alcoholism appears to be at least partially determined by genes; that is, having an alcoholic biological parent increases risk for alcoholism.
   b. if a person does not have an alcoholic biological parent, having an adopted parent with alcohol problems greatly increases risk for alcoholism.
   c. having the personality trait of "behavioral overcontrol" increases risk for alcoholism.
   d. only people with at least one alcoholic biological parent are at risk for alcoholism.

7. Sam currently drinks large amounts of alcohol on a daily basis. He plans his day around when alcohol will be available to him. He drives a certain route home from work that passes two liquor stores to ensure that liquor will be available each evening. His weekend activities are planned around availability of alcohol, and he will not attend social functions where alcohol is absent. Which term best describes his condition?
    a. binge drinker
    b. controlled drinker
    c. psychological dependence
    d. pre-alcoholic drinker

8. In most states, the current legal limit of alcohol concentration for driving is
    a. 50 mg percent.
    b. 100 mg percent.
    c. 150 mg percent.
    d. 200 mg percent.

9. One reason that risk for substance dependence is increased in elderly people is that
    a. the elderly demonstrate a reduced sensitivity to drug toxicity and therefore require higher drug dosages.
    b. adult children often encourage their elderly parents to use drugs to control their nerves.
    c. the elderly use prescribed psychoactive drugs more frequently than other age groups and are more sensitive to drug toxicity.
    d. in fact, there is little risk for substance dependence in the elderly.

10. A person who has legal problems because of his or her drug use and cannot function at work would be diagnosed with
    a. substance dependence.
    b. a recreational drug user.
    c. intoxicated.
    d. substance abuse.

11. A principal assumption of Alcoholics Anonymous (AA) is that
    a. people need to relapse several times before they will learn to take their alcohol problem seriously.
    b. individuals cannot recover on their own.
    c. individuals need to remove themselves from the stressful situations that trigger alcohol use.
    d. with enough help, people can develop effective methods of controlled drinking.

12. Which of the following statements is accurate regarding the definition of substance dependence in the DSM-IV-TR?
    a. No tolerance or withdrawal can be evident.
    b. The individual must exhibit several characteristics that describe a pattern of compulsive use.
    c. The person must exhibit characteristics of problematic substance use for at least two years.
    d. A prior diagnosis of substance abuse is required before the diagnosis of substance dependence may be considered.

13. Which would not be considered an example of a common alcohol expectancy?
    a. Alcohol decreases power and aggression.
    b. Alcohol enhances social and physical pleasure.
    c. Alcohol enhances sexual performance.
    d. Alcohol increases social assertiveness.

14. Which hallucinogenic substance can damage brain neurons permanently and has been linked with some fatalities?
    a. LSD
    b. mescaline
    c. MDMA
    d. psilocybin

15. What percentage of those who have ever used alcohol will develop serious problems resulting from prolonged alcohol consumption?
    a. 10 percent
    b. 20 percent
    c. 30 percent
    d. 40 percent

16. Which of the following statements is true regarding the presence of alcohol dependence over a long period of time?
    a. Alcohol dependence always results in dementia.
    b. Alcohol dependence follows opiate dependence and cocaine dependence in terms of potential negative health consequences.
    c. Nutritional disturbances caused by alcohol dependence can be controlled through appropriate medication.
    d. Alcohol dependence has more negative health consequences than does abuse of any other substance except nicotine.

17. Which of the following statements regarding tolerance is true?
    a. Individuals can develop tolerance to all psychoactive drugs over time.
    b. Certain hallucinogens may not lead to the development of tolerance.
    c. The most substantial tolerance effects are found among cannabis users.
    d. Heroin and CNS stimulants do not lead to the development of tolerance.

18. Rates of alcohol abuse are significantly lower among
    a. Jews.
    b. Catholics.
    c. Native Americans.
    d. Protestants.

19. Which of the following statements is true regarding alcohol expectancies?
    a. Negative expectancies appear to be less powerful than positive expectancies in influencing alcohol use.
    b. Adolescents do not appear to have strong beliefs about alcohol prior to taking their first drink.
    c. Expectations regarding alcohol do not predict drinking behaviors.
    d. Portrayal of alcohol in the mass media does not appear to influence individuals' alcohol expectancies.

20. Which of the following symptoms are side effects of alcohol withdrawal?
    a. hand tremors, sweating, and nausea
    b. anxiety and insomnia
    c. convulsions and hallucinations
    d. all of the above

21. One model for the biological basis of alcoholism examines alcohol's effect on the reward pathways in the brain which regulate natural rewards, such as food and sex, by increasing the level of which of the following neurotransmitters?
    a. dopamine
    b. serotonin
    c. epinephrine
    d. norepinephrine

22. The relapse prevention model
    a. focuses on the expectancies people have when drinking alcohol.
    b. focuses on anger management training.
    c. focuses on the brain's reward pathway.
    d. gives the person a way to cope with guilt and loss of control experienced at having a slip in abstinence.

23. Which of the following factors is a predictor of long-term successful treatment outcome for alcoholism?
    a. the availability of residential alcohol treatment programs in the area
    b. the alcoholic's participation in AA
    c. taking antidepressants
    d. the availability of social support

SHORT ANSWER
Answer the following short answer questions. Compare your answers to the material presented in the text.

1. Explain the theory of Type 1 and Type 2 alcoholism. What do you believe to be the weaknesses of this model? What further type of research is necessary to support or disconfirm this theory?

2. Describe the balanced placebo design. Why is it a useful research design to study of the effects of alcohol on behavior?

3. Discuss the ways that genetics and environmental factors interact to affect a person's alcohol dependence.

4. Discuss the issue of risk and risk factors in research.

ANSWER KEY

MATCHING I

1. g
2. b
3. t
4. n
5. l
6. w
7. k
8. q
9. y
10. e
11. x
12. p
13. f
14. c
15. h
16. i
17. m
18. a
19. u
20. v
21. d
22. j
23. o
24. r
25. s
26. cc
27. z
28. aa
29. bb

MATCHING II

a. 5
b. 17
c. 2
d. 1
e. 20
f. 9
g. 25
h. 18
i. 21
j. 3
k. 22
l. 11
m. 10
n. 7
o. 8
p. 16
q. 14
r. 15
s. 26
t. 24
u. 4
v. 12
w. 6
x. 23
y. 13
z. 19
aa. 29
bb. 27
cc. 28

MATCHING III

1. c

2. a

3. b

CONCEPT REVIEW

1.	true		30.	antisocial personality disorder, mood disorder; anxiety disorder
2.	false		31.	false
3.	control over drinking		32.	20
4.	alcohol, nicotine, heroin, cocaine, amphetamines		33.	2 to 1
5.	cannabinoids and hallucinogens		34.	disapproval
6.	caffeine		35.	true
7.	the liver		36.	24 percent
8.	false		37.	10.3 percent
9.	false		38.	false
10.	true		39.	use of alcohol in small amounts in religious ceremonies and disapproval of those who drink to intoxication
11.	true		40.	false
12.	false		41.	Asian
13.	true		42.	true
14.	true		43.	false
15.	euphoria		44.	false
16.	false		45.	false
17.	antidepressant		46.	dopamine
18.	arousal		47.	stressful
19.	medical device		48.	aggression; sexual
20.	adolescence		49.	positive
21.	heroin		50.	false
22.	true		51.	true
23.	false		52.	false
24.	depression		53.	2 in 3
25.	false		54.	temporary
26.	true		55.	better
27.	false		56.	Antabuse; Naltrexone
28.	abstinence		57.	nonconfrontational
29.	six			

MULTIPLE CHOICE

1. c	6. a	11. b	16. d	21. a
2. d	7. c	12. b	17. b	22. d
3. a	8. b	13. a	18. a	23. d
4. b	9. c	14. c	19. a	
5. b	10. d	15. b	20. d	

CHAPTER TWELVE

SEXUAL AND GENDER IDENTITY DISORDERS

CHAPTER OUTLINE

OBJECTIVES

You should be able to:

1. Discuss the role of cultural and religious values in the examination of sexual disorders.
2. Discuss the contributions of Freud, Kinsey, and Masters and Johnson in the study of human sexuality.
3. Distinguish hypoactive sexual desire from sexual aversion disorder.
4. Define male erectile disorder, female arousal disorder, premature ejaculation, dyspareunia, and female orgasmic disorder.
5. Discuss the prevalence of sexual disorders.
6. Discuss the biological and psychological causes of sexual disorders.
7. Describe sensate focus as a treatment technique for sexual disorders.
8. Identify the major forms of paraphilias.
9. Describe the etiology of paraphilias.
10. Discuss differences between sexual disorders and disorders of gender identity.

MATCHING I

Answers are found at the end of this chapter. Match these terms and concepts with the definitions that follow:

a.	Sexual dysfunctions	k.	Hypoactive sexual desire disorder
b.	Paraphilias	l.	Sexual aversion disorder
c.	Gender identity	m.	Erectile dysfunction
d.	Gender identity disorder	n.	Impotence
e.	Excitement	o.	Female sexual arousal disorder
f.	Orgasm	p.	Male erectile disorder
g.	Resolution	q.	Inhibited sexual arousal
h.	Refractory period	r.	Hypothetical construct
j.	Operational definition		

1. _____ sudden intensely pleasurable release of sexual tension
2. _____ a strong and persistent identification with the opposite sex coupled with a sense of discomfort with one's anatomical sex
3. _____ a disorder in which a person has an extreme aversion to and avoidance of genital sexual contact with a partner
4. _____ persistent or recurrent erectile dysfunction
5. _____ engorgement of blood vessels in an organ
6. _____ forms of sexual disorder that involve inhibitions of sexual desire or interference with the physiological responses leading to orgasm
7. _____ a procedure used to measure a theoretical construct
8. _____ period of time after orgasm the person is unresponsive to further sexual stimulation
9. _____ forms of sexual disorder that involve sexual arousal in association with unusual objects and situations
10. _____ persistent or recurrent inability to attain or maintain an adequate lubrication-swelling response of sexual excitement even in the presence of sexual desire
11. _____ a person's sense of being male or female
12. _____ third stage of Masters and Johnson's human sexual response cycle where the body returns to its resting state
13. _____ disorder characterized by diminished desire for sexual activity and reduced frequency of sexual fantasies
14. _____ first stage of Masters and Johnson's human sexual response cycle involving physiological responses and subjective feelings
15. _____ inability to attain or maintain an adequate lubrication-swelling response of sexual excitement
16. _____ an older term for erectile dysfunction that is no longer used because of its negative implications
17. _____ events or states that reside within a person and are proposed to explain that person's behavior
18. _____ difficulty in obtaining an erection that is sufficient to accomplish intercourse or to satisfy self or partner during intercourse

MATCHING II

Answers are found at the end of this chapter. Match these terms and concepts with the definitions that follow:

1. Penile plethysmograph	11. Sensate focus
2. Vaginal photometer	12. Scheduling
3. Construct validity	13. Fetishism
4. Premature ejaculation	14. Sexual sadism
5. Female orgasmic disorder	15. Transvestite
6. Genital anesthesia	16. Transvestic fetishism
7. Dyspareunia	17. Drag queens
8. Vaginismus	18. Transvestic fetishism with gender dysphoria
9. Excessive sexual drive	19. Sexual masochism
10. Performance anxiety	

a. _____ the extent to which a measure produces results consistent with the theoretical construct it is purported to assess

b. _____ a procedure for measuring male sexual arousal

c. _____ a diagnosis included in the ICD but not the DSM

d. _____ a person who dresses in the clothing of the other gender

e. _____ a paraphilia in which sexual arousal is associated with the actual act of being humiliated, beaten, bound, or otherwise made to suffer

f. _____ cross-dressing for sexual arousal with eventual persistent discomfort with gender identity

g. _____ involuntary muscular spasm preventing sexual intercourse

h. _____ setting aside specific time for sexual activity

i. _____ a treatment for sexual dysfunction that involves a series of simple exercises in which the couple spends time in a quiet, relaxed setting, learning to touch each other

j. _____ a paraphilia in which sexual arousal is associated with desires to inflict physical or psychological suffering or humiliation on another person

k. _____ absence of genital sensations during sexual activity

l. _____ a procedure for measuring female sexual arousal

m. _____ association of sexual arousal with nonliving objects

n. _____ persistent genital pain during or after intercourse

o. _____ gay men who engage in cross-dressing for reasons other than sexual arousal

p. _____ inability to achieve orgasm even though a person experiences uninhibited sexual arousal

q. _____ a disorder in which a man is unable to delay ejaculation long enough to accomplish intercourse

r. _____ fear of failure

s. _____ cross-dressing for the purpose of sexual arousal

MATCHING III

Answers are found at the end of this chapter. Match these terms and concepts with the definitions that follow:

a. Exhibitionism	e. Incest
b. Voyeurism	f. Rape
c. Frotteurism	g. Acquaintance rape
d. Pedophilia	h. Sadistic rapists

i.	Nonsadistic rapists	o.	Sexual predator laws
j.	Vindictive rapists	p.	Sex roles
k.	Opportunistic rapists	q.	Transexualism (gender dysphoria)
l.	Lovemap	r.	Pseudohermaphroditism
m.	Aversion therapy	s.	Sex-reassignment surgery
n.	Community notification laws		

1. _____ a paraphilia characterized by distress over, or acting on, urges to expose one's genitals to an unsuspecting stranger

2. _____ rape committed by someone known to the victim

3. _____ sexual activity between close blood relatives

4. _____ a category of rapist who is preoccupied with sadistic sexual fantasies, whose actions are brutal and violent

5. _____ a paraphilia characterized by distress over or acting on urges involving sexual activity with a prepubescent child

6. _____ discomfort with one's anatomical sex

7. _____ characteristics, behaviors, and skills that are defined within a culture as being either masculine or feminine

8. _____ surgery in which the person's genitals are changed to match his or her gender identity

9. _____ a category of rapist whose actions are intended to degrade and humiliate the victim

10. _____ being genetically male but lacking a hormone responsible for shaping the penis and scrotum, resulting in ambiguous external genitalia

11. _____ a paraphilia characterized by recurrent, intense sexual urges involving touching and rubbing against a nonconsenting person

12. _____ a paraphilia in which a person becomes sexually aroused by observing unsuspecting people while they are undressing or involved in sexual activity

13. _____ a category of rapist with distorted views of sexuality and women, feelings of inferiority, and poor social skills

14. _____ a treatment where the therapist repeatedly presents the stimulus that elicits inappropriate sexual arousal in association with an aversive stimulus

15. _____ acts involving nonconsensual sexual penetration obtained by physical force, threat of bodily harm, or when the victim is incapable of giving consent

16. _____ a mental picture representing a person's ideal sexual relationship

17. _____ laws designed to keep some criminals in custody indefinitely

18. _____ a category of rapist with impulsive, unplanned actions who seeks immediate gratification

19. _____ laws that require the distribution of information to the public regarding the presence of child molesters and sexually violent offenders when they are released from prison

MATCHING IV

Answers are found at the end of this chapter. Match these names with the descriptions of their contributions to the study of abnormal psychology:

a. Alfred Kinsey   b. William Masters and Virginia Johnson   c. John Money

1. _____ proposed a model of the human sexual response cycle and developed treatments for sexual dysfunctions

2. _____ applied scientific methods to the study of sexuality

3. _____ studied the etiology of paraphilias; developed the concept of lovemaps

CONCEPT REVIEW

Answers are found at the end of this chapter. After you have read and reviewed the material, test your comprehension by filling in the blanks or circling the correct answer.

1. Male and female orgasm have different numbers of stages: **true   false**

2. Women typically have a longer refractory period than men: **true   false**

3. Women are capable of multiple orgasms while men are typically not: **true   false**

4. Sexual problems are best seen as problems of the individual: **true   false**

5. Early scientific approaches to sexual behavior were strongly influenced by the idea that the exclusive goal of sexuality was _____.

6. Kinsey rejected the distinction between _____ and _____ sexual behavior and saw differences as quantitative rather than qualitative.

7. Men report that their sexual partners have orgasms more often than women report having orgasms:

   true false

8. The only factor important to sexual satisfaction, especially among women, is experiencing an orgasm:

   true false

9. Failure to reach orgasm is not considered a disorder unless it is _____ and results in _____.

10. Viagra has been documented to be effective in the treatment of erectile dysfunction: **true   false**

11. Viagra has been associated with some deaths: **true   false**

12. Hypoactive sexual desire disorder can be diagnosed by comparing a person's interest level with a chart of normal levels of sexual interest: **true   false**

13. People with low sexual desire often have _____ disorders.

14. There are high correlations between subjective and physiological measures of arousal in normal women: **true   false**

15. Almost all clinicians will identify the response of ejaculating before or upon_____ as indicative of premature ejaculation.

16. Dyspareunia is more common in   **men   women.**

17. What is the most frequent form of male sexual dysfunction?

   _____

18. There is a cultural prejudice against sexual activity among older_____.

19. Older men achieve erections   **more quickly   more slowly.**

20. The subjective experience of the intensity of orgasm **increases   decreases**   with age.

21. Frequency of sexual dysfunction among men typically   **increases   decreases**   with age.

22. Frequency of sexual dysfunction among women typically **increases** **decreases** with age.

23. The influence of male sex hormones on sexual behavior is thought to be on sexual _____ rather than on sexual _____.

24. Men who smoke cigarettes are more likely to have problems with

_____.

25. Antidepressants can include the side effect of difficulty achieving orgasm: **true** **false**

26. Performance anxiety, or fear of _____, appears to be more common among men with erectile difficulties.

27. Changing the way people think about sex is a major aspect of sex therapy: **true** **false**

28. Paraphilias are only diagnosed if the person has _____ the urges or is _____ by them.

29. Most of the people in treatment for sexual disorders are people with paraphilias: **true** **false**

30. The central feature of paraphilia is that sexual arousal is dependent on images that are detached from _____ relationships with another adult.

31. Paraphilias are similar to **addictions** **anxiety disorders** **mood disorders**.

32. Masochists tend to be disproportionately represented among poorer groups of people:

true **false**

33. Most exhibitionists are women: **true** **false**

34. A voyeur is not aroused by watching people who know they are being observed: **true** **false**

35. Most pedophiles are homosexual: **true** **false**

36. Rape is not included as a paraphilia because it is not always motivated by

_____.

37. Many rapists in one study had a history of paraphilias: **true** **false**

38. Most people with a paraphilia exhibit other paraphilias as well: **true** **false**

39. About what percent of people who seek treatment for paraphilias are men?

60 percent 75 percent 95 percent

40. Damage to what part of the brain can lead to unusual sexual behaviors?

_____

41. _____ skills may play as important a role in paraphilias as sexual arousal.

42. A surprising number of people involved in masochism had what type of experience as children?

_____

43. Most people in treatment for paraphilias are there _____.

44. Cognitive-behavioral treatment was found to be   **more   less**   effective than aversion therapy in treating paraphilia.

45. Gender identity disorders are relatively   **rare   common**.

46. Pseudohermaphrodites typically make a quick and fairly easy transition from a childhood female to an adult male gender identity: **true   false**

47. Results of sex-reassignment surgery have mostly been negative: **true   false**

MULTIPLE CHOICE
Answers are found at the end of this chapter. These multiple choice questions will test your understanding of the material presented in the chapter. Read each question and circle the letter representing the best answer.

1. All of the following types of medication have been used to treat paraphilias except
    a. antipsychotic medications.
    b. antidepressants.
    c. antianxiety medications.
    d. drugs that reduce levels of testosterone.

2. All of the following factors may increase the probability that a person might experiment with unusual types of sexual stimulation or employ maladaptive sexual behaviors except
    a. ignorance and poor understanding of human sexuality.
    b. lack of diverse sexual experiences.
    c. lack of self-esteem.
    d. lack of confidence and ability in social interactions.

3. With regard to the context of occurrence, which of the following terms indicates that the sexual dysfunction is not limited only to certain situations or partners?
    a. situational
    b. lifelong
    c. acquired
    d. generalized

4. Recent revisions of the DSM reflect the following important changes in society's attitudes toward sexual behavior except
    a. growing acceptance of women of their own sexuality.
    b. tolerance for greater variety in human sexuality.
    c. an increasing focus on sexual aberrations rather than on sexual satisfaction.
    d. increased recognition that the main purpose of sexual behavior need not be reproduction.

5. The sexual dysfunction that involves the muscles of the vagina involuntarily spasming and interfering with intercourse is called
    a. vaginismus.
    b. dyspareunia.
    c. female orgasmic disorder.
    d. sexual aversion disorder.

6. The sexual dysfunction of pain with intercourse is called
    a. vaginismus.
    b. dyspareunia.
    c. female orgasmic disorder.
    d. sexual aversion disorder.

7. This involves the use of nonliving objects for the purpose of sexual arousal.
    a. frotteurism
    b. pedophilia
    c. fetishism
    d. sexual masochism

8. Sex-reassignment surgery is the process whereby a person's genitals are changed to match his or her
    a. gender identity.
    b. sex role.
    c. sexual identity.
    d. gender role.

9. According to your text, _____ may be the most common neurologically-based cause of impaired erectile responsiveness among men.
    a. depression
    b. coronary heart disease
    c. diabetes
    d. cancer

10. All of the following are treatment options for sexual dysfunctions except
    a. sensate focus.
    b. cognitive restructuring.
    c. communication training.
    d. aversion therapy.

11. What percentage of those who seek treatment for paraphilia disorders are men?
    a. 40 percent
    b. 60 percent
    c. 75 percent
    d. 95 percent

12. _____ and _____ have been the best-known sex therapists and researchers in the United States since the late 1960s.
    a. William Masters; Virginia Johnson
    b. Alfred Kinsey; Havelock Ellis
    c. Sigmund Freud; Richard von Krafft-Ebing
    d. Robert Spitzer; Helen Singer Kaplan

13. The sense of being either male or female is known as
    a. sexual identity.
    b. gender dysphoria.
    c. gender identity.
    d. sex roles.

14. Premature ejaculation may be the most frequent form of sexual dysfunction, affecting nearly one in every
    a. three adult men.
    b. ten adult men.
    c. fifteen adult men.
    d. twenty adult men.

15. The treatment approach used for paraphilias in which the therapist repeatedly presents a stimulus eliciting inappropriate sexual arousal in association with an aversive stimulus is called
    a. counterconditioning.
    b. aversion therapy.
    c. flooding.
    d. systematic desensitization.

16. Research on sexual behavior across the life span shows that
    a. younger men have difficulty regaining an erection if it is lost before orgasm, while older men can only maintain erections for a short period of time.
    b. older adults are not interested in, or capable of, performing sexual behaviors.
    c. differences between younger and older people are mostly a matter of degree.
    d. as women get older, the clitoris becomes more responsive.

17. Men with this problem may report feeling aroused, but the vascular reflex mechanism fails, and sufficient blood is not pumped to the penis.
    a. sexual aversion disorder
    b. premature ejaculation
    c. male orgasmic disorder
    d. erectile dysfunction

18. Exhibitionists often seek
    a. to shock their victim.
    b. to be arrested.
    c. to be chased by a witness of the exposure.
    d. to be accepted and liked by their victim in spite of their behavior.

19. About _____ of people seeking treatment for hypoactive sexual desire report other forms of sexual dysfunction.
    a. 25 percent
    b. 40 percent
    c. 60 percent
    d. 75 percent

20. In order to meet diagnostic criteria, all categories of sexual dysfunction require all of the following except
    a. the sexual dysfunction is associated with atypical stimuli and the person is preoccupied with, or consumed by, these activities.
    b. the disturbance causes marked distress or interpersonal difficulty.
    c. the sexual dysfunction is not better accounted for by another Axis I disorder (such as major depression).
    d. the sexual dysfunction is not due to direct physiological effects of a substance or a general medical condition.

21. The unresponsiveness of most men to further sexual stimulation for a period of time after reaching orgasm is called
    a. sensation of suspension.
    b. pulsation.
    c. sexual aversion.
    d. refractory period.

22. The correct order for the phases of the sexual response cycle is
    a. resolution—excitement—orgasm.
    b. excitement—orgasm—resolution.
    c. excitement—resolution—orgasm.
    d. resolution—orgasm—excitement.

23. A man rubbing his penis against a woman's buttocks on a crowded train is engaging in
    a. exhibitionism.
    b. voyeurism.
    c. fetishism.
    d. frotteurism.

24. All of the following refer to a sense of discomfort with one's anatomical sex except
    a. gender identity disorder.
    b. transvestic fetishism.
    c. gender dysphoria.
    d. transsexualism.

25. Which of the following characterizes an individual who is genetically male, but is unable to produce a hormone that is responsible for shaping the penis and scrotum in the fetus, and is therefore born with external genitalia that are ambiguous in appearance?
    a. transsexualism
    b. secondary sexual characteristic disorder
    c. transvestic fetishism
    d. pseudohermaphroditism

26. This involves the act of observing an unsuspecting person who is naked, in the process of disrobing, or engaging in sexual activity:
    a. sexual sadism.
    b. voyeurism.
    c. exhibitionism.
    d. fetishism.

27. Which paraphilia do men and women have in equal numbers?
    a. voyeurism
    b. exhibitionism
    c. masochism
    d. pedophilia

28. Which of the following is not one of the reasons for opposition to the proposed diagnostic category of excessive sexual drive?
    a. It is very rare.
    b. Its definition is circular.
    c. Problems controlling sexual impulses can be characteristic of several other disorders.
    d. It is unclear whether it represents a meaningful diagnostic category.

SHORT ANSWER
Answer the following short answer questions. Compare your work to the material presented in the text.

1. Compare and contrast the treatment of paraphilias with the treatment of sexual dysfunction. Select two types of paraphilias and two types of sexual dysfunctions. Discuss which type of treatment would be most effective for each.

2. Discuss Barlow's studies comparing sexually dysfunctional men with control subjects in laboratory settings. What were his findings? What are several limitations to these studies? Discuss several applications of his findings.

3. Compare and contrast different perspectives regarding the etiology of paraphilias. Which perspectives do you believe best explain the etiology of paraphilias? Why?

4. Discuss what is meant by a hypothetical construct. Why is sexual arousal considered a hypothetical construct?

ANSWER KEY

MATCHING I

1. f	6. a	11. c	16. n
2. d	7. j	12. g	17. r
3. l	8. h	13. k	18. m
4. p	9. b	14. e	
5. i	10. o	15. q	

MATCHING II

a. 3	f. 18	k. 6	p. 5
b. 1	g. 8	l. 2	q. 4
c. 9	h. 12	m. 13	r. 10
d. 15	i. 11	n. 7	s. 16
e. 19	j. 14	o. 17	

MATCHING III

1. a	7. p	13. i	19. n
2. g	8. s	14. m	
3. e	9. j	15. f	
4. h	10. r	16. l	
5. d	11. c	17. o	
6. q	12. b	18. k	

MATCHING IV

1. b	2. a	3. c

CONCEPT REVIEW

1.	true		14.	false
2.	false		15.	insertion
3.	true		16.	women
4.	false		17	premature ejaculation
5.	reproduction		18.	women
6.	normal; abnormal		19.	more slowly
7.	true		20.	decreases
8.	false		21.	increases
9.	persistent; distress		22.	decreases
10.	true		23.	appetite; performance
11.	true		24.	erection
12.	false		25.	true
13.	mood		26.	failure

27. true
28. acted on; distressed
29. false
30. loving
31. the addictions
32. false
33. false
34. true
35. false
36. sexual arousal
37. true

38. true
39. 95 percent
40. temporal lobe
41. Interpersonal
42. traumatic disease and painful medical procedures
43. involuntarily
44. more
45. rare
46. true
47. false

MULTIPLE CHOICE

1. a	6. b	11. d	16. c	21. d	26. b
2. b	7. c	12. a	17. d	22. b	27. c
3. d	8. a	13. c	18. a	23. d	28. a
4. c	9. c	14. a	19. d	24. b	
5. a	10. d	15. b	20. a	25. d	

CHAPTER THIRTEEN

SCHIZOPHRENIC DISORDERS

CHAPTER OUTLINE

Overview
Symptoms
      Positive Symptoms
      Negative Symptoms
      First Person Account of Delusional Beliefs
      Disorganization
Diagnosis
      Brief Historical Perspective
      DSM-IV-TR
      Subtypes
      Related Psychotic Disorders
      Course and Outcome
Frequency
      Gender Differences
      Cross-Cultural Comparisons
Causes
      Biological Factors
      Social Factors
      Psychological Factors
      Interaction of Biological and Environmental
      The Search for Markers of Vulnerability
Treatment
      Antipsychotic Medication
      Psychosocial Treatment
Summary

OBJECTIVES

You should be able to:
1.   Distinguish between positive symptoms, negative symptoms, and disorganization.
2.   Discuss the phases of schizophrenia.
3.   Define and describe hallucinations, delusional beliefs, and disorganized speech.
4.   Provide examples of motor disturbances, affective and emotional disturbances, and avolition.
5.   Discuss the contributions of Kraepelin and Bleuler in defining schizophrenia.
6.   Distinguish between disorganized, catatonic, paranoid, undifferentiated, and residual types of schizophrenia.
7.   Describe characteristics of schizoaffective, delusional, and brief psychotic disorder.
8.   Discuss the epidemiology of schizophrenia.
9.   Discuss the diathesis-stress model as it relates to schizophrenia.
10.   Describe current brain research regarding the etiology of schizophrenia.

11. Explain the dopamine hypothesis and current beliefs about the role of dopamine in schizophrenia.
12. Identify several social and psychological factors that may contribute to the development and maintenance of schizophrenia.
13. Discuss the identification of cognitive and eye-tracking dysfunctions in schizophrenics and biological relatives.
14. Describe the effectiveness of medications in the treatment of schizophrenia.
15. Describe family-oriented aftercare programs, social skills training, and the use of token economies in the treatment of those with schizophrenia.

MATCHING I

Answers are found at the end of this chapter. Match these terms and concepts with the definitions that follow:

a	Negative symptoms		m.	Tangentiality
b.	Positive symptoms		n.	Perseveration
c.	Dementia praecox		o.	Alogia
d.	Catatonic type		p.	Poverty of speech
e.	Disorganized type		q.	Thought disorder
f.	Prodromal phase		r.	Catatonia
g.	Residual phase		s.	Delusions
h.	Hallucinations		t.	Blunted affect
i.	Disorganized speech		u.	Anhedonia
j.	Stuporous state		v.	Inappropriate affect
k.	Derailment		w.	Avolition
l.	Loose associations			

1. _____ disturbance in thought patterns that manifests in disorganized speech
2. _____ impoverished thinking marked by nonfluent or barren speech
3. _____ after positive symptoms: continued deterioration of role functioning
4. _____ reflect loss of normal functions
5. _____ immobility and marked muscular rigidity, or excitement and overactivity
6. _____ another term for loose associations—shifting topics abruptly during conversation
7. _____ an early grouping of several types of psychosis now seen as schizophrenia
8. _____ reflect a distortion of normal functions, like psychosis
9. _____ inability to experience pleasure
10. _____ remarkable reductions in the amount of speech
11. _____ schizophrenia characterized by disorganized speech, disorganized behavior, and flat or inappropriate affect
12. _____ shifting topics too abruptly
13. _____ schizophrenia characterized by symptoms of motor immobility or excessive and purposeless motor activity
14. _____ sensory experiences not caused by actual external stimuli
15. _____ idiosyncratic beliefs that are rigidly held despite their preposterous nature
16. _____ indecisiveness, ambivalence, and loss of willpower
17. _____ generally reduced responsiveness
18. _____ persistently repeating the same word or phrase over and over again
19. _____ prior to positive symptoms, marked by deterioration in role functioning
20. _____ a flattening or restriction of a person's nonverbal display of emotion

21. _____ incongruity and lack of adaptability in emotional expression
22. _____ severe disruptions of verbal communication involving the form of speech
23. _____ replying to a question with an irrelevant response

MATCHING II

Answers are found at the end of this chapter. Match these terms and concepts with the definitions that follow:

1. Paranoid type
2. Undifferentiated type
3. Residual type
4. Schizoaffective disorder
5. Delusional disorder
6. Brief psychotic disorder
7. Extrapyramidal symptoms
8. Antipsychotic drugs
9. Vulnerability marker
10. Endophenotypes

11. Working memory
12. Assertive community treatment
13. Token economies
14. Dopamine hypothesis
15. Social causation hypothesis
16. Social selection hypothesis
17. Social skills training
18. Expressed emotion
19. Atypical antipsychotics
20. Tardive dyskinesia

a. _____ harmful events associated with membership in the lowest social classes play a causal role in the development of schizophrenia

b. _____ a syndrome caused by prolonged treatment with antipsychotic drugs consisting of involuntary movements of the mouth and face as well as spasmodic movements of the limbs and trunk of the body

c. _____ another term for vulnerability markers

d. _____ new class of antipsychotic medications that does not cause as many extrapyramidal symptoms and has a lower risk of tardive dyskinesia

e. _____ side effects including muscular rigidity, tremors, restless agitation, peculiar involuntary postures, and motor inertia

f. _____ drugs that reduce the severity of or eliminate psychotic symptoms

g. _____ social learning programs that reinforce desired behaviors

h. _____ focuses on the function of specific dopamine pathways in the limbic area of the brain as having a role in the etiology of schizophrenia

i. _____ schizophrenia characterized by psychotic symptoms but that does not fit any one subtype

j. _____ schizophrenia in partial remission, with no active phase symptoms

k. _____ an intervention combining psychological treatments with medication

l. _____ schizophrenia characterized by systematic delusions with persecutory or grandiose content

m. _____ a specific measure that might be useful in identifying people who are vulnerable to a disorder

n. _____ an episode of symptoms of both schizophrenia and a mood disorder

o. _____ people with schizophrenia experience downward social mobility

p. _____ a structured, educational approach that involves modeling, role playing, and reinforcement for appropriate behaviors

q. _____ does not meet the criteria of schizophrenia but are preoccupied for at least one month with delusions that are not bizarre

r. _____ people who exhibit psychotic symptoms for at least a day but less than a month

s. _____ negative or intrusive attitudes displayed by relatives of schizophrenics

t. _____ the ability to maintain and manipulate information for a short period of time

MATCHING III

Answers are found at the end of this chapter. Match these names with the descriptions of their contributions to the study of abnormal psychology:

a. Emil Kraeplin   c. Gordon Paul   e. Irving Gottesman
b. Eugen Bleuler   d. Leonard Heston

1. _____ one of the world's leading experts on genetic factors and schizophrenia
2. _____ grouped together several psychotic disorders into the category of dementia praecox, an early term for schizophrenia
3. _____ coined the term schizophrenia, which means splitting of mental associations
4. _____ conducted the first adoption study of schizophrenia
5. _____ developed behavioral treatments for chronic schizophrenic patients

CONCEPT REVIEW

Answers are found at the end of this chapter. After you have read and reviewed the material, test your comprehension by filling in the blanks or circling the correct answer.

1. What are the three symptom categories of schizophrenia? _____,

_____, and _____

2. What is the period of risk for the development of a first episode of schizophrenia? _____ years old to

_____ years old

3. After the onset of schizophrenia, most people return to their previous levels of functioning:

true false

4. What is the most common type of hallucination? _____

5. Delusions are typically shared by the patient's family: **true**   **false**

6. Disorganized speech breaks all the rules of grammar: **true**   **false**

7. During a state of stupor, schizophrenic patients remain aware of what is happening around them:

true false

8. Many people with schizophrenia evidence social withdrawal: **true**   **false**

9. Schizophrenia is a sort of multiple personality disorder: **true**   **false**

10. Schizophrenia follows a predictable course among most patients: **true**   **false**

11. What is the lifetime prevalence of schizophrenia? _____ percent

12. Women typically have an earlier age of onset than men: **true**   **false**

13. Men typically have more negative symptoms than women: **true**   **false**

14. Women typically respond better to treatment than men: **true**   **false**

15. Schizophrenia is very rare in non industrialized countries: **true**   **false**

16. People with schizophrenia have a better outcome if they live in a developing country rather than a developed country: **true   false**

17. What is the lifetime risk of developing schizophrenia if your identical twin has the disorder? ____ percent

18. What is the lifetime risk of developing schizophrenia if your fraternal twin has the disorder? ____ percent

19. Genetic factors do not play a role in the etiology of schizophrenia: **true   false**

20. Adoption studies indicate that environmental factors cause schizophrenia: **true   false**

21. The data suggest that genes may increase vulnerability to schizophrenia by affecting dopamine transmission in the prefrontal cortex: **true   false**

22. People with schizophrenia are more likely to have experienced difficulties during and prior to their birth: **true   false**

23. Severe _____ of the mother during the early part of pregnancy increases the child's later risk for schizophrenia.

24. People with schizophrenia were more likely to be born during what season?

    _____

25. People with schizophrenia have been found to have _____ lateral ventricles in the brain.

26. People with schizophrenia are more likely to show a decrease in the size of what brain structure?

    _____

27. One MZ twin pair discordant for schizophrenia involved one brother who was a successful businessman and another who was severely impaired with schizophrenia. Whose lateral ventricles were five times larger?

    _____

28. What other neurotransmitter besides dopamine may be involved in schizophrenia?

    _____

29. Which hypothesis has received support in the research literature, the social causation hypothesis or the social selection hypothesis? _____

30. Rates of schizophrenia among people who have migrated from the Caribbean to the United Kingdom are **higher   lower**   than either the populations living in the Caribbean or the established population in the United Kingdom.

31. Parents and schizophrenic children have abnormal relationships, which are believed to play a causal role in the development of the schizophrenia: **true   false**

32. Men with schizophrenia were **more** **less** likely to return to the hospital if they were discharged to live with their wives or parents rather than their siblings or strangers.

33. What seems to be the important component of expressed emotion?

_____

34. Lots of contact with relatives high on EE **helps** **hurts** patients with schizophrenia; lots of contact with relatives low on EE **helps** **hurts** patients with schizophrenia.

35. High EE is **more** **less** common in Western countries.

36. Schizophrenic patients have **better** **worse** performance than normal people in working memory.

37. Relatives of schizophrenic patients have **better** **worse** performance than normal people in working memory.

38. _____-tracking performance may be associated with a predisposition to schizophrenia.

39. Neuroleptic medications take _____ to have an effect.

40. All people with schizophrenia respond to neuroleptic medications given in the correct dose:

   true **false**

41. What causes tardive dyskinesia?

_____

42. Continued maintenance on neuroleptic drugs after recovery significantly reduces relapse:

   true **false**

43. Second-generation antipsychotics like Clozaril, Zyprexa, and Risperdal are **more** **less** likely to cause tardive dyskinesia than the first-generation antipsychotics.

44. Patients who do not respond to neuroleptic medication do not improve with any type of treatment:

   true **false**

MULTIPLE CHOICE

Answers are found at the end of this chapter. These multiple choice questions will test your understanding of the material presented in the chapter. Read each question and circle the letter representing the best answer.

1. Research on the relationship between expressed emotion (EE) and schizophrenia supports which of the following?
   a. The presence of expressed emotion is only associated with the onset of an individual's initial episode of schizophrenia.
   b. Among the various types of comments that contribute to a high EE rating, criticism is typically most associated with the likelihood of relapse.
   c. The influence of expressed emotions is unique to schizophrenia.
   d. all of the above

2. The trend in the DSM-IV-TR diagnosis of schizophrenia over time has been which of the following?
   a. include more affective symptoms
   b. omit subtyping of the disorder
   c. move from a broader to narrower definition of schizophrenia
   d. move from a more restrictive to less restrictive duration criterion

3. Which of the following would not be considered a positive symptom of schizophrenia?
   a. hallucinations
   b. blunted affect
   c. delusions
   d. disorganized speech

4. The distribution of schizophrenia within families is probably best explained by which of the following genetic models?
   a. polygenic
   b. single dominant gene
   c. single recessive gene
   d. environment only

5. A difference between schizophrenia and delusional disorder is that
   a. patients with schizophrenia display less impairment in their daily functioning than patients with delusional disorder.
   b. patients with delusional disorder display more negative symptoms during the active phase of their illness.
   c. the behavior of patients with schizophrenia is considerably less bizarre.
   d. patients with delusional disorder are preoccupied with delusions that are not necessarily bizarre.

6. In the search to identify people who are vulnerable to schizophrenia, several potential vulnerability markers have been considered. Which of the following would not be considered a good criterion for a vulnerability marker?
   a. The marker should be able to distinguish between people who are already schizophrenic and people who are not.
   b. The marker should be a characteristic that is stable over time.
   c. The marker should be able to identify more people who are relatives of schizophrenics than people in the general population.
   d. The marker should be able to predict the likelihood of relapse for people who have already experienced their first episode of schizophrenia.

7. Individuals who exhibit psychotic symptoms for less than a month that cannot be attributed to other disorders such as substance abuse or mood disorder would be diagnosed with
   a. delusional disorder.
   b. schizophreniform disorder.
   c. brief psychotic disorder.
   d. schizoaffective disorder.

8. Tangentiality is an example of which type of disturbance?
   a. motor disturbance
   b. affective disturbance
   c. disorganized speech
   d. delusional belief

9. Which of the following statements is true regarding the use of neuroleptic medication?
   a. Beneficial effects are noticed within twenty-four hours after beginning the medication.
   b. They appear to be particularly effective for relief of the positive symptoms associated with schizophrenia.
   c. Almost all schizophrenic patients are considered to be complete responders to this type of medication.
   d. Schizophrenic patients with the most severe symptoms respond best to them.

10. Research on schizophrenic twins and adopted-away offspring of schizophrenics suggests which of the following?
   a. Vulnerability to schizophrenia is consistently manifested by the same symptoms of this disorder across relatives.
   b. Vulnerability to schizophrenia is expressed through a variety of different symptom patterns, including depressive and anxiety syndromes.
   c. Vulnerability to schizophrenia is consistently manifested by the same symptoms of this disorder only when male relatives are affected.
   d. Vulnerability to schizophrenia is sometimes manifested by schizophrenic-like personality traits and non-schizophrenic psychotic disorders.

11. Studies investigating the relationship between social class and schizophrenia indicate that risk for the disorder
   a. is associated with adverse social and economic circumstances.
   b. is not associated with circumstances most likely to be present in the lives of people who are economically disadvantaged.
   c. is associated with unique types of circumstances most frequently affiliated with high social class.
   d. is most associated with religious involvement.

12. Reduction in the amount of the patient's speech is called
   a. alogia.
   b. disorganized speech.
   c. catatonia.
   d. perseveration.

13. A restriction of an individual's nonverbal display of his or her emotional responses is referred to as
   a. blunted affect.
   b. affective loosening.
   c. anhedonia.
   d. inappropriate affect.

14. An interesting and consistent result across numerous MRI studies is that some people with schizophrenia have
    a. an enlarged hypothalamus.
    b. enlarged lateral ventricles.
    c. enlarged temporal lobes.
    d. less cerebrospinal fluid.

15. The inability to experience pleasure, seen among schizophrenic patients, is called
    a. apathy.
    b. alogia.
    c. avolition.
    d. anhedonia.

16. Which statement about the course of schizophrenia is true?
    a. A significant number of individuals experience their first episode between 35–50 years of age.
    b. The onset of the disorder typically occurs during adolescence or early adulthood.
    c. The active phase of illness is always the longest of the three phases.
    d. The premorbid phase of illness usually lasts no longer than six months.

17. Which of the following is not a characteristic of disorganized speech?
    a. derailment
    b. perseveration
    c. tangentiality
    d. stuperous state

18. Which of the following is not included in the DSM-IV-TR as a subtype of schizophrenia?
    a. paranoid
    b. residual
    c. undifferentiated
    d. negative

19. Joshua's behavior has been observed in the hospital ward for several hours. He has been sitting perfectly still in one position. Furthermore, he has been completely mute (has not spoken a single word) since admission. Which subtype of schizophrenia best represents Joshua's behavior?
    a. disorganized
    b. paranoid
    c. catatonic
    d. undifferentiated

20. Which unusual type of affect would not be a typical feature of schizophrenia?
    a. an expressionless face
    b. laughing at something to which laughter is an inappropriate response
    c. excessive rage
    d. unresponsiveness

21. A conclusion of twin studies and their persuasive evidence for the role of genetic factors in schizophrenia is that
    a. DZ and MZ twin concordance rates are approximately equal, suggesting that genetic factors are less important than environmental factors.
    b. MZ twin concordance rates are higher than DZ twin concordance rates, implicating genetic factors.
    c. the studies determining concordance rates are flawed because they do not take into account the birth order of the MZ twins.
    d. the concordance rates for MZ twins for schizophrenia has fluctuated dramatically across studies.

22. The potentially exciting part of eye-tracking dysfunction and the possibility of this characteristic being a vulnerability marker for schizophrenia is that
    a. eye-tracking dysfunction appears to be influenced by genetic factors and is apparently a stable trait.
    b. eye-tracking dysfunction appears to be present only in patients with schizophrenia.
    c. approximately 90 percent of the first-degree relatives of schizophrenic individuals show this characteristic.
    d. the eye-tracking dysfunction only appears during episodes of schizophrenia.

23. Research suggests that the outcome of schizophrenia may be best described by which of the following statements?
    a. Very few patients recover completely.
    b. Some people recover and others do not.
    c. With appropriate treatment, most recover completely.
    d. Negative symptoms usually are cured, but not positive symptoms.

24. When Samuel grins as he talks about the loss of his father in a traumatic accident, he is displaying
    a. disorganized affect.
    b. avolition.
    c. catatonia.
    d. inappropriate affect.

25. The theory that harmful events associated with being a member of the lowest social class (e.g. poor nutrition, social isolation) play a role in the development of schizophrenia is called
    a. the social class hypothesis.
    b. the social causation hypothesis.
    c. the social impairment hypothesis.
    d. the social selection hypothesis.

26. The usefulness of subtyping schizophrenia has been criticized because
    a. some individuals do not fit the traditional subtype descriptions.
    b. some individuals display the symptoms of more than one subtype simultaneously.
    c. the symptoms of some individuals change from one episode to the next, reflecting subtype instability.
    d. all of the above

27. The average concordance rate for monozygotic twins for schizophrenia is
    a. 22 percent.
    b. 36 percent.
    c. 48 percent.
    d. 72 percent.

28. Perhaps the most unpleasant side effect of neuroleptics is
    a. the fact that the drugs must be taken for two to four months before the patient experiences relief from symptoms.
    b. potentially toxic reactions to the drugs if the patient's diet is not carefully monitored.
    c. the presence of extrapyramidal symptoms.
    d. acute gastrointestinal symptoms (e.g. nausea, vomiting) during the first few weeks of use.

29. Research on gender differences in schizophrenia supports that
    a. men experience their first episode of schizophrenia about five years later than women.
    b. women typically display better premorbid social competence prior to their first episode of schizophrenia.
    c. men typically display a less chronic course compared to women.
    d. women display more negative symptoms.

30. Which of the following describe tardive dyskinesia?
    a. tongue protrusion and writhing fingers
    b. a stuporous state
    c. immobility
    d. weight gain and obesity

SHORT ANSWER

Answer the following short answer questions. Compare your work with the material presented in the text.

1. You are on a committee that will be responsible for developing the diagnostic criteria for schizophrenia for DSM-V. What would you consider to be the most appropriate criteria to be included? Explain.

2. Discuss the diathesis-stress model of schizophrenia. Which factors would represent the diathesis? Which factors would represent stress?

3. What issues must be addressed as a researcher designs a research project in psychopathology? What are the issues involved in the selection of subjects?

4. Describe and compare several forms of psychosocial approaches shown to be effective for the treatment of schizophrenia. What are their advantages and disadvantages?

ANSWER KEY

MATCHING I

1.	q	7.	c	13.	d	19.	f
2.	o	8.	b	14.	h	20.	t
3.	g	9.	u	15.	s	21.	v
4.	a	10.	p	16.	w	22.	i
5.	r	11.	e	17.	j	23.	m
6.	k	12.	l	18.	n		

MATCHING II

a.	15	g.	13	m.	9	s.	1
b.	20	h.	14	n.	4		8
c.	10	i.	2	o.	16	t.	1
d.	19	j.	3	p.	17		1
e.	7	k.	12	q.	5		
f.	8	l.	1	r.	6		

MATCHING III

1.	e	3.	b	5.	c
2.	a	4.	d		

CONCEPT REVIEW

1. positive symptoms; negative symptoms; disorganization
2. 15; 35
3. false
4. auditory
5. false
6. false
7. true
8. true
9. false
10. false
11. 1
12. false
13. true
14. true
15. false
16. true
17. 48
18. 17

19. false
20. false
21. true
22. true
23. malnutrition
24. winter
25. larger
26. left temporal lobe
27. the businessman
28. serotonin
29. both
30. higher
31. false
32. more
33. criticism
34. hurts; helps
35. more
36. worse
37. worse

38. Eye   medications
39. several weeks   42. true
40. true   43. less
41. prolonged treatment with antipsychotic   44. false

MULTIPLE CHOICE

1. b	7. c	13. a	19. c	25. b
2. c	8. c	14. b	20. c	26. d
3. b	9. b	15. d	21. b	27. c
4. a	10. d	16. b	22. a	28. c
5. d	11. a	17. d	23. b	29. b
6. d	12. a	18. d	24. d	30. a

CHAPTER FOURTEEN

DEMENTIA, DELIRIUM, AND AMNESTIC DISORDERS

CHAPTER OUTLINE

OBJECTIVES

You should be able to:

1. Describe the characteristics of dementia, delirium, and amnestic disorders.
2. Distinguish between retrograde and anterograde amnesia.
3. Describe the primary symptoms of aphasia, apraxia, and agnosia.
4. Discuss the role of neuropsychological assessment in the diagnosis of dementia.
5. Identify the contributions of Korsakoff, Alzheimer, and Kraepelin in the diagnosis and understanding of cognitive disorders.
6. Describe the features of Alzheimer's, Pick's, Huntington's, Parkinson's, and vascular diseases.
7. Describe the role of genetics, neurotransmitters, viral infections, and environmental factors in the development of cognitive disorders.
8. Discuss the importance of an accurate diagnosis in the treatment of dementia.
9. Discuss the importance of environmental and behavioral management, caregiver support, and respite programs in treatment patients with cognitive disorders.

MATCHING
Answers are found at the end of this chapter. Match these terms and concepts with the definitions:

a.	Dementia	p.	Neurofibrillary tangles
b.	Delirium	q.	Amyloid plaques
c.	Amnestic disorders	r.	Beta-amyloid
d.	Neurologists	s.	Frontotemporal dementia (Pick's disease)
e.	Neuropsychologists		
f.	Retrograde amnesia	t.	Pick's bodies
g.	Association analysis	u.	Huntington's disease
h.	Dementia with Lewy bodies (DLB)	v.	Chorea
		w.	Parkinson's disease
i.	Anterograde amnesia	x.	Infarct
j.	Aphasia	y.	Vascular dementia
k.	Apraxia	z.	Pseudodementia
l.	Agnosia	aa.	Genetic linkage
m.	Neuropsychological assessment	bb.	Lewy bodies
n.	Dyskinesia	cc.	Stroke
o.	Alzheimer's disease		

1. _____ a gradually worsening loss of memory and related cognitive functions
2. _____ inability to learn or remember new material after a particular point in time
3. _____ severe interruption of blood flow to the brain
4. _____ problems identifying stimuli in the environment
5. _____ deposits found in neurons of patients with Parkinson's disease and dementia
6. _____ a confusional state that develops over a short period of time and is often associated with agitation and hyperactivity
7. _____ involuntary movements such as tics and tremors
8. _____ using cases and controls to compare them on the frequency of a particular gene
9. _____ psychologists with expertise in the assessment of specific types of cognitive impairment
10. _____ various types of loss or impairment in language caused by brain damage
11. _____ evaluation of performance on psychological tests to indicate whether a person has a brain disorder
12. _____ physicians who deal primarily with diseases of the brain and nervous system
13. _____ a cognitive disorder characterized by limited memory impairments
14. _____ difficulty performing purposeful movements in response to verbal commands
15. _____ unusual involuntary muscle movements
16. _____ loss of memory for events prior to the onset of an illness or traumatic event
17. _____ may be the second most common form of dementia, characterized by progressive decline with fluctuations in ability as well as hallucinations
18. _____ a protein material
19. _____ a lesion consisting of a central core of homogenous protein material surrounded by clumps of debris left over from destroyed neurons
20. _____ a distinctive ballooning of nerve cells
21. _____ a form of dementia associated with atrophy in the frontal and temporal lobes of the brain
22. _____ a close association between two genes on a chromosome
23. _____ disorder of the motor system caused by a degeneration of the *substantia nigra* and loss of dopamine but rarely including dementia
24. _____ symptoms of dementia actually produced by a major depressive disorder

25. _____ a form of dementia characterized by the presence of unusual involuntary muscle movements as well as personality changes

26. _____ a form of dementia in which cognitive impairment appears gradually and deterioration is progressive

27. _____ the area of dead tissue produced by a stroke

28. _____ a form of dementia associated with strokes

29. _____ when the structural network of some neurofibrils becomes highly disorganized

CONCEPT REVIEW

Answers are found at the end of this chapter. After you have read and reviewed the material, test your comprehension by filling in the blanks or circling the correct answer.

1. Delirium can fluctuate throughout the day: **true   false**

2. Delirium is less common among the elderly: **true   false**

3. Dementia can be cured: **true   false**

4. Changes in cognitive processes are not a normal part of aging: **true   false**

5. Which of the following typically show a decline with age: **fluid intelligence   wisdom**

6. Neuropsychological tests can sometimes be used to infer the location of a brain lesion: **true   false**

7. Hallucinations and delusions are seen in what percentage of dementia cases? _____

8. Korsakoff's syndrome may be caused in part by a _____ deficiency.

9. Which types of dementia are most common? **differentiated   undifferentiated**

10. A definitive diagnosis of Alzheimer's disease can only be made after _____.

11. Huntington's disease is caused by _____.

12. Vascular dementia often results in   **unilateral   bilateral**   impairment.

13. Almost _____ percent of people over 90 years of age exhibit symptoms of moderate or severe

    dementia: **20   40   60**

14. Average time between the onset of Alzheimer's disease and death is _____ years.

15. Genetic factors have been shown to play a role in dementia: **true   false**

16. Alzheimer's disease has been linked to what birth defect? _____.

17. Alzheimer's disease may involve dysfunction of the _____ system.

18. There is currently no treatment to return an Alzheimer's disease patient to previous levels of

    functioning: **true   false**

19. Medications for Alzheimer's disease focus on the action of which neurotransmitter?

    _____

20. People with higher educational levels are less likely to develop Alzheimer's disease: **true   false**

21. Patients with dementia benefit from _____ environments.

22. Patients with dementia who remain active have less _____.

23. Dementia with Lewy bodies involves fluctuations in cognitive performance: **true**   **false**

24. Prevalence rates for dementia may be   **lower   higher**   in developing countries.

25. Elderly people who have been knocked unconscious as adults have a **higher lower**   risk of developing Alzheimer's disease.

26. What type of dementia is the second most common after Alzheimer's disease?

_____

27. Pseudodementia is when a case of _____ is mistaken for dementia.

28. _____ can be caused by medications.

MULTIPLE CHOICE
Answers are found at the end of this chapter. These multiple choice questions will test your understanding of the material presented in the chapter. Read the questions and circle the best answer.

1. All of the following are goals in designing an environment conducive to patients with dementia except
    a. keep the patients relatively inactive in order to prevent them from hurting themselves.
    b. facilitate the patient's knowledge of the environment through labeled rooms, hallways, etc.
    c. keep the environment negotiable (i.e. keep areas that a person will use often visible from their room if they cannot be remembered).
    d. stay abreast of safety and health issues.

2. The _____is probably the best known neuropsychological assessment procedure that involves the examination of performance on psychological tests to indicate whether a person has a brain disorder.
    a. Halstead-Reitan
    b. Wechsler
    c. Symptoms Checklist-90 (SCL-90)
    d. *Minnesota Multiphasic Personality Inventory-2* (MMPI-2)

3. All of the following are typical symptoms of Parkinson's disease except
    a. tremors.
    b. postural abnormalities.
    c. gradual dementia.
    d. reduction in voluntary movements.

4. Which of the following appears to be the most common type of dementia?
    a. Pick's disease
    b. Huntington's disease
    c. Alzheimer's disease
    d. vascular dementia

5. _____ is a type of motor dysfunction that involves jerky, semi-purposeful movements of the person's face and limbs.
    a. Anoxia
    b. Myotonia
    c. Chorea
    d. Apraxia

6. A _____ deals primarily with diseases of the brain and the nervous system.
    a. neurologist
    b. psychiatrist
    c. psychologist
    d. cardiologist

7. Which of the following diagnoses depends on the presence of a positive family history for the disorder?
    a. Parkinson's disease
    b. Alzheimer's disease
    c. Pick's disease
    d. Huntington's disease

8. Two general aspects of mental functioning are
    a. dementia and delirium.
    b. reading and writing.
    c. fluid intelligence and wisdom.
    d. plaques and tangles.

9. The DSM-IV-TR currently classifies dementia and related clinical phenomena as
    a. organic mental disorders.
    b. biological mental disorders.
    c. psychological disorders with organic etiology.
    d. cognitive disorders.

10. Hallucinations and delusions are seen in about _____ of dementia cases.
    a. 10 percent
    b. 20 percent
    c. 30 percent
    d. 40 percent

11. All of the following are frequently associated with dementia except
    a. personality changes.
    b. emotional difficulties.
    c. a high frequency of drug abuse.
    d. motivational problems.

12. A definite diagnosis of Alzheimer's disease requires the observation of
    a. neurofibrillary tangles and senile plaques.
    b. degeneration of the substantia nigra.
    c. enlargement of the hypothalamus.
    d. all of the above.

13. One theory regarding Korsakoff's syndrome suggests that lack of _____ leads to atrophy of the medial thalamus.
    a. zinc
    b. vitamin C
    c. vitamin B1 (thiamin)
    d. potassium

14. Which of the following is a state of confusion that develops over a short period of time and is often associated with agitation and hyperactivity?
    a. delirium
    b. amnesia
    c. dementia
    d. Alzheimer's disease

15. Betty's physician handed her a hairbrush and said "Show me what you do with this object." She took the brush and brushed her hair with it, but was unable to name the object. She is most likely suffering from which of the following?
    a. agnosia
    b. aphasia
    c. apraxia
    d. ataxia

16. The most effective form of treatment for improving cognitive functioning in dementia of the Alzheimer's type is
    a. cognitive therapy.
    b. cognitive-behavioral therapy.
    c. rational-emotive therapy (RET).
    d. No form of treatment is presently capable of improving cognitive functioning in dementia of the Alzheimer's type.

17. Dementia with Lewy bodies is not associated with
    a. hallucinations.
    b. variations in performance.
    c. a slow, gradual course.
    d. muscular rigidity.

18. In order to qualify for a diagnosis of dementia, the person must exhibit memory impairment and which of the following?
    a. aggressive behavior
    b. problems in abstract thinking
    c. a previous episode of delirium
    d. age of at least sixty-five years

19. All of the following are true of delirium except
    a. it usually has a rapid onset.
    b. speech is typically confused.
    c. the person usually remains alert and responsive to the environment.
    d. it can be resolved.

20. Parkinson's disease is primarily a disorder of the motor system that is caused by a loss of dopamine and a degeneration of this specific area of the brain stem:
    a. *substantia nigra*
    b. thalamus
    c. fomix
    d. superior colliculi

21. Epidemiologic investigations have discovered that some types of dementia, especially Alzheimer's disease, may be related to all of the following except
    a. genes.
    b. head injury.
    c. level of educational experience.
    d. caffeine.

22. The incidence of dementia will be much greater in the near future because
    a. diagnostic criteria are more loosely defined.
    b. the average age of the population is increasing steadily.
    c. more people are being exposed to the environmental factors that have been shown to cause dementia.
    d. dementia is now striking people at a much earlier age.

23. Which of the following can be distinguished from other types of dementia listed in the DSM-IV-TR on the basis of speed of onset (i.e. cognitive impairment appears gradually, and the person's cognitive deterioration is progressive)?
    a. vascular dementia
    b. Huntington's disease
    c. Alzheimer's disease
    d. substance-induced persisting dementia

24. Which of the following is caused by an autosomal dominant gene?
    a. Huntington's disease
    b. Alzheimer's disease
    c. vascular dementia
    d. HIV

25. Some studies have confirmed an association between Alzheimer's disease and
    a. dependent personality disorder.
    b. vascular dementia.
    c. Korsakoff's syndrome.
    d. Down syndrome.
    e.

26. Almost _____ of people over ninety years of age exhibit symptoms of moderate or severe dementia.
    a. 25 percent
    b. 40 percent
    c. 65 percent
    d. 80 percent

27. What is the goal of treatment for patients with Alzheimer's disease?
    a. to keep the patient from infecting others
    b. to return the patient to work
    c. to cure the underlying pathology and halt the progression of the disease
    d. to maintain the current level of functioning as long as possible

28. _____ is a disorder that can be mistaken for dementia.
    a. Bipolar disorder
    b. Depression
    c. Schizophrenia
    d. Multiple personality disorder

29. All of the following are true of delirium except
    a. it typically fluctuates throughout the day and is usually worse at night.
    b. the delirious person loses the ability to learn new information or becomes unable to recall previously learned information.
    c. the delirious person is likely to be disoriented with relation to time or place.
    d. the primary symptom is clouding of consciousness, which might also be described as a person's reduced awareness of his or her surroundings.

SHORT ANSWER
Answer the following short answer questions. Compare your work to the material in your text.

1. Discuss how the behavioral effects of a stroke are different from those of dementia.

2. Discuss several environmental factors linked to dementia. What do you see as problematic with these findings? Why must we be cautious when interpreting this data?

3. Discuss the similarities and differences of dementia and depression. Provide an example of when it may be difficult to distinguish these apart.

4. Describe delirium, Korsakoff's syndrome, Alzheimer's disease, and Huntington's disease.

5. What is a genetic linkage? Provide an example.

ANSWER KEY

MATCHING

1.	a	9.	e	17.	h	25.	u
2.	i	10.	j	18.	r	26.	o
3.	cc	11.	m	19.	q	27.	x
4.	l	12.	d	20.	t	28.	y
5.	bb	13.	c	21.	s	29.	p
6.	b	14.	k	22.	aa		
7.	n	15.	v	23.	w		
8.	g	16.	f	24.	z		

CONCEPT REVIEW

1.	true	15.	true
2.	false	16.	Down Syndrome
3.	false	17.	immune
4.	false	18.	true
5.	fluid intelligence	19.	acetylcholine
6.	true	20.	true
7.	20 percent	21.	structured
8.	vitamin	22.	depression
9.	undifferentiated	23.	true
10.	death	24.	lower
11.	a gene	25.	higher
12.	unilateral	26.	dementia with Lewy bodies
13.	40	27.	depression
14.	eight	28.	delirium

MULTIPLE CHOICE

1. a	9. d	17. c	25. d
2. a	10. b	18. b	26. b
3. c	11. c	19. c	27. d
4. c	12. a	20. a	28. b
5. c	13. c	21. d	29. b
6. a	14. a	22. b	
7. d	15. b	23. c	
8. c	16. d	24. a	

CHAPTER FIFTEEN

MENTAL RETARDATION AND PERVASIVE DEVELOPMENTAL DISORDERS

CHAPTER OUTLINE

Overview
Mental Retardation
      Symptoms of Mental Retardation
      Measuring Intelligence
      Diagnosis of Mental Retardation
      Frequency of Mental Retardation
      Causes of Mental Retardation
      Normal Genetic Variation
      Treatment: Prevention and Normalization
Autism and Pervasive Development Disorders
      Symptoms of PDD
      Diagnosis of Autism and PDD
      Frequency of Autism and PDD
      Causes of Autism
      Treatment of PDD
Summary

OBJECTIVES

You should be able to:
1.   Describe the defining characteristics of mental retardation and autism.
2.   Distinguish between intelligence and adaptive skills.
3.   Identify the classification of mental retardation in DSM-IV-TR.
4.   Discuss the biological causes of mental retardation.
5.   Distinguish between primary, secondary, and tertiary prevention efforts as they relate to mental retardation.
6.   Describe the types of difficulties autistic children have with social interactions.
7.   Define dysprosody, echolalia, and pronoun rehearsal as they apply to impaired communication in autism.
8.   Discuss the epidemiology of autism.
9.   Discuss evidence pertaining to the biological basis of autism.
10.   Discuss the advantages and disadvantages of behavior modification in the management of children with autism.

MATCHING I
Answers are found at the end of this chapter. Match the terms and concepts with their definitions:

a.	Mental retardation	e.	Mild mental retardation
b.	Intelligence quotient (IQ)	f.	Moderate mental retardation
c.	Normal distribution	g.	Severe mental retardation
d.	Standard deviation	h.	Profound mental retardation

i. Down syndrome
j. Fragile-X syndrome
k. Klinefelter syndrome
l. XYY syndrome
m. Turner syndrome
n. Phenylketonuria (PKU)
o. Autistic spectrum disorders
p. Tay-Sachs disease
q. Hurler syndrome

r. Lesch-Nyhan syndrome
s. Cytomegalovirus
t. Toxoplasmosis
u. Rubella
v. Syphillis
w. Genital herpes
x. Encephalitis
y. Meningitis
z. Fetal alcohol syndrome

1. _____ an infection of the membranes that line the brain, which can lead to inflammation that can damage the brain
2. _____ a relatively common and usually harmless infection that can be passed to the fetus and can cause mental retardation
3. _____ a chromosomal abnormality transmitted genetically that sometimes leads to mental retardation or learning disabilities
4. _____ characterized by mental retardation and self-mutilation
5. _____ substantial limitations in present functioning characterized by significantly subaverage intellectual functioning, limitations in adaptive skills, and an onset before age eighteen
6. _____ motor skills, communication, and self-care are severely limited: constant supervision required
7. _____ a bacterial sexually transmitted disease which, if untreated, can be passed to the fetus and can result in physical and sensory handicaps in the fetus, including mental retardation
8. _____ a protozoan infection caused by ingestion of infected raw meats or from contact with infected cat feces that can cause brain damage to a fetus
9. _____ an intelligence test's rating of an individual's intellectual ability
10. _____ can generally function at the second grade level academically, require close training and supervision in work activities, and need family or group home supervision
11. _____ pervasive developmental disorders
12. _____ also called German measles, a viral infection that can cause severe mental retardation or death in a fetus
13. _____ caused by a recessive gene, this disorder involves the absence of an enzyme that metabolizes phenylalanine, an amino acid in certain foods, which leads to brain damage that results in mental retardation
14. _____ once thought to increase criminality but now recognized to be linked with social deviance and a mean IQ 10 points lower than average
15. _____ a measure of dispersion of scores around the mean
16. _____ an extra X chromosome in males that leads to low normal to mildly mentally retarded intellectual functioning
17. _____ results in gross physical abnormalities, including dwarfism, humpback, bulging head, and clawlike hands
18. _____ a bell-shaped frequency distribution
19. _____ a rare recessive-gene disorder that eventually results in death during the infant or preschool years that is particularly common among Jews of Eastern European heritage
20. _____ can be transmitted to the baby at birth and cause mental retardation, blindness, or death
21. _____ a missing X chromosome in females that leads to failure to develop sexually and intelligence near or within the normal range
22. _____ a disorder characterized by retarded physical development, a small head, narrow eyes, cardiac defects, and cognitive impairment

23. _____ can generally function at the sixth grade level academically, acquire vocational skills, and live in the community without special supports
24. _____ typically have abnormal motor development, sharply limited communicative speech, and require close supervision for community living
25. _____ a brain infection that can cause permanent brain damage in about 20 percent of cases
26. _____ a chromosomal disorder characterized by a distinctively abnormal physical appearance and mental retardation typically in the moderate to severe range

MATCHING II

Answers are found at the end of this chapter. Match the terms and concepts with their definitions:

1.	Mercury poisoning	14.	Autistic disorder (autism)
2.	Lead poisoning	15.	Gaze aversion
3.	Rh incompatibility	16.	Dysprosody
4.	Premature birth	17.	Echolalia
5.	Anoxia	18.	Pronoun reversal
6.	Epilepsy	19.	Self-stimulation
7.	Cultural-familial retardation	20.	Apparent sensory deficit
8.	Heritability ratio	21.	Self-injurious behavior
9.	Reaction range	22.	Savant performance
10.	Amniocentesis	23.	Asperger's disorder
11.	Normalization	24.	Childhood disintegrative
12.	Mainstreaming		disorder
13.	Pervasive developmental	25.	Rett's disorder
	disorders	26.	Nondisjunction

a. _____ a diagnostic procedure in which fluid is extracted from the amniotic sac that protects the fetus and genetic tests are run on the fluid to identify genetic abnormalities
b. _____ proposes that heredity determines the upper and lower limits of IQ and experience determines the extent to which people fulfill their genetic potential
c. _____ a person's repetition of phrases that are spoken to them
d. _____ a failure of chromosomes to separate during cell division: the cause of Down syndrome
e. _____ can produce severe physical, emotional, and intellectual impairments
f. _____ disturbance in rate, rhythm, and intonation of speech production
g. _____ an index to measure the extent of genetic contribution to a characteristic
h. _____ a disorder similar to autism but that does not involve language delay
i. _____ at least five months of normal development followed by a deceleration in head growth, loss of purposeful hand movements, loss of social engagement, and language delay
j. _____ profound problems in social interaction, communication, and stereotyped behavior, interests, and activities
k. _____ confusion of pronouns, such as between "you" and "I"
l. _____ active avoidance of eye contact
m. _____ an exceptional ability in a highly specialized area of functioning
n. _____ cases of mental retardation with no known etiology that run in families and are linked with poverty
o. _____ seizure disorder that can result in mental retardation
p. _____ at toxic levels can produce behavioral and cognitive impairments, including mental retardation

q. _____ means that people with mental retardation are entitled to live as much as possible like other members of society

r. _____ unresponsiveness to auditory, tactile, or visual sensations even though there is no impairment in the sensory organ

s. _____ unusual psychological problems that begin early in life and involve severe impairments in a number of areas of functioning

t. _____ keeping mentally retarded children in regular classrooms as much as possible

u. _____ problems in social interaction and communication, as well as stereotyped behavior, with an onset following at least two years of normal development

v. _____ poses a risk for subsequent pregnancies because the mother's body produces antibodies that attack the developing fetus unless treated with an antibiotic

w. _____ ritual actions such as flapping a string or spinning a top that seem to serve no other purpose than to provide sensory feedback

x. _____ can result in sensory impairments, poor physical development, and mental retardation: worse outcomes are typically associated with lower birth weights

y. _____ often repeated head banging or biting of fingers

z. _____ oxygen deprivation that can lead to brain damage

MATCHING III

Answers are found at the end of this chapter. Match the terms and concepts with their definitions:

a. Culture bias
b. Trisomy 21
c. Mean
d. Median
e. Mode
f. Standard scores
g. Variance
h. Phenylalanine
i. Intelligence test
j. Culture-fair tests
k. Flynn effect

l. Deinstitutionalization
m. Eugenics
n. Neuropeptides
o. Endorphins
p. Applied Behavior Analysis (ABA)
q. Gene therapy
r. Theory of mind
s. Facilitated communication
t. Thimerosal
u. Mirror neurons

1. _____ intensive behavior modification using operant conditioning techniques
2. _____ moving care from institutions to the community
3. _____ a term for Down syndrome that describes the chromosomal abnormality
4. _____ neurons that fire both when individuals perform an action and when they see another performing the same action: problems with them may be linked to autism
5. _____ understanding of another person's perspective or point of reference
6. _____ a movement to alter the genetic variability of humans
7. _____ a treatment shown to be ineffective in which a facilitator helps the child with autistic disorder type on a keyboard
8. _____ sum of the squared differences from the mean
9. _____ test items are geared toward the language and knowledge of majority groups
10. _____ midpoint of a frequency distribution
11. _____ substances that affect neurotransmitter action
12. _____ possible future treatment for people with genetic disorders
13. _____ internally-produced opioids

14. ____ a compound that used to be in the MMR vaccine that was incorrectly implicated as a cause for autistic disorder
15. ____ IQ scores are increasing across generations
16. ____ allows for the comparison of scores from different frequency distributions
17. ____ an amino acid that individuals with PKU cannot metabolize, which builds up and causes brain damage
18. ____ a standardized measure for assessing intellectual ability
19. ____ the arithmetic average
20. ____ tests that contain material that is equally familiar to people of different ethnic or cultural backgrounds
21. ____ the most frequent score

MATCHING IV

Answers are found at the end of this chapter. Match these names with the descriptions of their contributions to the study of abnormal psychology:

a. Alfred Binet   c. Langdon Down   e. Hans Asperger
b. O. Ivar Lovaas   d. Leo Kanner

1. ____ first described autism
2. ____ first described a subgroup of children with a chromosomal disorder later named after him
3. ____ described a subgroup of people with a disorder similar to autism but not involving mental retardation
4. ____ developed the first successful IQ test
5. ____ applied behavioral techniques to the management of people with autism

CONCEPT REVIEW

Answers are found at the end of this chapter. After you have read and reviewed the material, test your comprehension by filling in the blanks or circling the correct answer.

1. Most people with pervasive developmental disorders also have mental retardation: **true** **false**

2. Intelligence is _____ distributed in the general population.

3. Intelligence tests have a mean of _____ and a standard deviation of _____.

4. The IQ of a particular person changes significantly over time: **true** **false**

5. IQ tests measure potential for _____.

6. According to the American Association on Mental Retardation, adaptive skills include _____, _____, and _____ skills.

7. The disparity among ethnic groups on IQ test scores appears to be shrinking: **true** **false**

8. More people fall into the **lower** **upper** range of the curve of IQs than would be predicted by a normal distribution.

9. What are the two categories of etiology of mental retardation?

_____ and _____

10. The incidence of Down syndrome is related to maternal _____.

11. Intensive intervention with people with Down syndrome has been shown to be beneficial to their achievement: **true   false**

12. People with Down syndrome typically die in their forties: **true   false**

13. Fragile-X syndrome is more likely to lead to mental retardation in boys than in girls: **true   false**

14. There is no known treatment for phenylketonuria: **true   false**

15. Pregnant women who drink one ounce of alcohol per day or less are not putting their fetus at risk for fetal alcohol syndrome: **true   false**

16. Babies exposed to crack cocaine during the prenatal stage are more likely to be born _____.

17. Today in the United States, the primary way that fetuses are exposed to mercury—which can cause cognitive damage—is when their mothers eat _____.

18. Children living in dilapidated housing are at increased risk for ingesting paint chips containing

    _____.

19. Rh incompatibility is only a potential danger to children of mothers who are Rh

    negative   positive.

20. The IQs of adopted children are more highly correlated to the IQs of their   **adoptive**

    biological parents.

21. What is the most impoverished age group in the United States? _____

22. Environment has been shown to have little effect on IQ: **true   false**

23. Children who participate in Head Start are less likely to _____ or

    _____.

24. The use of neuroleptics to manage aggression and uncontrolled behavior among mentally retarded patients in institutions is recommended: **true   false**

25. People with autism have unusual physical appearances: **true   false**

26. Autism is not usually identified until the child reaches kindergarten: **true   false**

27. Children with autism tend to be very affectionate: **true   false**

28. Many children with autism remain mute: **true   false**

29. People with autism have problems in their capacity for social _____.

30. People with autism **resist   require**   routine.

31. People with autism have superior intelligence: **true   false**

32. When a person with autistic disorder has savant performance, his or her overall intelligence is in the superior range: **true   false**

33. Autism is more common among the upper social classes: **true   false**

34. Autism is more common among   **boys   girls**.

35. Siblings of people with autism are likely to have autism: **true   false**

36. Autism is likely caused by some combination of poor parenting and biological factors:

    true   false

37. MZ twins show higher concordance for autism than DZ twins: **true   false**

38. Most people grow out of autism: **true   false**

39. A number of teens with autism develop _____ disorders.

40. A number of medications show promise in improving functioning of autistic patients: **true   false**

41. Behavioral treatments to reduce self-injurious behavior in autistic patients are controversial because
    they involve _____.

42. The only form of treatment found to be effective in increasing the functioning of autistic patients is
    _____ operant behavior therapy.

MULTIPLE CHOICE

Answers are found at the end of this chapter. These multiple choice questions will test your understanding of the material presented in the chapter. Read each question and circle the best answer.

1. Which of the following teratogens presents the greatest threat to a fetus?
    a. nicotine
    b. alcohol
    c. lead
    d. mercury

2. Mild mental retardation is diagnosed for individuals with deficits in adaptive skills and IQ scores
    between which of the following?
    a. 20–25 and 40
    b. 35–40 and 50
    c. 50–55 and 70
    d. 65–70 and 90

3. All but which of the following are central symptoms of autism?
    a. impaired communication abilities
    b. impairments in social interaction
    c. abnormalities of the eyes, nose, and ears
    d. stereotyped patterns of behavior, interests, and activities

4. As outlined in your text, which of the following has been suggested as an interpretation for pronoun
    reversal as documented in some cases of autism?
    a. pronoun reversal demonstrates a lack of understanding of speech
    b. pronoun reversal is a result of faulty neurotransmitters
    c. pronoun reversal results from damage to specific areas in the frontal lobe
    d. pronoun reversal is due to the autistic child's disinterest in other people

5. Autism is considered to be a _____ disorder, with approximately _____ out of every 10,000 children qualifying for the diagnosis.
   a. rare; 4–60
   b. rare; 150–200
   c. common; 1,000–1,500
   d. common; 3,000–3,500

6. Which of the following is one of the most important current secondary prevention efforts in preventing cultural-familial retardation?
   a. amniocentesis
   b. prenatal care
   c. Head Start
   d. prenatal evaluation

7. Treatment for self-injurious behavior that is sometimes seen in autistic children is controversial because
   a. there is no empirical support to back up the treatment.
   b. the treatment typically involves punishment (e.g. slap or mild electric shock).
   c. the treatment has been relatively ineffective.
   d. the treatment has been used without guardian consent.

8. The reaction range concept of IQ proposed that _____ determines the upper and lower limits of IQ, and _____ determines the extent to which people fulfill their genetic potential.
   a. heredity; experience
   b. experience; heredity
   c. parental IQ; age
   d. age; parental IQ

9. Mental retardation with a specific, known organic cause
   a. is typically more common among families living in poverty.
   b. generally is more common among Hispanics and African Americans.
   c. is most prevalent among the upper class.
   d. generally has an equal prevalence among all social classes.

10. Which of the following was the original developer of IQ tests?
    a. Biklin
    b. Binet
    c. Kanner
    d. Lovaas

11. All but which of the following is true of autistic children?
    a. Most are normal in physical appearance.
    b. Physical growth and development are generally normal.
    c. Their body movements are typically grossly uncoordinated.
    d. They sometimes have unusual actions and postures.

12. Premature birth is defined either as a birth weight of less than five and a half pounds or as birth before _____ weeks of gestation.
    a. thirty-five
    b. thirty-six
    c. thirty-seven
    d. thirty-eight

13. The most common form of self-injury that can accompany autism and other pervasive developmental disorders is
    a. head banging.
    b. repetitive hitting of objects with one's fists.
    c. dare-devil behaviors (i.e. skydiving, bungee jumping, etc.).
    d. cutting of oneself with sharp objects.

14. All but which of the following are diagnostic criteria for autism?
    a. lack of social or emotional reciprocity
    b. a prior diagnosis of Rett's disorder
    c. apparently compulsive adherence to specific, nonfunctional routines or rituals
    d. lack of varied spontaneous make-believe play or social imitative play appropriate to developmental level

15. Autism is believed to be caused by
    a. poor parenting.
    b. an abusive environment.
    c. neurological abnormalities.
    d. there is no known etiology for autism.

16. Almost _____ of all children in the United States are born to teenage mothers.
    a. 10 percent
    b. 15 percent
    c. 20 percent
    d. 25 percent

17. Savant performance is not typical in which of the following areas?
    a. artistic
    b. mathematical
    c. musical
    d. athletic

18. According to the text, which of the following interpretations of self-stimulation is the most plausible?
    a. It is a way for the autistic child to feel similar to others.
    b. It serves the purpose of increasing stimulation to the autistic child who receives too little sensory input.
    c. It serves the function of making a terrifying world more constant and predictable and therefore less frightening.
    d. It is merely a repetitive behavior that serves no function.

19. According to the American Association of Mental Retardation's definition, mental retardation manifests before age
    a. five.
    b. eight.
    c. thirteen.
    d. eighteen.

20. Which of the following is an infectious disease that is the result of infection of the brain and produces inflammation and permanent damage in approximately 20 percent of all cases?
    a. meningitis
    b. rubella
    c. encephalitis
    d. cytomegalovirus

21. Which of the following is caused by the presence of an extra chromosome and is characterized by a distinctively abnormal physical appearance which includes slanting eyes, small head and stature, protruding tongue, and a variety of organ, muscle, and skeletal abnormalities?
    a. Down syndrome
    b. fetal alcohol syndrome
    c. Phenylketonuria (PKU)
    d. multiple sclerosis

22. Severe mental retardation accounts for approximately _____ of the mentally retarded.
    a. 1–2 percent
    b. 3–4 percent
    c. 8–10 percent
    d. 12–15 percent

23. Which of the following is the most promising approach to treating autism?
    a. intensive behavior modification using operant conditioning techniques
    b. antidepressant medication
    c. psychodynamic therapy that focuses on providing a nurturing, supportive environment
    d. None of the above have been effective in treating autism.

24. Both mental retardation and pervasive developmental disorders include all of the following except
    a. they are either are present at birth or begin early in life.
    b. serious disruptions in many areas of functioning, often including an inability to care for oneself independently.
    c. gross physical abnormalities.
    d. often, but not always, a below-average IQ

25. Autism is usually first noticed
    a. early in life.
    b. in adolescence.
    c. in adulthood.
    d. late in life.

26. Which of the following terms was used for several years to classify autism together with other severe forms of childhood psychopathology?
    a. childhood dissociation
    b. disruptive childhood behaviors
    c. psychopathology first evident in childhood
    d. childhood schizophrenia

27. On which Axis is mental retardation coded?
    a. Axis I
    b. Axis II
    c. Axis III
    d. Axis IV

28. Allen is a six-year-old boy who has been diagnosed with autism. Frequently, when asked "would you like a drink?" Allen will repeat the question over and over again. This is an example of
    a. pronoun reversal.
    b. dysprosody.
    c. echolalia.
    d. self-stimulation.

SHORT ANSWER

Answer the following short answer questions. Compare your work to the material presented in the text.

1. Despite the value of IQ tests in predicting academic performance, one controversial question is whether intelligence tests are culturally fair. Discuss your views on this topic.

2. Currently, mental retardation is classified according to the American Association on Mental Retardation and by the DSM-IV-TR. Discuss the similarities and differences in classification of these two approaches.

3. Discuss several etiological considerations regarding autism. Which hypotheses seem most plausible to you. Why? What research supports these hypotheses?

4. Discuss the ethical debate regarding the use of behavior modification techniques to reduce self-injurious behaviors in children with autism. Do you believe these treatments to be unethical? What may be several alternatives to this behavioral approach?

5. Discuss what is meant by a measure of central tendency. Provide an example. Why is this type of measure of importance in research?

ANSWER KEY

MATCHING I

1.	y	8.	t	15.	d	22.	z
2.	s	9.	b	16.	k	23.	e
3.	j	10.	f	17.	q	24.	g
4.	r	11.	o	18.	c	25.	x
5.	a	12.	u	19.	p	26.	i
6.	h	13.	n	20.	w		
7.	v	14.	l	21.	m		

MATCHING II

a.	10	h.	23	o.	6	v.	3
b.	9	i.	25	p.	2	w.	19
c.	17	j.	14	q.	11	x.	4
d.	26	k.	18	r.	20	y.	2
e.	1	l.	15	s.	13	z.	5
f.	16	m.	22	t.	12		
g.	8	n.	7	u.	24		

MATCHING III

1.	p	7.	s	13.	o	19.	c
2.	l	8.	g	14.	t	20.	j
3.	b	9.	a	15.	k	21.	e
4.	u	10.	d	16.	f		
5.	r	11.	n	17.	h		
6.	m	12.	q	18.	i		

MATCHING IV

1.	d	4.	a	
2.	c	5.	b	
3.	e			

CONCEPT REVIEW

1.	true	8.	lower
2.	normally	9.	biological factors; normal genetic variation
3.	100; 15		
4.	false	10.	age
5.	school achievement	11.	true
6.	conceptual; social; practical	12.	true
7.	true	13.	true

14. false
15. false
16. premature
17. certain types of fish like tuna and swordfish
18. lead
19. negative
20. biological
21. children
22. false
23. repeat a grade; be placed in special education classes
24. false
25. false
26. false
27. false

28. true
29. imitation
30. require
31. false
32. false
33. false
34. boys
35. true
36. false
37. true
38. false
39. seizure
40. false
41. punishment
42. intensive

MULTIPLE CHOICE

1. b	6. c	11. c	16. a	21. a	26. d
2. c	7. b	12. d	17. d	22. b	27. b
3. c	8. a	13. a	18. c	23. a	28. c
4. a	9. d	14. b	19. d	24. c	
5. a	10. b	15. c	20. c	25. a	

CHAPTER SIXTEEN

PSYCHOLOGICAL DISORDERS OF CHILDHOOD

CHAPTER OUTLINE

Overview
Externalizing Disorders
      Symptoms of Externalizing Disorders
      Diagnosis of Externalizing Disorders
      Frequency of Externalizing Disorders
      Causes of Externalizing Disorders
      Treatment of Externalizing Disorders
Internalizing and Other Disorders
      Symptoms of Internalizing Disorders
      Diagnosis of Internalizing and Other Disorders
      What Are Learning Disorders?
      Frequency of Internalizing Disorders
      Causes of Internalizing Disorders
      Treatment of Internalizing Disorders
Summary

OBJECTIVES

You should be able to:

1. Distinguish between externalizing and internalizing disorders of childhood.
2. State several factors considered in the evaluation of externalizing symptoms.
3. Compare separation anxiety with separation anxiety disorder.
4. Differentiate between children's psychological problems and adult disorders.
5. Describe the characteristics of pica, rumination disorder, Tourette's disorder, selective autism, reactive attachment disorder, stereotypic movement disorder, encopresis, and enuresis.
6. Describe the defining characteristics of conduct disorder, oppositional defiant disorder, and attention-deficit/hyperactivity disorder.
7. Understand how attachment theory attempts to explain disorders of childhood.
8. State and describe the four parenting styles and explain how inconsistent parenting leads to externalizing symptoms in children.
9. Compare adolescent-limited with life-course-persistent antisocial behavior.
10. List and describe genetic and biological evidence, both positive and negative, concerning the etiology of childhood disorders.
11. Describe the ways in which behavioral family therapy is utilized in the treatment of externalizing disorders.
12. Identify the common course and outcome of the primary childhood disorders.
13. Understand the importance of developmental norms in evaluating children's difficulties.

MATCHING I

Answers are found at the end of this chapter. Match these terms and concepts with the definitions that follow:

a.   Externalizing disorders
b.   Attention-deficit/hyperactivity disorder
c.   Oppositional-defiant disorder
d.   Conduct disorder
e.   Internalizing disorders
f.   Learning disorders
g.   Continuous performance test
h.   Separation anxiety
i.   Separation anxiety disorder
j.   School refusal
k.   Peer sociometrics
l.   Pica
m.   Rumination disorder

n.   Tourette's disorder
o.   Stereotypic movement disorder
p.   Selective mutism
q.   Reactive attachment disorder
r.   Encopresis
s.   Enuresis
t.   Hyperkinesis
u.   Index offenses
v.   Juvenile delinquency
w.   Status offenses
x.   Representative sample
y.   Attachment theory
z.   Anaclitic depression

1.   _____   crimes against people or property that are illegal at any age
2.   _____   consistent failure to speak only in certain social situations
3.   _____   describes the development of attachments and the adverse consequences of troubled attachment relationships
4.   _____   a legal classification determined by a judge
5.   _____   a disorder characterized by persistent and excessive worry for the safety of an attachment figure, fears of separation, nightmares with separation themes, and refusal to be alone
6.   _____   an outdated term for hyperactivity
7.   _____   a lack of social responsiveness found in infants without a consistent attachment figure
8.   _____   normal distress at separation from a caregiver that peaks at about fifteen months of age
9.   _____   repeated motor and verbal tics
10.   _____   acts that are illegal only because of the youth's status as a minor
11.   _____   an empirically derived category of disruptive child behavior problems that create problems
          for the external world
12.   _____   the repeated regurgitation and rechewing of food
13.   _____   a disorder defined primarily by behavior that is illegal as well as antisocial
14.   _____   characterized by severely disturbed and developmentally inappropriate social relationships
15.   _____   a sample that accurately represents some larger group of people
16.   _____   an extreme reluctance to go to school, accompanied by symptoms of anxiety
17.   _____   a laboratory task that requires the subject to monitor and respond to numbers or letters presented on a computer screen
18.   _____   a group of educational problems characterized by academic performance that is notably below academic aptitude
19.   _____   a method of assessing children's social relationships and categorizing children's social standing by obtaining information on who is "liked most" and who is "liked least" from a group of children who know each other
20.   _____   self-stimulation or self-injurious behavior that is serious enough to require treatment
21.   _____   inappropriately controlled defecation
22.   _____   a disorder characterized by hyperactivity, inattention, and impulsivity
23.   _____   the persistent eating of nonnutritive substances
24.   _____   inappropriately controlled urination

25. _____ a disorder characterized by negative, hostile, and defiant behavior
26. _____ an empirically derived category of psychological problems of childhood that affect the child more than the external world

MATCHING II

Answers are found at the end of this chapter. Match these terms and concepts with the definitions that follow:

a. Secure attachments
b. Anxious attachments
c. Anxious avoidant attachments
d. Anxious resistant attachments
e. Disorganized attachments
f. Resilience
g. Authoritative parenting
h. Authoritarian parenting
i. Indulgent parenting
j. Neglectful parenting
k. Coercion
l. Time-out
m. Temperament

n. Salicylates
o. Delay of gratification
p. Emotion regulation
q. Psychostimulants
r. Strattera
s. Behavioral family therapy
t. Parent training
u. Negotiation
v. Multisystemic therapy
w. Recidivism
x. Rehabilitation
y. *Parens patriae*
z. Diversion

a. _____ an anxious attachment where the infant is wary of exploration, not easily soothed by the attachment figure, and angry or ambivalent about contact
b. _____ an anxious attachment where the infant responds inconsistently because of conflicting feelings toward an inconsistent caregiver who is the source of both reassurance and fear
c. _____ a food additive that controlled research has found to be unrelated to ADHD
d. _____ a norepinephrine reuptake inhibitor which is the only nonstimulant drug approved for the treatment of ADHD
e. _____ parenting that is unconcerned with both the child's emotional needs and needs for discipline
f. _____ repeat offending
g. _____ learning to identify, evaluate, and control one's feelings based on the reactions, attitudes, and advice of others in the social world
h. _____ combines family treatment with coordinated interventions in other important contexts of the troubled child's life
i. _____ teaching parents discipline strategies
j. _____ parenting that is affectionate but lax in discipline
k. _____ parenting that is strict, often harsh and undemocratic, as well as lacking in warmth
l. _____ keeping problem youths out of the juvenile justice system
m. _____ a technique of briefly isolating a child following misbehavior
n. _____ infants with these attachments are fearful about exploration and are not easily comforted by their attachment figures, who respond inadequately or inconsistently to the child's needs
o. _____ infants with these attachments separate easily and explore away from their attachment figure but seek comfort when threatened
p. _____ a child's inborn behavioral characteristics, such as activity level, emotionality, and sociability

q. _____ a form of family treatment that trains parents to use the principles of operant conditioning to improve child discipline

r. _____ parents and children reciprocally reinforce child misbehavior and parent capitulation

s. _____ an anxious attachment where the infant is generally unwary of strange situations and shows little preference for the attachment figure over others

t. _____ the adaptive ability to defer smaller but immediate rewards for larger long-term benefits

u. _____ the goal of treatment for delinquent youths

v. _____ a process in which young people are actively involved in defining rules

w. _____ the ability to bounce back from adversity

x. _____ the state as parent

y. _____ a term for medications used to treat children with ADHD

z. _____ parenting that is both loving and firm

MATCHING III

Answers are found at the end of this chapter. Match these terms and concepts with the definitions that follow:

a. Developmental psychopathology
b. Developmental norms
c. Executive functioning
d. Hyperactivity
e. Sustained attention
f. Attention deficits
g. Adolescent-limited
h. Life-course-persistent
i. Attention-deficit disorder
j. Socialization
k. Developmental deviations
l. Clonidine

m. Internal working models
n. Inhibited to the unfamiliar
o. Self-control
p. Low self-esteem
q. Dyslexia
r. Dysgraphia
s. Discalculia
t. Problem-solving skills training
u. Family therapy
v. Negative attention
w. Bell and pad
x. Role reversal

1. _____ intervention with the entire family rather than just the child
2. _____ writing problems
3. _____ behavior that ends with the teen years
4. _____ a device that awakens children by setting off an alarm when they begin to wet the bed
5. _____ behavior that is typical for children of a particular age
6. _____ a DSM-III term
7. _____ the internal direction of behavior
8. _____ expectations about relationships derived from early attachment experiences
9. _____ arithmetic problems
10. _____ teaches children to slow down, evaluate a problem, and consider alternatives before acting
11. _____ reading problems
12. _____ distractibility, frequent shifts from one activity to another, carelessness, poor organization
13. _____ where children care for the parent
14. _____ feelings of low worth
15. _____ the internal regulation of behavior
16. _____ staying on task
17. _____ attempts at punishment sometimes inadvertently reinforce the child's misbehavior
18. _____ significant departures from age-appropriate norms in an area of functioning
19. _____ shaping children's behavior and attitudes to conform to the expectations of society

20. ____ behavior that continues into adult life
21. ____ overactivity suspected to be due to biological abnormalities
22. ____ classifying behavior as abnormal when it deviates from age-typical behavior
23. ____ a high-blood-pressure medication used to treat ADHD
24. ____ a temperamental style characterized by easy crying and fearfulness which is associated with childhood anxiety disorders

MATCHING IV
Answers are found at the end of this chapter. Match these names with their contributions to psychology:

a. Mary Ainsworth   c. John Bowlby   e. Gerald Patterson
b. Michael Rutter   d. Lawrence Kohlberg   f. Benjamin Feingold

1. ____ developed the family adversity index
2. ____ conducted many empirical studies on attachment theory
3. ____ developed the concept of coercion
4. ____ proposed that food additives caused hyperactivity
5. ____ studied moral development in children
6. ____ developed attachment theory

CONCEPT REVIEW
Answers are found at the end of this chapter. After you have read and reviewed the material, test your comprehension by filling in the blanks or circling the correct answer.

1. Which of the following disorders involves violations of laws?

oppositional defiant disorder   **conduct disorder**

2. What percentage of arrests for index offenses are of juveniles under 21 years of age?

7 percent   30 percent   63 percent

3. Adult antisocial behavior is better predicted by information about the person during:

childhood   adolescence

4. In adolescence, violations of rules is _____.

5. Impulsivity is acting before _____.

6. Where is hyperactivity particularly noticeable? _____

7. The behavioral problems that characterize ADHD are largely   **intentional   unintentional**.

8. Assessment of children's feelings is   **straightforward   difficult**.

9. Parents are very good at detecting their children's depression: **true   false**

10. If in error, parents are likely to   **overestimate   underestimate**   their children's depression.

11. Fears in children are a symptom of some emotional disorder: **true   false**

12. School refusal often indicates a child's fear of _____.

13. Which category of peer ratings is the most correlated with psychological disorders?

    _____

14. What type of norms are essential in assessing abnormal behavior in children?

    _____ norms

15. A learning disorder is defined as one or two standard deviations between

    _____ and _____ .

16. There is a high degree of comorbidity between learning disorders and which two psychological

    disorders? _____ and _____

17. Learning disorders are easily treated: **true   false**

18. Encopresis and enuresis are usually   **causes of   reactions to**   psychological distress.

19. The bell and pad is a device that is effective in treating _____ .

20. The current DSM-IV-TR is probably   **overinclusive   underinclusive**   in its listing of

    childhood psychological disorders.

21. Hyperactivity is the result of inattention: **true   false**

22. ADHD and oppositional defiant disorder are separate but _____

    disorders.

23. More   **boys   girls**   are treated for psychological disorders. More   **men   women**

    enter into therapy.

24. Teenage girls are more likely to have _____ problems, and young boys are

    more likely to have _____ problems.

25. Risk for _____ problems increase substantially when more than one family

    adversity risk factor is present.

26. What is the third leading cause of death among teenagers? _____

27. Genetic influence is **stronger   weaker**   for early- than late-onset antisocial behavior.

28. Children with serious conduct problems often have had what type of parenting?

    _____

29. Negative attention is sometimes _____ to children.

30. Crime rates are about the same in the United States and in Europe: **true   false**

31. Research has shown that critical and demanding parenting is the   **cause   result**   of hyperactive

    child behavior.

32. A certain temperamental style, inhibited to the unfamiliar, has been linked to _____

    disorders in adulthood.

33. Genetic factors appear to be strongly linked to ADHD: **true   false**

34. In coercion, the parent **positively** **negatively** reinforces a child's misbehavior by giving in to the child's demands, and the child **positively** **negatively** reinforces the parent's giving in by stopping the obnoxious behavior when the parent gives in.

35. Research has shown that sugar increases hyperactive behavior: **true** **false**

36. Children with externalizing disorder have problems with _____ control.

37. Aggressive children demonstrate immaturity in moral development: **true** **false**

38. Children with mothers who are depressed are more likely to develop

_____.

39. Children usually grow out of internalizing disorders: **true** **false**

40. Antidepressants are just as effective in treating children with depression as with adults:

true **false**

41. Research has found that antidepressants combined with _____ is the most effective treatment approach for adolescents.

42. The conclusion about whether or not antidepressants increase the risk for suicide among adolescents more than they decrease the risk by treating the depression is that the risks **do** **do not** outweigh the benefits.

43. Psychostimulants are effective in treating children with ADHD: **true** **false**

44. Psychostimulants have a paradoxical effect on children with ADHD, which demonstrates the biological underpinnings of the disorder: **true** **false**

45. Psychostimulants are taken for a couple of weeks and their effects last for several months at a time:

true **false**

46. Medication is more helpful in the treatment of ADHD than behavioral family therapy:

true **false**

47. When juveniles are diverted from the juvenile justice system, they show higher rates of recidivism:

true **false**

48. Psychostimulant use among preschoolers has significantly increased: **true** **false**

MULTIPLE CHOICE
Answers are found at the end of this chapter. These multiple choice questions will test your understanding of the material presented in the chapter. Read each question and circle the letter representing the best answer.

1. In his study on family adversity, Michael Rutter found that all of the following were predictors of behavior problems among children except
   a. low income.
   b. overcrowding in the home.
   c. conflict between parents.
   d. paternal depression.

2. In all but which of the following are there major problems in evaluating children's internalizing symptoms?
   a. There are insufficient self-report measures to assess internalizing symptoms in children.
   b. It is much more difficult for adults to assess children's inner experiences than it is to observe children's behavior.
   c. Children often are not reliable or valid informants about their internal life.
   d. Children's capacity to recognize emotions in themselves emerges slowly over the course of development and therefore they may not be aware of their own emotional turmoil.

3. Reactive attachment disorder is most likely caused by which of the following?
   a. It appears to have genetic origins.
   b. an unstable home environment in which caregivers are frequently changing
   c. extremely neglectful parenting
   d. Its etiology is unknown.

4. All but which of the following are major subtypes of externalizing disorders?
   a. attention-deficit/hyperactivity disorder
   b. conduct disorder
   c. depression
   d. oppositional defiant disorder

5. Which of the following is the most helpful for scientists in predicting adult antisocial behavior?
   a. information obtained during birth and infancy
   b. information obtained during childhood
   c. information obtained during adolescence
   d. information obtained during adulthood

6. According to a panel of experts assembled by the National Academy of Sciences, at least _____ percent of the sixty-three million children living in the United States suffer from a mental disorder.
   a. five
   b. twelve
   c. seventeen
   d. twenty-three

7. Which of the following is a sample that accurately depicts a larger group of people?
   a. representative sample
   b. random sample
   c. convenience sample
   d. heterogeneous sample

8. _____ is thought to have environmental origins, while _____is thought to have a biological cause.
   a. Attention-deficit/hyperactivity disorder; oppositional defiant disorder
   b. Oppositional defiant disorder; attention-deficit/hyperactivity disorder
   c. Conduct disorder; oppositional defiant disorder
   d. Oppositional defiant disorder; conduct disorder

9. Separation anxiety disorder is typically associated with all of the following except
   a. fears of getting lost or being kidnapped.
   b. refusal to be alone.
   c. persistent and excessive worry for the safety of an attachment figure.
   d. refusal to interact with others when the attachment figure is not present.

10. The attachment figure for an infant with an anxious attachment responds to the infant in which of the following ways?
    a. appropriately attends to the infant's needs
    b. inadequately or inconsistently attends to the infant's needs
    c. immediately attends to the infant's needs
    d. is completely unresponsive to the infant's needs

11. The FBI reports that about _____ percent of arrests for major crimes including murder, forcible rape, and robbery are of juveniles under the age of 21.
    a. 10
    b. 20
    c. 30
    d. 40

12. Which of the following is a well-known treatment device that awakens children with enuresis by setting off an alarm as they begin to wet the bed?
    a. bell and pad
    b. light and alarm
    c. sensitive signal seat
    d. responsive wetting device

13. Which of the following is characterized by self-stimulation or self-injurious behavior?
    a. conduct disorder
    b. developmental coordination disorder
    c. Tourette's disorder
    d. stereotypic movement disorder

14. ADHD is characterized by all but which of the following symptoms?
    a. impulsivity
    b. hyperactivity
    c. aggression
    d. inattention

15. Family therapy combined with coordinated interventions in other aspects of the child's life, like school and peer groups, is called
    a. multisystemic therapy.
    b. behavioral family therapy.
    c. problem-solving skills training.
    d. a residential program.

16. Which of the following gender differences is not true in respect to internalizing and externalizing problems?
    a. More adult men enter into therapy than do adult women.
    b. Boys are treated more for psychological problems than girls.
    c. By early adult life, more females report psychological problems than males.
    d. Boys have far more externalizing disorders than girls.

17. According to the "peer sociometric method" of assessing children's relationships, which of the following groups is characterized by a high frequency of "liked least" ratings and a low frequency of "liked most" ratings?
    a. average
    b. neglected
    c. rejected
    d. controversial

18. All but which of the following are internalizing symptoms?
    a. somatic complaints
    b. fears
    c. aggressive behavior
    d. sadness

19. Which term refers to acts that are only illegal when performed by a minor?
    a. index offenses
    b. conduct disorder
    c. juvenile delinquency
    d. status offenses

20. Infants typically develop a fear of _____ around the age of seven to eight months.
    a. strangers
    b. the dark
    c. monsters
    d. unfamiliar environments

21. Which of the following is the process of shaping children's behavior and attitudes to conform to the expectations of parents, teachers, and society?
    a. modeling
    b. socialization
    c. conditioning
    d. vicarious learning

22. Brandon is a three-year-old who frequently throws a tantrum in the grocery store if he does not get what he wants. Because this is such an embarrassing situation for his mother, she will give Brandon whatever he desires in order to get his cooperation. In this case, Brandon is being _____ while his mother is being _____.
   a. positively reinforced; negatively reinforced
   b. negatively reinforced; positively reinforced
   c. classically conditioned; punished
   d. positively reinforced; punished

SHORT ANSWER
Answer the following short answer questions. Compare your work to the material presented in the text.

1. Discuss the challenges of identifying internalizing problems in children. How do different sources of information (e.g. parents, teachers) vary on their estimation of internalizing problems?

2. Discuss the role of context in the etiology and maintenance of children's psychological problems. Provide one example.

3. Compare attention-deficit/hyperactivity disorder, oppositional defiant disorder, and conduct disorder. Describe the overlap between these disorders.

4. Why must a sample be representative of a general population? Provide one example.

ANSWER KEY

MATCHING I

1. u	8. h	15. x	22. b
2. p	9. n	16. j	23. l
3. y	10. w	17. g	24. s
4. v	11. a	18. f	25. c
5. i	12. m	19. k	26. e
6. t	13. d	20. o	
7. z	14. q	21. r	

MATCHING II

a. 4	h. 22	o. 1	v. 21
b. 5	i. 20	p. 13	w. 6
c. 14	j. 9	q. 19	x. 25
d. 18	k. 8	r. 11	y. 17
e. 10	l. 26	s. 3	z. 7
f. 23	m. 12	t. 15	
g. 16	n. 2	u. 24	

MATCHING III

1. u	7. c	13. x	19. j
2. r	8. m	14. p	20. h
3. g	9. s	15. o	21. d
4. w	10. t	16. e	22. a
5. b	11. q	17. v	23. l
6. i	12. f	18. k	24. n

MATCHING IV

1. b	3. e	5. d
2. a	4. f	

CONCEPT REVIEW

1. conduct disorder	10. underestimate
2. 30 percent	11. false
3. childhood	12. leaving a parent
4. common	13. rejected
5. thinking	14. developmental
6. in the classroom	15. aptitude; achievement
7. unintentional	16. ADHD; oppositional defiant disorder
8. difficult	17. false
9. false	18. causes of

19. enuresis
20. overinclusive
21. false
22. overlapping
23. boys; women
24. internalizing; externalizing
25. externalizing
26. suicide
27. stronger
28. neglectful
29. reinforcing
30. false
31. result
32. anxiety
33. true

34. positively; negatively
35. false
36. self
37. true
38. depression
39. false
40. false
41. cognitive behavior therapy
42. do not
43 true
44. false
45. false
46. true
47. false
48. true

MULTIPLE CHOICE

1. d
2. a
3. c
4. c
5. b
6. b
7. a
8. b
9. d
10. b
11. c
12. a
13. d
14. c
15. a
16. a
17. c
18. c
19. d
20. a
21. b
22. a

CHAPTER SEVENTEEN

ADJUSTMENT DISORDERS AND LIFE-CYCLE TRANSITIONS

CHAPTER OUTLINE

Overview
    Symptoms
    Diagnosis
    Brief Historical Perspective
    Contemporary Classification
The Transition to Adulthood
    Symptoms of the Adult Transition
    Diagnosis of Identity Conflicts
    Frequency of Identity Conflicts
    Causes of Identity Conflicts
    Treatment during the Transition to Adult Life
Family Transitions
    Symptoms of Family Transitions
    Diagnosis of Troubled Family Relationships
    Frequency of Family Transitions
    Causes of Difficulty in Family Transitions
    Treatment during Family Transitions
The Transition to Later Life
    Ageism
    Symptoms
    Diagnosis of Aging
    Frequency of Aging
    Causes of Psychological Problems in Later Life
    Treatment of Psychological Problems in Later Life
Summary

OBJECTIVES

You should be able to:
1. Define life-cycle transition.
2. Discuss the role of life-cycle transitions in the development of psychopathology.
3. Describe Erikson's psychosocial moratorium and identity crisis.
4. Define Marcia's four identity statuses.
5. Describe several common gender differences that occur in the transition to adulthood.
6. Identify ways in which power struggles, intimacy struggles, affiliation, interdependence, and scapegoating impact family structure.
7. Describe Gottman's four communication problems.
8. Describe several premarital and marital therapy treatment programs.
9. Compare Bowlby's and Kubler-Ross's model of grieving.
10. Identify typical psychological and physiological processes in young-old, old-old, and oldest-old adults.
11. Describe several gender differences in later life regarding relationships.

MATCHING I

Answers are found at the end of this chapter. Match these terms and concepts with their definitions:

a.	Adjustment disorders	k.	Identity crisis
b.	Psychological pain	l.	Intimacy versus self-absorption
c.	Life-cycle transitions	m.	Generativity versus stagnation
d.	Transition to adult life	n.	Integrity and despair
e.	Family transitions	o.	Family life cycle
f.	Transition to later life	p.	Early adult transition
g.	Interpersonal diagnoses	q.	Midlife transition
h.	Crisis of the healthy personality	r.	Late adult transition
i.	Identity	s.	Social clocks
j.	Identity versus role confusion		

1. ____ the challenge in establishing intimate relationships, balanced between closeness and independence

2. ____ clinically significant symptoms in response to stress that are not severe enough to warrant classification as another mental disorder

3. ____ career and family accomplishments with purpose or direction as opposed to lacking purpose or direction

4. ____ struggles in the process of moving from one social or psychological stage of adult development into a new one

5. ____ a series of normal conflicts related to change as the comfortable and predictable conflicts with the fearsome but exciting unknown

6. ____ becoming less driven by internal and external demands and developing more compassion for ourselves and others

7. ____ classification of psychological problems that reside within the context of human relationships rather than within an individual

8. ____ age-related goals for ourselves

9. ____ a period of basic uncertainty about self

10. ____ the challenge of adolescence and young adulthood: this stage involves integrating various role identities into a global sense of self

11. ____ difficult but normal emotions that can result from difficult life transitions

12. ____ looking back on one's life with either a sense of acceptance and pride or anger and despair

13 ____ global sense of self

14. ____ the changing roles and relationships of later life

15. ____ the developmental course of family relationships throughout life

16. ____ in the middle years of life: includes birth of first child and divorce

17. ____ in the late teens and early twenties: struggling with identity, career, and relationship issues

18. ____ moving away from family and assuming adult roles

19. ____ major changes in life roles like retirement, grief over the death of loved ones, and aging and facing mortality

MATCHING II

Answers are found at the end of this chapter. Match these terms and concepts with their definitions:

1. Moratorium	14. Gene-environment correlation
2. Identity diffusion	15. Cognitive behavioral couple therapy
3. Identity foreclosure	16. Scapegoat
4. Identity moratorium	17. Heritability
5. Identity achievement	18. Heritability ratio
6. Alienated identity achievement	19. Criticism
7. Empty nest	20. Contempt
8. Power struggles	21. Defensiveness
9. Intimacy struggles	22. Stonewalling
10. Reciprocity	23. Androgynous couples
11. Demand and withdrawal pattern	24. Moving against
12. Rational suicide	25. Moving toward
13. Assisted suicide	26. Moving away

a. ____ an elderly adult choosing to end his or her life

b. ____ couples in which both husbands and wives have high levels of masculinity and femininity

c. ____ the adjustment that occurs when adult children leave the family home

d. ____ an identity status common in the 1960s, where one's definition of self is alienated from many values held by the larger society

e. ____ attacking someone's personality rather than his or her actions

f. ____ emphasizes the couple's moment-to-moment interaction, focusing on exchange of positive and negative behaviors, style of communication, and strategies for problem-solving

g. ____ where the wife becomes increasingly demanding and the husband withdraws further and further as time passes

h. ____ a statistic used for summarizing the genetic contributions to behavioral characteristics

i. ____ being in the middle of an identity crisis and actively searching for adult roles

j. ____ a form of self-justification, such as denying responsibility or blaming the other person

k. ____ social exchange of cooperation and conflict

l. ____ a pattern of isolation and withdrawal

m. ____ attempts to change dominance relations

n. ____ a time of uncertainty about self and goals

o. ____ a family member who is held to blame for all of a family's troubles

p. ____ attempts to alter the degree of closeness in a relationship

q. ____ having questioned childhood identity but not actively searching for new adult roles

r. ____ a nonrandom association between inborn characteristics and environmental experience

s. ____ having questioned one's identity and successfully decided on long-term goals

t. ____ an insult motivated by anger and intended to hurt the other person

u. ____ a medical professional helping a disabled person end his or her life

v. ____ the relative contribution of genes to behavioral characteristics

w. ____ having never questioned oneself or one's goals but proceeding along the predetermined course of one's childhood commitments

x. ____ fulfills needs for power and dominance

y. ____ fulfills needs for love and acceptance

z. ____ fulfills needs for independence and efficacy

MATCHING III
Answers are found at the end of this chapter. Match these terms and concepts with their definitions:

a. Ageism
b. Menopause
c. Estrogen
d. Hormone replacement therapy
e. Reminiscence
f. Integrative reminiscence
g. Instrumental reminiscence
h. Transitive reminiscence
i. Escapist reminiscence
j. Narrative reminiscence

k. Obsessive reminiscence
l. Living wills
m. Grief
n. Bereavement
o. Gerontology
p. Young-old adults
q. Old-old adults
r. Oldest-old adults
s. Behavioral gerontology

1. _____ the cessation of menstruation
2. _____ descriptive rather than interpretive
3. _____ misconceptions and prejudices about aging
4. _____ the recounting of personal memories of the distant past
5. _____ the multidisciplinary study of aging
6. _____ a female sex hormone that fluctuates during menopause
7. _____ the emotional and social process of coping with a separation or loss
8. _____ adults ages eighty-five and older
9. _____ an attempt to achieve a sense of self-worth, coherence, and reconciliation with the past
10. _____ preoccupation with failure: full of guilt, bitterness, and despair
11. _____ adults roughly between the ages of sixty-five and seventy-five; those in good health and active in their communities
12. _____ a sub-discipline of health psychology and behavioral medicine that focuses on the study and treatment of behavioral components of health and illness among older adults
13. _____ a specific form of grieving in response to the death of a loved one
14. _____ the administration of artificial estrogen
15. _____ full of glorification of the past and deprecation of the present
16. _____ includes both direct moral instruction and storytelling with clear moral implications: serves the function of passing on cultural heritage and personal legacy
17. _____ adults roughly between the ages of seventy-five and eighty-five: those who suffer from major physical, psychological, or social problems and require some routine assistance in living
18. _____ the review of goal-directed activities and attainments reflecting a sense of control and success in overcoming life's obstacles
19. _____ legal documents that direct health care professionals not to perform procedures to keep a terminally ill patient alive

MATCHING IV

Answers are found at the end of this chapter. Match these names with the descriptions of their contributions to the study of abnormal psychology:

a.	Erik Erikson	c.	Karen Horney	e.	John Gottman
b.	Daniel Levinson	d.	Elisabeth Kubler-Ross		

1. _____ theorized that people have competing needs to move toward, away from, and against others
2. _____ widened the emphasis of adult development to social as well as psychological tasks
3. _____ developed a stage theory of grieving in bereavement
4. _____ developed a stage theory of psychosocial development from birth to death
5. _____ focused on communication patterns in marital interaction

CONCEPT REVIEW

Answers are found at the end of this chapter. After you have read and reviewed the material, test your comprehension by filling in the blanks or circling the correct answer.

1. The DSM-IV-TR has a comprehensive, detailed section on adjustment disorders and other conditions besides mental disorders that may be the focus of psychotherapy: **true**   **false**

2. Erikson focused more on the _____ side of "psychosocial" development, while Levinson focused more on the _____ aspects.

3. Research has shown that   **adolescents**   **adults**   experience more intense emotions.

4. In non-Western cultures, the transition to adult life is characterized by **more**   **less**   uncertainty and conflict than in the United States.

5. The "forgotten half" refers to youth who do not _____.

6. Research suggests that the most successful young adults have parents who strike a balance between continuing to provide support and _____ and allowing their children increasing _____.

7. For women in traditional roles, identity often develops out of _____.

8. Marital satisfaction   **increases**   **decreases**   following the birth of the first child.

9. Family members with happy relationships _____ negative comments and _____ positive ones.

10. Happy couples are more likely to use the pronoun   **I**   **you**   when interacting over their conflicts.

11. About _____ of all existing marriages will end in divorce.

12. **Whites**   **blacks**   are more likely to remarry following divorce.

13. Androgynous couples had marriages that were   **higher**   **lower**   in satisfaction than nonandrogynous couples.

14. Research indicates that the Premarital Relationship Enhancement Program **is** **is not** effective in increasing marital satisfaction over time.

15. Behavioral marital therapy has been shown to be more effective than other therapy approaches: **true** **false**

16. Couples therapy can be effective in alleviating a person's depression: **true** **false**

17. **Men** **women** have a shorter life expectancy.

18. Older people are less satisfied with their lives: **true** **false**

19. Personality has been found to be consistent from middle age to old age: **true** **false**

20. Physical activity and physical health are some of the best predictors of psychological well-being among older adults: **true** **false**

21. Hormone replacement therapy increases the risk for cancer: **true** **false**

22. Visual acuity actually increases with age: **true** **false**

23. Older adults report fewer positive relationships and a decreased sense of mastery over their environment than young and middle age adults: **true** **false**

24. Researchers have found support for the stages of bereavement proposed by Kubler-Ross: **true** **false**

25. Less intense bereavement predicts better long-term adjustment: **true** **false**

26. The prevalence of mental disorders increases with age: **true** **false**

27. The risk of completed suicide is higher among the elderly: **true** **false**

28. Men apparently benefit more from **marriage** **happy relationships** while women benefit more from **marriage** **happy relationships.**

MULTIPLE CHOICE
Answers are found at the end of this chapter. These multiple choice questions will test your understanding of the material presented in the chapter. Read each question and circle the best answer.

1. The decline in the divorce rate is mostly the result of
    a. more people completing marital therapy.
    b. the changing age of the U.S. population.
    c. divorce being less acceptable.
    d. people most prone to divorce not marrying in the first place.

2. Which of the following groups has the highest suicide rate?
    a. teenagers
    b. young adults
    c. middle-aged adults
    d. adults over the age of sixty-five

3. On the average, marital happiness declines following_____.
    a.   the death of a family member
    b.   the birth of the first child
    c.   the emptying of the family nest
    d.   the fifth year of marriage

4. Approximately _____ of couples seen in behavioral marital therapy do not improve significantly.
    a.   30 percent
    b.   40 percent
    c.   50 percent
    d.   60 percent

5. Which of the following includes various struggles in the process of moving from one social or psychological "stage" of adult development into a new stage?
    a.   life cycle transitions
    b.   transition to adult life
    c.   developmental tasks of adult life
    d.   family transitions

6. According to Erikson, which of the following stages is the major challenge of adolescence and young adulthood?
    a.   integrity versus despair
    b.   generativity versus stagnation
    c.   intimacy versus self-absorption
    d.   identity versus role confusion

7. Which of the following refers to youth who do not attend college and who often assume marginal roles in U.S. society?
    a.   "Transient Youth"
    b.   "Generation X"
    c.   "Alienated Youth"
    d.   "Forgotten Half"

8. When reviewing the various models of adult development, which of the following must be taken into consideration?
    a.   History, culture, and personal values influence views about which kinds of "tasks" are normal during adult development.
    b.   Transitions or "crises" may not be as predictable as the models imply.
    c.   Some people may not pass through a particular stage of development.
    d.   all of the above

9. Research indicates that in happy relationships, family members _____ each other's positive actions, and _____ each other's negative behavior.
    a.   reciprocate; overlook
    b.   overlook; reciprocate
    c.   reciprocate; reciprocate
    d.   overlook; overlook

10. The ratio of men to women _____ at older ages.
    a. increases
    b. decreases
    c. is approximately equal
    d. stays relatively the same across the age span

11. Erik Erikson highlighted _____ as a common theme that occurs throughout life cycle transitions.
    a. uncertainty
    b. conflict
    c. remorse
    d. acceptance

12. Estimates indicate that about _____ of today's marriages will end in divorce.
    a. 30 percent
    b. 50 percent
    c. 40 percent
    d. 60 percent

13. Epidemiological evidence indicates that the prevalence of mental disorders is _____ among people sixty-five years of age and older as compared to younger adults.
    a. lower
    b. higher
    c. about the same
    d. it is unknown due to the difficulty in studying this population

14. Which of the following identifies people who are in the middle of an identity crisis and who are actively searching for adult roles?
    a. alienated identity achievement
    b. identity moratorium
    c. identify diffusion
    d. identity foreclosure

15. All of the following are emphasized by behavioral marital therapy except
    a. the couple's moment-to-moment interactions.
    b. strategies for solving problems.
    c. extensive clinical interview of relationship patterns in the couple's families.
    d. the couple's style of communication.

16. Family life cycle theorists classify adult development according to which of the following?
    a. the tasks and transitions of family life
    b. the adult's memories of their childhood and adolescence
    c. the tasks and transitions of psychological challenges of adulthood
    d. all of the above

17. Psychological research suggests that the most successful young adults have which kind of parents?
    a. parents who are strict and authoritarian
    b. parents who are supportive and could be characterized as their children's "best friend"
    c. parents who strongly encourage individuation and provide opportunities for their children to take on numerous responsibilities at an early age
    d. parents who strike a balance between continuing to provide support and supervision of their children while allowing them increasing independence

18. Which of the following individuals theorized that people have competing needs to move toward, away from, and against others?
    a. Erikson
    b. Levinson
    c. Horney
    d. Kubler-Ross

19. _____ struggles are attempts to change dominance relations, whereas _____ struggles are attempts to alter the degree of closeness in a relationship.
    a. Intimacy; power
    b. Power; intimacy
    c. Conflict; relational
    d. Relational; conflict

20. Which of the following is not a normal change of aging?
    a. decline in hearing ability
    b. decline in visual acuity
    c. decline in muscle strength
    d. decline in happiness

21. All of the following are true of the "V codes" in the DSM-IV-TR except
    a. they do not include an extensive summary of life difficulties.
    b. they are similar to other diagnoses in the DSM in that they are diagnosed as mental disorders.
    c. they include issues such as bereavement, identity problems, and phase of life problems.
    d. All of the above are true of "V codes."

22. Lisa and Mike have been married for four years. Recently, they have been arguing more than usual. Whenever they get into an argument, Lisa engages in a pattern of isolation and withdrawal, ignoring Mike's complaints and virtually ending all communication with him. According to Gottman, Lisa is engaged in which of the following?
    a. stonewalling
    b. contempt
    c. defensiveness
    d. criticism

23. All but which all of the following are true of hormone replacement therapy?
    a. It alleviates some of the psychological strains associated with adverse physical symptoms of menopause.
    b. It reduces the subsequent risk for heart and bone disease.
    c. It increases the risk for cancer.
    d. It decreases symptoms of depression, which are often associated with menopause.

24. Alternative lifestyles not withstanding, evidence indicates that _____ of the adults in the United States get married during their adult lives.
    a. 40 percent
    b. 60 percent
    c. 75 percent
    d. 90 percent

25. One criticism of Erikson's theories is that
    a. the stages are inappropriate for certain developmental levels.
    b. the theories are too broad and general, and are not applicable to a large proportion of the population.
    c. they are not very accurate in outlining developmental stages.
    d. the theories focus on men to the exclusion of women.

26. Which of the following is associated with less successful adjustment in later life?
    a. obsessive reminiscence
    b. transitive reminiscence
    c. instrumental reminiscence
    d. integrative reminiscence

27. Family therapists and family researchers often blame difficulties in negotiating family transitions on which of the following?
    a. low motivation
    b. problems with communication
    c. difficulty identifying problem areas
    d. all of the above

28. Which of the following is not a stage of adult development in Erikson's model?
    a. intimacy versus self-absorption
    b. integrity versus despair
    c. assurance versus apprehension
    d. generativity versus stagnation

29. Research on identity achievement indicates that _____ may have rejecting and distant families, while _____ may have overprotective families.
    a. identity diffusers; identity foreclosers
    b. identity foreclosers; identity diffusers
    c. identity achievers; alienated identity achievers
    d. alienated identity achievers; identity achievers

30. All but which of the following are stages included in the Family Developmental Tasks through the Family Life Cycle?
    a. childbearing
    b. launching center
    c. aging family members
    d. death and dying

31. Girls who grow up with an unrelated male in their household have been found to reach menarche at earlier ages. Instead of being an evolutionary mechanism, this finding may be due to a gene-environment correlation where the girls
    a. have higher-fat diets that affect estrogen levels and lead to earlier menstruation.
    b. inherited their absent father's gene for risk-taking.
    c. inherited their mothers' gene for early menarche, which made their mothers more likely to enter risky relationships which were more likely to break up.
    d. lived in environments characterized by high levels of violence.

SHORT ANSWER
Answer the following short answer questions. Compare your work to the material presented in the text.

1. Discuss the stages of Erikson's model of adult development. What do you consider to be the strengths of this model? What are some of its weaknesses?

2. Outline the psychological, social, and biological factors that may contribute to difficulties in family transitions. Which factors do you think are most important when identifying the etiology of family transition difficulties?

3. Review the categories of reminiscence identified by Wong and Watt. Which categories appear to be related to successful aging? Which appear to be associated with less successful adjustment in later life? Which category do you think will best describe your reminiscence later in life? Why?

4. Discuss categories of identity conflicts. Do you identify with any of these? Explain.

ANSWER KEY

MATCHING I

1. l	6. q	11. b	16. e
2. a	7. g	12. n	17. d
3. m	8. s	13. i	18. p
4. c	9. k	14. r	19. f
5. h	10. j	15. o	

MATCHING II

a. 12	h. 18	o. 16	v. 17
b. 23	i. 4	p. 9	w. 3
c. 7	j. 21	q. 2	x. 24
d. 6	k. 10	r. 14	y. 25
e. 19	l. 22	s. 5	z. 26
f. 15	m. 8	t. 20	
g. 11	n. 1	u. 13	

MATCHING III

1. b	6. c	11. p	16. h
2. j	7. m	12. s	17. q
3. a	8. r	13. n	18. g
4. e	9. f	14. d	19. l
5. o	10. k	15. i	

MATCHING IV

1. c	4. a
2. b	5. e
3. d	

CONCEPT REVIEW

1.	false	11.	40 percent
2.	psychological; social	12.	whites
3.	adolescents	13.	higher
4.	less	14.	is
5.	attend college	15.	false
6.	supervision; independence	16.	true
7.	relationships	17.	men
8.	decreases	18.	false
9.	ignore; reciprocate	19.	true
10.	I	20.	true

21.	true	25.	true
22.	false	26.	false
23.	false	27.	true
24.	false	28.	marriage; happy relationships

MULTIPLE CHOICE

1. d	6. d	11. b	16. a	21. b	26. a	31. c
2. d	7. d	12. b	17. d	22. a	27. b	
3. b	8. d	13. a	18. c	23. d	28. c	
4. c	9. a	14. b	19. b	24. d	29. a	
5. a	10. b	15. c	20. d	25. d	30. d	

MENTAL HEALTH AND THE LAW

CHAPTER OUTLINE

OBJECTIVES

You should be able to:

1. Discuss the issues of free will and determinism as they relate to the insanity defense.
2. Distinguish between the M'Naghten test, the irresistible impulse test, the product test, and the American Law Institute legislation for determining insanity.
3. Discuss the "guilty but mentally ill" verdict and explain the consequences of this verdict.
4. Distinguish between the verdict of NGRI with that of a "guilty" verdict.
5. Discuss the issue of competence and its role in the legal system.
6. Contrast the libertarian position with the paternalist position regarding involuntary psychiatric commitment.
7. Discuss issues of reliability as they relate to predictions of dangerousness and suicide risk.
8. Describe the issues involved in a patient's right to treatment, a least restrictive alternative environment, and right to refuse treatment.
9. Discuss problems associated with deinstitutionalization.
10. Describe the role of mental health practitioners in child custody disputes.
11. Discuss the most common types of malpractice cases filed against mental health practitioners.
12. List situations in which psychologists are legally bound to break confidentiality.

MATCHING I

Answers are found at the end of this chapter. Match these terms and concepts with the definitions that follow:

a.	Free will	m.	Standard of proof
b.	Criminal responsibility	n.	Expert witnesses
c.	Determinism	o.	Battered woman syndrome
d.	Insanity	p.	Temporary insanity
e.	Insanity defense	q.	Competence
f.	M'Naghten test	r.	Miranda warning
g.	Not guilty by reason of insanity	s.	Moral treatment
h.	*Parens patriae*	t.	Deinstitutionalization movement
i.	Mitigation evaluation	u.	Sexual predator laws
j.	Product test	v.	Incompetent to stand trial
k.	Guilty but mentally ill (GBMI)	w.	Civil commitment
l.	Burden of proof		

1. ____ a defendant's ability to understand the legal proceedings that are taking place against him or her and to participate in his or her own defense
2. ____ a legal term referring to a defendant's state of mind while committing a crime
3. ____ the state as parent
4. ____ specialists allowed to testify about specific matters of opinion within their area of expertise
5. ____ a person being held accountable when he or she breaks the law
6. ____ the attempt to care for the mentally ill in their communities
7. ____ the idea that people have the capacity to make choices and act freely on them
8. ____ the finding by a court that a person committed a crime, was mentally ill at the time it was committed, but was not legally insane at that time
9. ____ unable to exercise the right to participate in one's own trial defense
10. ____ the psychological effects of being chronically abused by a husband or lover
11. ____ the involuntary hospitalization of the mentally ill
12. ____ the principle for determining insanity of whether the person is prevented from knowing the wrongfulness of his or her actions by a mental disease or defect
13. ____ the stress of an event temporarily causes a person to be legally insane
14. ____ the idea that an accused person is not criminally responsible if the unlawful act was the product of a mental disease or defect
15. ____ a movement founded on a basic respect for human dignity
16. ____ the police must inform a suspect during arrest of his or her rights to remain silent and to have an attorney present during police questioning
17. ____ the idea that human behavior is determined by biological, psychological, and social forces
18. ____ a thorough review of factors that may have been relevant to the commission of a crime, such as mental illness and duress at the time of the crime
19. ____ the degree of certainty required
20. ____ the finding by a court that a person is not criminally responsible for his or her actions because of a mental disease or defect
21. ____ laws designed to keep sexual offenders imprisoned indefinitely
22. ____ whether the prosecution or the defense has the obligation to prove guilt
23. ____ an attempt to prove that a person with a mental illness did not meet the legal criteria for sanity at the time of committing a crime

MATCHING II

Answers are found at the end of this chapter. Match these terms and concepts with the definitions that follow:

1. Emergency commitment procedures
2. Formal commitment procedures
3. Base rates
4. Outpatient commitment
5. Termination of parental rights
6. Informed consent
7. Substituted judgment
8. Revolving door phenomenon
9. Child custody
10. Physical custody
11. Legal custody
12. Sole custody
13. Joint custody

14. Munchausen-by-proxy syndrome
15. Confidentiality
16. Divorce mediation
17. Child abuse
18. Physical child abuse
19. Child sexual abuse
20. Child neglect
21. Psychological abuse
22. Foster care
23. Professional responsibilities
24. Negligence
25. Malpractice

a. _____ where the children will live at what times
b. _____ a court order that allows an individual to be involuntarily committed to a mental hospital for a long period of time, such as six months
c. _____ population frequencies
d. _____ repeated denigration in the absence of physical harm
e. _____ a legal decision that involves determining where children will reside and how parents will share legal rights and responsibilities for child rearing
f. _____ the ethical obligation not to reveal private communications
g. _____ a form of physical child abuse in which the parent induces illness in the child
h. _____ more patients are admitted to psychiatric hospitals more frequently but for shorter periods of time
i. _____ parents meet with a neutral third party who helps them identify, negotiate, and resolve their disputes during a divorce
j. _____ a temporary placement of the child outside of his or her home
k. _____ appointing an independent guardian to provide informed consent when a person is not competent to provide it for himself or herself
l. _____ when professional negligence results in harm to patients
m. _____ the requirement that a clinician tell a patient about a procedure and its risks, the patient understand the information and freely consents to the treatment, and the patient be competent to give consent
n. _____ allow an acutely disturbed individual to be confined in a mental hospital for a few days
o. _____ how the parents will make separate or joint decisions about their children's lives
p. _____ the patient is court-ordered to comply with outpatient treatment
q. _____ involves placing children at risk for serious physical or psychological harm by failing to provide basic and expected care
r. _____ a situation in which only one parent retains custody of the children
s. _____ involves sexual contact between an adult and child
t. _____ a situation in which both parents retain custody
u. _____ a legal decision that a parent or other responsible adult has inflicted damage or offered inadequate care to a child
v. _____ when a professional fails to perform in a manner that is consistent with the level of skill exercised by other professionals in the field
w. _____ nonvoluntary removal of any right a parent has to care for his or her child

x. _____ involves the intentional use of physically painful and harmful actions

y. _____ a professional's obligations to meet the ethical standards of the profession and to uphold the laws of the states in which he or she practices

MATCHING III

Answers are found at the end of this chapter. Match these names with their contributions to psychology:

a.	Thomas Szasz	c.	Lenore Walker
b.	John Monahan	d.	Henry Kempe

1. _____ researched the relationship between violence, mental illness, and predicting dangerousness
2. _____ wrote about the "battered child syndrome"
3. _____ asserted that the concept of mental illness is a myth, and argued that abnormal behavior must be defined relative to some social or moral standard
4. _____ coined the term "the battered woman syndrome"

CONCEPT REVIEW

Answers are found at the end of this chapter. After you have read and reviewed the material, test your comprehension by filling in the blanks or circling the correct answer.

1. Mental health professionals typically assume which view?   **free will**   **determinism**

2. Criminal law assumes which view?   **free will**   **determinism**

3. One possible solution to improve testimony by expert witnesses would be to have one _____ expert testify rather than an expert for each side.

4. The views of Szasz are widely accepted in the psychiatric community: **true**   **false**

5. The irresistible impulse test and the product test   **narrowed**   **broadened**   the grounds for determining insanity.

6. The problem of circular reasoning was introduced when mental health professionals decided to include _____ disorder as one of the mental diseases that could be the basis of an insanity defense.

7. In federal courts today, the burden of proof of a defendant's insanity lies with the **prosecution defense**.

8. There is strong research evidence to support the existence of the battered woman syndrome: **true false**

9. Substance abuse lowers a psychiatric inpatient's risk of committing violence: **true**   **false**

10. About _____ percent of all criminal cases involve the insanity defense.

11. Most defendants who are found not guilty by reason of insanity spend substantially less time in a mental hospital than they would have spent in prison: **true**   **false**

12. The goal of commitment following an NGRI verdict is _____.

13. Competence refers to the defendant's _____ mental state and insanity refers to the defendant's state of mind at the time of _____.

14. The poor conditions of mental institutions were publicized shortly after World War II by

_____.

15. Mitigating factors that would result in not applying the death penalty include mental _____

and mental _____.

16. What percentage of the mentally disturbed have no history of violence? _____

17. Clinicians can usually predict violence quite accurately: **true   false**

18. Staff at hospital where minors are committed qualify as independent fact finders to verify the need for

involuntary commitment, but they have a clear _____ interest in committing the minor.

19. Clinicians' accuracy at predicting violence is no better than the flip of a coin: **true   false**

20. *Wyatt v. Stickney* established that hospitalized mental patients have a right to _____.

21. *Lake v. Cameron* established the patient's right to be treated in the _____.

22. The development of resources to treat people in their communities grew rapidly with the

deinstitutionalization movement: **true   false**

23. Many community mental health centers do not offer services to the seriously mentally ill:

true   false

24. Many patients who would have been institutionalized before are now in jail or are homeless:

true   false

25. Mental health law is mostly based on the state's _____, and family law is mostly

based on the state's _____.

26. Parents and the legal system may be undermining a child's best _____ by fighting for

them in a custody battle.

27. Research evidence suggest that conflict between parents is strongly related to maladjustment among

children following divorce: **true   false**

28. Mental health professionals are not permitted to break confidentiality, even to report child abuse:

true   false

29. _____ reduces the number of custody hearings, helps parents reach earlier decisions, is viewed

more favorably by parents, and results in nonresidential parents working better together twelve years

later.

30. The most common reasons for malpractice claims against mental health professionals are the inappropriate

use of ECT and medication, and the existence of a _____ relationship between the therapist

and the patient.

31. The Tarasoff case established a mental health professional's duty to _____ a potential victim of

their client.

MULTIPLE CHOICE

Answers are found at the end of this chapter. These multiple choice questions will test your understanding of the material presented in the chapter. Read each question and circle the letter representing the best answer.

1. Which of the following cases ruled that a state could not confine a non-dangerous individual who is capable of surviving safely on his or her own or with the help of willing and responsible family members or friends?
   a. *Washington v. Harper*
   b. *Parham v. J.R.*
   c. *O'Connor v. Donaldson*
   d. *Lake v. Cameron*

2. _____ commitment procedures allow an acutely disturbed individual to be temporarily confined in a mental hospital, typically for no more than a few days, while _____ commitment procedures can lead to involuntary hospitalization that is ordered by the court and typically lasts for much longer.
   a. Formal; emergency
   b. Emergency; formal
   c. Medical; crisis
   d. Crisis; medical

3. All but which of the following are true of the "guilty but mentally ill" (GBMI) verdict?
   a. It holds defendants criminally responsible for their crimes.
   b. It helps ensure that the defendant receives treatment for the mental disorder.
   c. It was designed as a compromise with the "not guilty by reason of insanity" (NGRI) verdict.
   d. A defendant found to be GBMI cannot be sentenced in the same manner as any criminal.

4. All but which of the following have been goals of deinstitutionalization?
   a. to prevent inappropriate mental hospital admissions through arranging community alternatives to treatment
   b. to release to the community all institutionalized patients who have been given adequate preparation for such a change
   c. to decrease the influx of patients by not allowing them continued access to mental hospitals and thus encouraging independence
   d. to establish and maintain community support systems for non-institutionalized people receiving mental health services in the community

5. Which of the following individuals argued that mental disorders are subjective "problems in living" rather than objective diseases, and thus believed that the concept of mental illness is a myth?
   a. Thomas Szasz
   b. E. Fuller Torrey
   c. Bertram Brown
   d. Henry Kempe

6. The majority of custody decisions are made by
   a. parents themselves.
   b. attorneys who negotiate for the parents outside of court.
   c. a judge and decided in court.
   d. mental health professionals who evaluate the case.

7. All but which of the following are true of the *parens patriae*?
   a. It is used to justify the state's supervision of minors and incapacitated adults.
   b. It is based on the state's duty to protect the public safety, health, and welfare.
   c. Commitment under this rationale was virtually unknown to the United States until the early 1950s.
   d. It refers to the concept of the "state as parent."

8. Following a civil commitment to a mental hospital, mental patients' rights include all of the following except
   a. the right to treatment.
   b. the right to design their own treatment plan.
   c. the right to refuse treatment.
   d. the right to treatment in the least restrictive alternative environment.

9. Evidence suggests that the insanity defense is used in approximately _____ of all criminal cases in the United States.
   a. 1 percent
   b. 4 percent
   c. 7 percent
   d. 10 percent

10. All but which of the following stages are part of Lenore Walker's stages of the "cycle of violence"?
    a. battering incident
    b. tension-building phase
    c. loving contrition
    d. verbal reprimands

11. On average, defendants who are found "not guilty by reason of insanity" (NGRI) spend _____ time confined in an institution as they would have in prison if they had been given a prison sentence instead.
    a. significantly less
    b. twice as much
    c. approximately the same
    d. roughly three times as much

12. Which of the following terms is defined as the ethical obligation not to reveal private communication and is basic to psychotherapy?
    a. confidentiality
    b. private communications
    c. classified information
    d. privileged communications

13. Mental disorders and the actions that result from them are typically viewed as
    a. choices.
    b. conditions that are outside of voluntary control.
    c. responsibilities that the mentally disordered individual must assume.
    d. a and c

14. The acquittal of John Hinckley prompted all of the following except
   a. the new verdict "guilty but mentally ill" (GBMI).
   b. a revised definition of the insanity defense.
   c. shifting the burden of proof from the prosecution to the defense in federal courts.
   d. the creation of a much stricter standard of proof for the defense in the majority of states.

15. All but which of the following are issues of special relevance regarding involuntary hospitalization of the severely mentally impaired?
   a. criminal record
   b. civil commitment
   c. patients' rights
   d. deinstitutionalization

16. Research indicates that approximately _____ of the mentally disturbed are not violent.
   a. 30 percent
   b. 50 percent
   c. 70 percent
   d. 90 percent

17. All but which of the following are grounds that tend to dominate commitment laws?
   a. being dangerous to others
   b. inability to care for self
   c. being dangerous to self
   d. inability to care for others

18. Over _____ of all reports of child abuse are found to be unsubstantiated after an investigation.
   a. one eighth
   b. one quarter
   c. one half
   d. two thirds

19. Which is not one of the major problems with deinstitutionalization as identified by Torrey?
   a. Patients are released from hospitals with no follow-up treatment.
   b. The treatment of the mentally ill does not reduce the likelihood of them being violent.
   c. The number of mentally ill people in jails is rising.
   d. Many mentally ill people are homeless.

20. Where the child will live after a marital separation is called
   a. physical custody.
   b. legal custody.
   c. joint custody.
   d. sole custody.

21. Which of the following is known as the "product test" that indicated "an accused is not criminally responsible if his unlawful act was the product of mental disease or defect"?
   a. *Parsons v. State*
   b. *O'Connor v. Donaldson*
   c. *Durham v. United States*
   d. *Parham v. J.R.*

22. One common malpractice claim against mental health professionals is
    a. the misuse of psychotherapeutic techniques.
    b. the inappropriate use of electroconvulsive therapy (ECT).
    c. the failure to disclose therapeutic interpretations to clients.
    d. inappropriate hospitalization.

23. Confidentiality between a therapist and a client can be broken under which of the following circumstances?
    a. The client is threatening to harm another person.
    b. The client has disclosed sexual or physical abuse of a child.
    c. The client is threatening to harm himself or herself.
    d. all of the above

24. Which of the following is not true of the legal definition of competence?
    a. It refers to the defendant's ability to understand criminal proceedings.
    b. It refers to the defendant's current mental status.
    c. It refers to the defendant's willingness to participate in criminal proceedings.
    d. The "reasonable degree" of understanding needed to establish competence is generally acknowledged to be fairly low.

25. In the case of *Wyatt* v. *Stickney*, the federal district court ruled that at a minimum, public mental institutions must provide all of the following except
    a. a humane psychological and physical environment.
    b. a sufficient number of qualified staff to administer adequate treatment.
    c. individualized treatment plans.
    d. "reasonable" rates for inpatient services.

26. Which of the following details a suspect's rights to remain silent and to have an attorney present during police questioning?
    a. Miranda warning
    b. informed consent
    c. confidentiality
    d. *parens patriae*

27. Evidence suggests that in child custody cases, mediation
    a. does not necessarily reduce the number of custody hearings in court.
    b. is more effective than the role mental health professionals play in custody cases, and thus mental health professionals should limit their involvement in the legal system.
    c. does not help parents reach decisions more quickly than if they were to go through custody hearings in court.
    d. is viewed by parents as more favorable than litigation, especially fathers.

28. Which of the following cases established the patient's right to be treated in the least restrictive alternative environment?
    a. *Lake v. Cameron*
    b. *Osheroff v. Chestnut Lodge*
    c. *O'Connor v. Donaldson*
    d. none of the above

29. Which of the following is true regarding the idea that mental disability should limit criminal responsibility?
    a. It is a relatively new concept among mental health professionals.
    b. It dates back to ancient Greek and Hebrew traditions and was evident in early English law.
    c. It has emerged in our legal system within the past fifty years.
    d. It surfaced following World War II, when large numbers of veterans experienced post-traumatic stress symptoms and committed violent acts.

30. In his research on the prediction of dangerousness, John Monahan has found which of the following to be several times higher among prison inmates as among the general population?
    a. major depression
    b. bipolar disorder
    c. schizophrenia
    d. all of the above

SHORT ANSWER
Answer the following short answer questions. Compare your work to the material presented in the text.

1. Brian is a thirty-five-year-old white male who was recently arrested for sexually abusing a seven-year-old girl. Although this is Brian's first offense, he has a history of addictive behavior. Explain how you think a criminal lawyer would conceptualize Brian's behavior and how a mental health professional would conceptualize his behavior. Discuss the similarities and differences of the two perspectives.

2. Discuss Szasz's position on free will, determinism, mental illness, and the insanity defense. Do you agree or disagree with Szasz? Why?

3. What are the underlying principles of libertarianism and paternalism? Which view do you agree with? Defend your position.

4. Discuss the implications of *Tarasoff* v. *Regents of the University of California*. If you had been Poddar's therapist, would you have handled the situation differently? Why?

5. What are base rates? Discuss their utility in research.

ANSWER KEY

MATCHING I

1. q
2. d
3. h
4. n
5. b
6. t
7. a
8. k
9. v
10. o
11. w
12. f
13. p
14. j
15. s
16. r
17. c
18. i
19. m
20. g
21. u
22. l
23. e

MATCHING II

a. 10
b. 2
c. 3
d. 21
e. 9
f. 15
g. 14
h. 8
i. 16
j. 22
k. 7
l. 24
m. 6
n. 1
o. 11
p. 4
q. 20
r. 12
s. 19
t. 13
u. 17
v. 25
w. 5
x. 18
y. 23

MATCHING III

1. b
2. d
3. a
4. c

CONCEPT REVIEW

1.	determinism	17.	false
2.	free will	18.	financial
3.	neutral	19.	false
4.	false	20.	treatment
5.	broadened	21.	least restrictive environment
6.	antisocial personality	22.	false
7.	defense	23.	true
8.	false	24.	true
9.	false	25.	police power; parens patriae
10.	1	26.	interests
11.	false	27.	true
12.	treatment	28.	false
13.	current; the crime	29.	mediation
14.	conscientious objectors	30.	sexual
15.	illness; retardation	31.	warn
16.	90 percent		

MULTIPLE CHOICE

1. c	6. b	11. c	16. d	21. c	26. a
2. b	7. c	12. a	17. d	22. b	27. d
3. d	8. b	13. b	18. c	23. d	28. a
4. c	9. a	14. d	19. b	24. c	29. b
5. a	10. d	15. a	20. a	25. d	30. d

NOTES

NOTES

NOTES

NOTES

NOTES

NOTES

NOTES

NOTES

NOTES

NOTES

NOTES